United Nations justice

United Nations justice:
Legal and judicial reform in governance operations

Calin Trenkov-Wermuth

**United Nations
University Press**

TOKYO · NEW YORK · PARIS

The views expressed in this publication are those of the author and do not necessarily reflect the views of the United Nations University.

United Nations University Press
United Nations University, 53-70, Jingumae 5-chome,
Shibuya-ku, Tokyo 150-8925, Japan
Tel: +81-3-5467-1212   Fax: +81-3-3406-7345
E-mail: sales@unu.edu   general enquiries: press@unu.edu
http://www.unu.edu

United Nations University Office at the United Nations, New York
2 United Nations Plaza, Room DC2-2062, New York, NY 10017, USA
Tel: +1-212-963-6387   Fax: +1-212-371-9454
E-mail: unuony@unu.edu

United Nations University Press is the publishing division of the United Nations University.

Cover design by Mea Rhee

Printed in Hong Kong

ISBN 978-92-808-1173-5

Library of Congress Cataloging-in-Publication Data

Trenkov-Wermuth, Calin.
United Nations justice : legal and judicial reform in governance operations /
Calin Trenkov-Wermuth.
    p. cm.
 Includes bibliographical references and index.
  ISBN 978-9280811735 (pbk. : alk. paper) 1. United Nations. 2. Justice,
Administration of—International cooperation. 3. Social justice—International
cooperation. I. Title.
K2100.T75 2010
341.5'2—dc22   2009038156

Endorsements

"Extensively researched and powerfully argued, *United Nations Justice* is a penetrating criticism of past efforts to bring the rule of law to conflict-ridden countries and an inspiring effort to identify better practices that can help the UN assist those countries in the creation of a sustainable peace."
***Michael W. Doyle**, Harold Brown Professor of International Affairs, Law and Political Science, Columbia University*

"Establishing sustainable justice systems in societies torn by civil strife is an enormously complex, sensitive, and ambitious task. Few have tried it, fewer have succeeded. United Nations Justice provides a candid assessment of two such efforts: the United Nations' attempts to nurture such transformations in Kosovo and East Timor. The author questions the UN's approach as much as its delivery. In doing so, he raises timely questions that demand further reflection by scholars, policy analysts, and practitioners alike. Not everyone will agree with his provocative conclusions, but we could all benefit from the debate that should ensue."
***Edward C. Luck**, Senior Vice President, International Peace Institute, and Professor of Practice, School of International and Public Affairs, Columbia University.*

"As Dr Trenkov-Wermuth argues in this important book, the UN's attempts to craft judicial and legal systems in the territories it has found itself administering has been deeply flawed, partly because they have been too ambitious and partly because they have too often failed to take

note of local custom and reality. His critique deserves to be read by all those, scholars and practitioners alike, with an interest in improving the process of post conflict reconstruction."
James Mayall, Emeritus Sir Patrick Sheehy Professor of International Relations, University of Cambridge.

"Calin Trenkov-Wermuth's book is a sobering assessment of the considerable obstacles and small victories, but also the avoidable fumbles and troubling legacies, of the UN's unprecedented efforts at comprehensive legal and judicial reform in Kosovo and East Timor – a remarkable and sorely needed memento for future operations."
Cesare P.R. Romano, co-Director, Project on International Courts and Tribunals and Loyola Law School Los Angeles

"This study marks an important new contribution to the scholarship on legal and judicial reform carried out under the auspices of the UN. It is highly relevant to scholars and practitioners from all disciplines who explore the relationship between international rule-of-law reform and local ownership."
Carsten Stahn, Leiden University & Grotius Centre for International Legal Studies, The Hague

"This important and timely book analyzes the very considerable deficiencies of international legal and judicial interventions. What the author demonstrates is that these failures are as much conceptual as programmatic, with outcomes that can undermine the very ideals that inspire them. The study is well grounded, unflinching in its findings and conclusions and provides compelling insights important for practitioners, planners and theorists."
Jim Whitman, Head, Department of Peace Studies, University of Bradford

To
my parents

In memory of
Khristo and Lilia Trenkov, and Max Wermuth

In gratitude to
Israel Almog, David and Sarah Evans, Gitta and Gee Martin, Georg and Renate Mestmacher, Marjorie Nieuwenhuis, Blagoe and Branka Petrović, Charles and Sally Svenson, Erwin and Martina Wendland, Anne and Allen Woolf

For man, when perfected, is the best of animals, but, when separated from law and justice, he is the worst of all...

Aristotle, *Politics*, Book I, Chapter 2

Contents

Acknowledgements

Writing a book requires the mental and physical exertions of one person, but the intellectual, financial and moral contributions of many. I therefore wish to thank the individuals and institutions who supported me while I researched, wrote and edited this work. First and foremost, I would like to thank Marc Weller, who supervised this research in its earlier guise as a PhD dissertation; I am very grateful for his expert guidance and rigorous feedback at all stages of the process, but also for providing me with the opportunity to expand my knowledge of the field through my involvement with the work of various research projects he directs. I also owe a debt of gratitude to Maurice Pearton, who read and commented on several drafts of all chapters, and whose editorial skill and moral support were invaluable for the completion of the project. The insightful comments and constructive feedback I received from my examiners, James Mayall and Jim Whitman, were also hugely beneficial in turning the thesis into a book.

Several individuals at the Centre of International Studies at the University of Cambridge were also particularly helpful: I am grateful to Geoffrey Edwards for his refreshing feedback on various chapters; Duncan Bell and Mette Eilstrup-Sangiovanni kindly offered their views on my methodology; Tarak Barkawi offered valuable criticism of several chapters I presented at the centre's colloquium; and Brendan Simms was supportive at several key junctures. Finally, Wendy Cooke and Wendy Slaninka provided the type of administrative support which students are not normally privileged to receive.

I also extend my gratitude to the members of several other faculties, at both Cambridge and other universities. Devon Curtis's advice on my methodology and on the general direction of the study proved to be invaluable. T. R. S. Allan clarified some questions on jurisprudence, and Oliver Ramsbotham helpfully commented on specific ideas and critiques I wished to propose. John Micgiel of the Harriman Institute provided me with an intellectual home during my stay at Columbia University, and Michael Doyle, Edward Luck, Simon Chesterman and Vivienne O'Connor offered many valuable insights on legal and judicial reform in governance operations. Kenneth Waltz helped and encouraged me to challenge my own preconceptions about the United Nations during his weekly graduate seminar. Finally, Geoffrey Hawthorn, Glen Rangwala and Mary Sarotte of the Faculty of Social and Political Sciences at Cambridge provided me with the opportunity to teach international politics, an experience which has in itself helped me to learn as much about my chosen subject as I did throughout all my prior education. In this respect, I would also like to express my gratitude to the students whom I have had the privilege to supervise over the course of four years, and whose intellect and curiosity helped my own intellectual growth.

Various aspects of my research were funded by different bodies, and I wish to acknowledge the contribution of these trusts and institutions. The Kurt Hahn Trust Scholarship offered by the University of Cambridge in conjunction with the Deutscher Akademischer Austausch Dienst (DAAD) and the Allen, Meek and Reed Award offered by the Board of Graduate Studies at Cambridge were very helpful for my research period; the International Studies Committee of the Gilbert Murray Trust made it possible for me to carry out research in New York; the Fitzwilliam Society Trust Research Fund enabled me to travel to Kosovo; and the Dick Haywood Trust and the Cambridge Board of Graduate Studies Worts Travelling Scholars Award helped me to undertake research in Geneva.

Most of the interviews conducted in the course of field research were confidential. While I do not directly cite anyone in the text, I wish to acknowledge those who kindly shared their time and candidly offered their wisdom in New York, Pristina and Geneva: Wendy Brafman, Jean-Christian Cady, Jack Christofides, Haki Demolli, Ahmet Hasolli, Neithart Hoefer-Wissing, Alex Hug, Robert Husbands, Philip Kanning, Isabella Karlowicz, Iain King, Nesrin Lushta, Henry McGowen, Beth Miller, Charles Nihan, Robert Pulver, Pranvera Recica, Mona Rishmawi, Annamyriam Roccatello, Elizabeth Rolando, Kirsti Samuels, Eileen Simpson, Neeraj Singh and Michael Steiner. Erwin and Martina Wendland in Geneva and Eileen Simpson in Pristina assisted me with the setting up of interviews, and offered generous hospitality.

Without the assistance of the staff of the libraries where much of the research for this dissertation was carried out, the task of researching would have been a far more daunting experience, and I therefore wish to thank those whose help remains all too often unacknowledged. They are the staffs of the Cambridge University Library, the Squire Law Library, the Social and Political Sciences faculty library, the Mill Lane Library and the Fitzwilliam College Library at the University of Cambridge; the Butler Library and the Lehman Social Sciences Library at Columbia University; the New York Public Library; the British Library; the Bibliothèque de Sciences-Po; the Bibliothèque Sainte-Geneviève; and the Bibliothèque publique d'information du Centre Pompidou.

I also wish to thank the Centre of International Studies at Cambridge for its institutional support, and Fitzwilliam College for its pastoral support. And I am very grateful to Vesselin Popovski for first introducing me to UNU Press, and to Robert Davis for his professionalism in guiding me through the publication process.

Finally, a number of friends and several family members contributed to this project, both directly and indirectly. Jehangir Khan supervised my first work experience at the United Nations, which inspired my interest to study the work of the organization further. My discussions with Patrick Lenta proved instrumental for the book's methodology and aided my understanding of legal theory. Cecile Mouly helped to clarify key concepts and theoretical debates regarding peace research. The interesting discussions I had with Axel Wennmann on UN politics and affairs gave me insight into the internal workings of the organization. Richard Moules offered his practical assistance on several occasions. Martin, Jenny, Emma and Chris Jones were my adoptive family in the United Kingdom, and I am grateful for their hospitality. Eleni Orfanidou helped me to understand more about life, love and friendship than I could have hoped for. My friends from Fitzwilliam College and beyond provided me with support and friendship that turned my experience of Cambridge, and of writing this study, into the most enjoyable and memorable years of my life. And I thank Cecily Campbell-Bezat for waking in me feelings, hopes and dreams I had when we were children.

In proofreading the entire draft, my stepfather, Peter Atkinson, offered invaluable editorial assistance. My father, Kamen Trenkov, who had a keen interest in my topic and my progress from the beginning, offered moral support. My brother and sister-in-law, Jassen and Ashley Trenkov, have been steadfast supporters throughout, and I am especially grateful to my brother for his technical assistance. But my greatest appreciation goes to my mother, Judith Wermuth-Atkinson, whose editorial assistance in the final days helped immensely, but more importantly who went beyond the usual call of a mother's duty in finding the courage to leave her old life behind and escape from communist Bulgaria 22 years ago, so that she could offer a life to my brother and myself that has now surpassed everything that we ever imagined to be possible.

Abbreviations

CIVPOL	civilian police
COMKFOR	Commander of KFOR
CPA	Coalition Provisional Authority (Iraq)
DMU	Detainee Management Unit (East Timor)
DPKO	UN Department of Peacekeeping Operations
ECHR	European Convention on Human Rights
EU	European Union
FALINTIL	Forcas Armadas de Libertacao Nacional de Timor Leste (National Armed Forces for the Liberation of East Timor)
FRY	Federal Republic of Yugoslavia
GC IV	Geneva Convention IV
HRFOR	UN Human Rights Field Operation in Rwanda
IAC	Interim Administrative Council (Kosovo)
ICC	International Criminal Court
ICCPR	International Covenant on Civil and Political Rights
ICRC	International Committee of the Red Cross
ICTR	International Criminal Tribunal for Rwanda
ICTY	International Criminal Tribunal for the Former Yugoslavia
IJPs	international judges and prosecutors
INTERFET	International Force for East Timor
JAC/PJA	Joint Advisory Council on Provisional Judicial Appointments
JIAS	Joint Interim Administrative Structure (Kosovo)
JSMP	Judicial System Monitoring Programme
JSAP	Judicial System Assessment Program (Bosnia)
KFOR	Kosovo Force
KLA	Kosovo Liberation Army

KTC	Kosovo Transitional Council
KWECC	Kosovo War and Ethnic Crimes Court
LSMS	Legal System Monitoring Section
LRA	Lord's Resistance Army
MICIVIH	UN/OAS International Civilian Mission in Haiti
NCC	National Consultative Council (East Timor)
NATO	North Atlantic Treaty Organization
NGO	non-governmental organization
OAS	Organization of American States
OCHA	UN Office for the Coordination of Humanitarian Affairs
OHCHR	UN Office of the High Commissioner for Human Rights
ONUC	UN Operation in the Congo
ONUSAL	UN Observer Mission in El Salvador
OSCE	Organisation for Security and Co-operation in Europe
PISG	Provisional Institutions of Self-Government (Kosovo)
RUF	Revolutionary United Front (Sierra Leone)
SC	UN Security Council
SCU	Serious Crimes Unit (East Timor)
SOC	State of Cambodia
SRSG	Special Representative of the Secretary-General
STL	Special Tribunal for Lebanon
TA	Transitional Administrator (East Timor)
TJSC	Transitional Judicial Service Commission (East Timor)
UDT	Uniao Democratica Timorense (Timorese Democratic Union)
UN	United Nations
UNAMET	UN Mission in East Timor
UNDP	UN Development Programme
UNHCR	UN High Commissioner for Refugees
UNITAF	Unified Task Force (Somalia)
UNMIBH	UN Mission in Bosnia and Herzegovina
UNMIK	UN Interim Administration Mission in Kosovo
UNMISET	UN Mission of Support in East Timor
UNOSOM	UN Operation in Somalia I & II
UNPOL	UN Police
UNTAC	UN Transitional Authority in Cambodia
UNTAES	UN Transitional Administration in Eastern Slavonia, Baranja and Western Sirmium
UNTAET	UN Transitional Administration in East Timor
UNTAG	UN Transitional Assistance Group (Namibia)
UNTEA	UN Temporary Executive Authority (West Irian)
USAID	US Agency for International Development

Introduction

For the first four decades of the existence of the United Nations, Cold War rivalries between the United States and the Soviet Union hampered the organization's work in many areas. Its conflict management activities were mainly limited to what came to be known as *peacekeeping operations*, a concept invented by the then Canadian Minister of Foreign Affairs, Lester Pearson, and UN Secretary-General Dag Hammarskjöld in response to the need to oversee the withdrawal of French, British and Israeli troops from Suez in 1956. Starting with the UN Emergency Force in Egypt in 1956, most peacekeeping operations until the late 1980s took a similar form: that of a lightly armed military corps, prohibited from the use of force, with the exception of self-defence needs, and from interfering in the domestic politics of the host state; traditionally their task was either to monitor a cease-fire agreement or to patrol a neutral buffer zone between adversaries.[1]

The territorial rivalries of the two superpowers ensured that there was little deviation from this basic model of UN engagement in the management of hostilities. The United States and the USSR wanted to maintain a dominant influence over any political developments in their respective spheres of influence, and were therefore keen to minimize any outside interference; thus, a new peacekeeping mission could be set up only to the extent that the strategic interests of either of the two powers were not significantly threatened.[2] Furthermore, apart from Article 2(7) of the UN Charter expressly prohibiting the organization's interference in matters that fall within the domestic jurisdiction of the state, the ideological

United Nations justice: Legal and judicial reform in governance operations
Trenkov-Wermuth, United Nations University Press, 2010, ISBN 978-92-808-1173-5

differences of the superpowers also ensured that the United Nations would stay out of the domestic politics of states, failing or not, because any such interference would be ideologically charged: it would either support the liberal democratic and market-oriented economic model of the United States, or the model of the Soviet Union, a one-party people's democracy with public ownership and control of the means of production.[3]

The end of the Cold War in the late 1980s, and the collapse of the Soviet Union in 1991, gave rise to a new era of international involvement in inter- and intra-state conflicts.[4] This was the case mainly for two reasons. Firstly, the end of the confrontation between the superpowers changed their perception of the international community's involvement in conflicts as a threat to their strategic interests; thus there was less reason for either the United States or Russia, as the successor to the Soviet seat on the Security Council, to block any UN moves to establish peace missions. And secondly, the end of the tensions also signalled the end of much of the military and economic aid which the superpowers had used to influence and prop up various regimes. On both grounds, the United States and Russia began to allow the international community to become involved in conflict resolution in areas that were no longer strategically significant to them.[5]

Nevertheless, the end of the Cold War itself sparked intra-state conflicts, allowing political problems hitherto suppressed to come to the fore: the dissolution of Yugoslavia, for instance, although brewing for at least 10 years after Tito's death in 1980, did not become a reality until 1991.[6] Furthermore, the end to external financing of certain regimes prevented the continued suppression of their internal political opposition, and ultimately led to violent civil conflicts. For this reason, once external aid for Somalia began to dry up in the early 1990s, Siad Barre's government was driven from office by his political enemies, who then went on to fight among each other for political control.[7] This not only led to a protracted civil conflict, but also to a large-scale humanitarian crisis.

Yet with the UN's newly found freedom to intervene in conflicts and regions where it was previously unable to help came increasingly complex mandates, which not only called for its traditional *peacekeeping* role, but also for the United Nations to *make, restore, enforce* or *build* peace. The "Agenda for Peace" of 1992 signalled a change in the organizational culture, from one that focused mainly on conflict management or resolution to one that also incorporated conflict *prevention* as a main goal of the organization.[8] In particular, the notion of *peacebuilding* entered the UN's official language, and was regarded as key in order for peacemaking and peacekeeping operations to be "truly successful".[9] *Peacebuilding* activities were defined by UN Secretary-General Boutros Boutros-Ghali as actions "to identify and support structures which will tend to consolidate peace"[10] in order "to prevent the recurrence of violence".[11] The *action* was to be undertaken through a set of mechanisms which included the disarmament of warring factions and the restoration of order, the gathering and potential destruction of weapons, the repatriation of refugees, the training of security personnel, the promotion of human rights, the reform and strengthening of government institutions and the enhancement of political participation through formal and informal procedures.[12]

The increasingly complex peacekeeping, peace-enforcement and peace-building demands of the early 1990s eventually culminated in mandates which called for the UN's outright governance of war-torn regions. Three territories came to be governed by the United Nations: Eastern Slavonia in 1996 (UNTAES), Kosovo in 1999 (UNMIK) and East Timor, also in 1999 (UNTAET). What made these three UN missions distinctive is that all sovereign powers traditionally associated with the state – executive, legislative and judicial – were vested in them; but while UNTAES focused on the peaceful reintegration of Eastern Slavonia into an existing polity, Croatia,[13] UNMIK and UNTAET had to set up new political entities. They had to govern all aspects of public life, from the running of schools and public utilities to fiscal management and law enforcement.[14] This exercise of sovereign power was an entirely different enterprise from any previous peacekeeping activities the United Nations had undertaken, no matter what their complexity,[15] and presented problems for which any precedents were not directly helpful.

One of the important areas of peacebuilding for the United Nations was rule-of-law reform. UN attention to this area was triggered by its experience in the transitional authority mission to Cambodia (UNTAC):[16] since that protracted conflict had left Cambodia's justice system in a debilitated state, the mission's mandate required the United Nations to assist Cambodia's Supreme National Authority with judicial reform and administration prior to national elections.[17] However, UNTAC failed to accord sufficient resources and attention to this task, which ended in disappointing and inconsequential results.[18] This negative experience led in 1993 to the then Australian Foreign Minister, Gareth Evans, proposing the introduction of UN *justice packages*, which "should be part of any peacekeeping and post-conflict peacebuilding exercises in countries where the rule of law, and the institutions needed to support it, have manifestly broken down".[19] Although the United Nations failed to adopt and in fact officially rejected the idea of the justice package a decade after its initial conception,[20] from 1993 onwards the organization began to pay more attention to rule-of-law reform.

While police reform in particular became a central and often successful feature of many of the UN's missions during the 1990s,[21] legal and judicial reform proved to be a much more challenging and controversial area of peacebuilding. In 2000 the report of the UN Panel on Peace Operations noted that:

> the United Nations has faced situations in the past decade where the Security Council has authorized the deployment of several thousand police in a peacekeeping operation but has resisted the notion of providing the same operation with even 20 or 30 criminal justice experts.[22]

But what the UN's experience has shown is that due to the interdependence of the "triad"[23] of the justice system – the police, the judiciary and the prisons – a failure to reform one of these sectors will undermine any achievements reached in any of the other sectors: in Haiti, for instance, the UN's human rights staff observed that the effectiveness of the newly reformed police force was undermined by the weakness of the judicial institutions and prisons.[24]

In addition to political and budgetary problems within the United Nations itself and among its membership regarding judicial and legal reform efforts, the organization had to contend with many technical, structural and substantive problems in the field. For instance, in countries that had been plagued and polarized by civil war, and that had little or no experience of democratic institutions, political influence over the judiciary was a common phenomenon.[25] Furthermore, the relatively low income of judicial officials in societies emerging from conflict and economic hardship allowed for extensive corruption in the judiciary. Both of these problems created a real challenge for the United Nations in establishing judicial independence. Haiti is a particular case in point. Its justice system had suffered greatly under the military dictatorship of Raoul Cédras between 1991 and 1993: the military dominated the judiciary, which was in itself corrupt; the judges and prosecutors lacked adequate legal training, and most facilities were in a state of disrepair; civilian and military leaders were immune to prosecution; and the people had little respect for rule-of-law officials.[26]

Furthermore, the grim reality of the sheer physical loss and damage to judicial institutions and materials, and the death or flight of qualified legal and judicial personnel, created a huge obstacle to UN reconstruction and reform. In Kosovo and East Timor the retreating Serb and Indonesian forces, respectively, left a trail of destruction; most court buildings in East Timor had been burned, and most court equipment and materials necessary for legal practice, such as legal texts and case files, had been looted, dislocated or burned.[27] In Kosovo many courtrooms had been booby-trapped or mined, records destroyed or dislocated and court and office equipment looted.[28]

Moreover, after Yugoslav President Slobodan Milošević had stripped Kosovo of its autonomy in 1989, he replaced many Albanian judges and prosecutors with Serbian appointees. Most of these left their posts along with the Serbian forces retreating from Kosovo in 1999. So Kosovo was left with only a few judges and prosecutors; many of them had last served in 1989, but now they had to fill important posts without adequate training or recent legal experience, a not uncommon scenario in UN missions. In East Timor all judges and prosecutors had been directly appointed from Indonesia, and after the withdrawal of the Indonesian forces, no jurists were left. The United Nations had to attempt to recruit individuals with any sort of legal experience by dropping leaflets from aircraft; even after these efforts, only a handful of individuals applied for judicial posts. Thus the United Nations was assigned the daunting task of building a judiciary entirely anew.[29]

In addition, the United Nations frequently had to contend with either the absence or the inadequacy of legal codes, and thus had somehow to fill the legal vacuum or the gaps in the law. In Cambodia the Vietnamese-drawn criminal and criminal procedure codes were not viable if the United Nations was to achieve its key objectives, and consequently UNTAC chose to draft and enact its own laws. This effort, however, was marred by the fact that these UN laws failed to live up to international standards: the absence of consent, for instance, was not included as a key factor in the offence of rape.[30] In Somalia the former Italian penal code was utilized,[31] and in Afghanistan the Bonn Agreement resurrected Afghanistan's 1964 constitution as the central legal document to guide the legal and political development of the country.[32] In East Timor the Indonesian legal code was chosen as the applicable law, and in Kosovo the laws of the Federal Republic of Yugoslavia were used for the first five months of the mission, until this unpopular decision was overturned, mainly as a result of effective protests by Kosovar jurists who favoured Kosovo's legal code of 1989 instead. The difficulty with these legal codes was that they were inadequate in addressing many *modern* crimes, and were unable to respond to the needs of a modern economy.

Finally, the task of reforming the legal and judicial systems in the respective missions was made significantly more difficult because of the lack of historical precedent for this type of assignment and thus adequate practical experience from which the United Nations might draw lessons. Given the organization's membership and prior involvement with decolonization, a consideration of colonial experience and practice may have been inappropriate. Furthermore, the United Nations was also not an occupying power, and certainly did not have the resources and financial means of one; thus drawing on historical examples such as US involvement with legal and judicial reforms in Germany and Japan after the Second World War would have yielded few useful lessons. The United Nations could and did adopt some of the guidelines on legal and judicial matters for territories under occupation, as outlined in the law on belligerent occupation, as part of its approach in its governance operations. However, applying the law of belligerent occupation to missions that did not have the resources of an occupying power, and whose mandate included not only judicial administration but by implication also the establishment of a sustainable legal system, did not prove to be useful.

For these reasons, and in particular the lack of a real model on which to base its approach, many of the UN's early decisions on justice sector reform and transitional justice were broadly taken *ad hoc*. But after some initial mishaps with its *ad hoc* decisions, after a decade of gruesome violence and after some sharp academic criticisms about its peacebuilding and justice sector reform endeavours, the United Nations began to develop certain assumptions on how best to restore the rule of law in post-conflict societies, how to address problems of transitional justice, and in this respect also how to undertake legal and judicial reform.

By the time the United Nations came to govern Kosovo and East Timor in 1999, some of these assumptions had taken a firm hold in the UN's thinking on justice sector reform, and the approach which emerged consisted of five key elements: firstly, the laws chosen for the beginning of a mission had to be based on previously applicable legal codes, and these codes had to be as comprehensive as possible; secondly, the chosen legal framework had to incorporate a complete human rights catalogue from the beginning of a mission; thirdly, the courts had to continue to function or be re-established in the same configuration as had existed previously in a territory from the beginning of the mission; fourthly, past atrocities needed to be addressed promptly, and wherever necessary through the local legal framework and court system; and fifthly, local participation in the judicial process was to be pursued from the start of the mission, and to the fullest extent possible.

The central argument of this book is that these five main elements of the UN's approach were not suited to the task of establishing a sustainable legal system, largely because they failed to address adequately some of the key tensions at the heart of such governance operations. These tensions stem firstly from a mission's need to balance the demands for order and security on the one hand and justice on the other hand, and secondly from a mission's need to govern a territory to a high standard while also helping to empower the local community through local ownership of institutional processes. The failure to take such tensions into account led to the violation of numerous legal principles and judicial norms, to frequent and major local opposition to various UN decisions, and in some instances to increased levels of violence and political destabilization. In essence, the approach confused the *ends* with the *means*: there appears to have been a naïve assumption that by starting with what should be the final product of the reform efforts, the desired results could be achieved. This assumption not only proved to be ineffectual, but also yielded an approach which threatened to undermine the fundamental goals of justice and the re-establishment of the rule of law.

It is clear that a sustainable legal system is vital for the rule of law in any society, and that the rule of law is vital for a sustainable peace. As Kofi Annan has acknowledged, the United Nations has "learned that the rule of law delayed is lasting peace denied and that justice is the hand-maiden of true peace".[33] Thus the failure to reform the legal framework and judicial institutions quickly and effectively, and thereby to aid in the creation of a sustainable legal system, has the potential to result in an eventual relapse into violence. In this respect, it is crucial to understand the failures of the UN's reform method, and how the UN's approach has itself contributed to problems in this area, since such an understanding may render any future governance operations with a justice sector reform mandate more effective and successful. While this study focuses predominantly on uncovering, analysing and assessing the UN's approach to legal and judicial reform in its governance operations, some of the alternative methods proposed in the literature, which may better balance the above-mentioned tensions, thus decreasing the likelihood that legal principles and judicial norms are violated in the reform process and increasing the likelihood that a sustainable legal system will be established, are analysed and evaluated in the final chapter.

Delay to the rule of law in early UN peacebuilding operations, starting with Namibia in 1989, resulted from the *ad hoc* basis of decisions on justice sector reform. But by the time the United Nations began administering Kosovo and East Timor, a decade's worth of failed peacebuilding experiences, together with academic developments in the areas of transitional justice and peacebuilding and the changing nature of the post–Cold War conflicts, had led the United Nations to adopt the assumptions about justice sector reform, and the particular approach to such reforms, discussed above. However, much of the literature on the subject presents the UN's reform decisions in a way which fails to account for these assumptions and the approach which they led to. Such accounts clearly lean towards an explanation of key decisions as having been taken on an *ad hoc* basis, depending on the particular circumstances and exigencies found in the territories under administration. The principal legal adviser to the UN Transitional Administration Mission in East Timor (UNTAET), Hansjoerg Strohmeyer, presents the UN's decision on the choice of law in Kosovo and East Timor as having been taken *ad hoc* for "practical" reasons,[34] an explanation which ignores the political context, the legal rationale and the theoretical basis underpinning this decision. Thus, in addition to highlighting the five key elements to the UN's approach to legal and judicial reform in both Kosovo and East Timor, this book will root these elements within their academic, political, legal and historical context.

It is undeniable that many of the difficulties which the United Nations encountered with its legal and judicial reform efforts resulted from inadequate funding and resources, and inappropriate decisions taken by particular individuals. But explanations of the difficulties based on these factors, however true, fail to relate to the key elements of the UN's approach and the assumptions which underpinned those decisions. Hence the solution to the problems lies not solely in better funding and more resources, as advocated in a number of articles and reports.[35] The UN's own approach contributed to and in part created the difficulties which the organization encountered in reforming the legal system in the territories it administered, and thus a better understanding of the way in which this occurred will lay the groundwork for an approach which leads to fewer complications.

To date, there is no comprehensive account and analysis of the UN's *approach* to legal and judicial reform in its governance operations. The issue of international territorial administration and the UN's governance of war-torn societies is treated in a number of books written on the subject.[36] There are also various articles and reports that focus broadly on the subject of international territorial administration, or more specifically on the UN's efforts to that end.[37] Legal and judicial reform as an aspect of rule-of-law reform, and of international territorial administration more broadly, is addressed in some of those works. There are articles which deal with particular aspects of legal and judicial reform in governance operations, e.g. the establishment of special courts, tribunals and internationalized panels for the addressing of past atrocities, the deployment of international judges and prosecutors, and various specific rule-of-law issues.[38] One book focuses exclusively on the new internationalized criminal courts.[39] Another deals with the challenges of addressing serious crimes in post-conflict societies.[40] A third deals with the establishment of the rule of law in UN governance operations in broad terms, but does not aim to focus on transitional justice as such.[41] Some authors try to tackle particular problems, such as how to address the legal vacuum in the immediate aftermath of a conflict, for instance focusing on model legal codes[42] or the role of legal advisers in international territorial administration;[43] others deal with the question of what lessons can be learned from legal and judicial reform efforts in multidimensional peace-keeping operations, and how to strengthen the rule of law in such operations.[44] However, such *lessons learned* accounts are broader in scope and draw lessons that apply more generally to rule of law reform in all types of multidimensional peace operations, whereas this study focuses more in depth on legal and judicial reform in operations where the UN has governed a territory. And the aforementioned articles, on the other hand, are too focused on particular aspects of the reform efforts. An attempt to discuss legal reform and judicial reconstruction in governance operations was made by an official directly involved with and responsible for many of the key reform decisions taken in Kosovo and East Timor, but he fails to discuss flaws and mistakes made during the operations.[45]

Furthermore, no article or study accounts for all key elements of the UN's approach, or attempts to link that approach to the intellectual assumptions which underpinned it and the theories which had an impact on it. Also, a number of the works have evaluated some aspects of that approach in terms of internationally accepted standards of justice, particularly as reflected in international human rights instruments, but an attempt to assess and evaluate it through legal theory is lacking. This book attempts a more comprehensive explanation of the UN's approach to legal and judicial reform in its governance operations, and also an assessment and evaluation of that approach through the lens of jurisprudence.

What renders this study important is the fact that the UN's experience with such reforms in its governance operations is likely to inform not only any similar future UN endeavours in international territorial administrations with a justice sector reform mandate, but also more broadly the conduct of such reforms in the UN's peace-assistance missions, and the conduct of such reforms undertaken by other bodies and organizations. While the international community has taken a step back from governance operations at the moment, as the *light-footprint*[46] approach which was adopted in Afghanistan in 2001 and in some of the UN's subsequent missions clearly illustrates, the history of international territorial administration throughout the twentieth century and the international community's most recent efforts to that end in Eastern Slavonia, Kosovo, East Timor and Bosnia teach us that the international community may sooner or later revert to the model of international governance again.[47] Given the challenges and difficulties which the United Nations faced with such reforms, it is important to undertake a comprehensive analysis and assessment of the UN's approach, so as to gain an insight into the ways in which that approach itself contributed to the problems, and the ways in which it must be adjusted so as to lead to a better and improved method in the future. However, even if no governance operations were ever undertaken again, it is clear that the UN's experience with legal and judicial reforms is likely to hold many valuable lessons for its own peace-assistance missions where such reforms have to be undertaken, as well as for the endeavours of other institutions involved with such reforms.

While many intergovernmental, regional, non-governmental and governmental organizations and bodies have become involved with justice sector reforms in recent years,[48] the particular interest here in UN practice stems from the fact that no other organization has been involved in such reforms to the same extent as the United Nations: only the United Nations has been mandated in recent years to establish a legal system in a post-conflict society virtually from the ground up; all other organizations have been involved in such reforms primarily in an advisory capacity, and have mostly dealt with a legal system that was already in place. Furthermore, the focus on UN operations is also because the United Nations has been involved in international territorial administration more than any other institution or body in the last 60 years. This fact has a bearing on the relevance of the study's focus on UN operations, since it serves as an indication that any potential future governance missions will more likely than not be led by the United Nations, and therefore UN practice and its particular methods of reforming the justice sector merit close scrutiny. And finally, focusing on legal and judicial reform in UN governance operations, rather than within a broader context, makes the subject more manageable within the given limits, and allows for sufficient breadth and depth in the case-study analysis.

It should be stressed here that the book will not consider any questions and issues relating to legal and judicial reform from an organizational or managerial perspective: for instance, questions about where within a UN mission, or the United Nations more broadly, decisions on such reforms should be made. The question as to which department or UN body plays or should play the leading role on issues of rule-of-law reform is very interesting indeed, and until relatively recently the matters were not clear-cut: the Office of the High Commissioner for Human Rights (OHCHR) was designated as the focal point for rule-of-law issues within the UN system for a long time. But while it undertook noble initiatives, such as the development of various rule-of-law tools for post-conflict states,[49] the relatively small size and budget of the institution did not place it in a position to undertake initiatives that go beyond the publishing of reports which offer practical guidance on the matter to field missions, and to become actively involved with rule-of-law reform in peace operations itself.

Most of the legal and judicial reform efforts have been run directly by the field missions themselves and thus also indirectly by the UN's Department of Peacekeeping Operations, which has been in charge of these missions. However, despite such a key responsibility and the department's extensive involvement with legal and judicial reform through its missions, it has employed in the past only a few criminal justice and rule-of-law experts, whose duties have been stretched well beyond capacity, frequently mandating them to be in several places at the same time.[50]

Furthermore, the UN's Office of Legal Affairs was consulted on some legal and judicial reform matters for the UN's governance operations, but it did not play a formal role in the reforms undertaken in the UN's missions. And while the crisis prevention and recovery efforts of the UN Development Programme (UNDP) have focused over the course of the past decade to no small extent on rule-of-law reform and transitional justice,[51] and the UNDP does have capacity and some funding for legal and judicial reform initiatives, it was not extensively involved in such reforms in the UN's governance operations.

It is evident that for many years the United Nations lacked clarity as to which of its departments, units or sister organizations should lead on rule-of-law reform matters. At one point more than 10 different UN departments or agencies claimed expertise in the rule-of-law area, and some of these were running competing law reform programmes, sometimes even in the same country.[52] This confusing and competitive approach led to various calls, from member states and experts alike, for a more coordinated and coherent approach to such reforms.[53] Since 2007, the Rule of Law Coordination and Resource Group, bringing together nine leading UN departments and agencies engaged in rule-of-law activities, and supported by a Rule of Law Unit, has attempted to improve the coordination of such efforts. Whether this coordination mechanism will be enough remains uncertain, but it is a positive step step in the right direction. But while the question of how to best coordinate rule of law reform efforts is highly interesting, this book will not broach this subject. Such questions, as well as questions about where decisions and advice on matters of legal and judicial reform within a particular mission should originate, would best be answered in a study that focuses on organizational management – something which this work does not aspire to do.

There are a few other areas that this book will not touch upon: since this is essentially not a *legal* study, it does not concern itself with any major discussions on subject matter jurisdiction, legal procedures, specific issues related to substantive criminal or procedural law, or any overly legalistic accounts of legal frameworks, institutional structures and judicial mechanisms. While each of these topics is touched upon to a certain extent, a competent discussion on these matters requires the expertise of a lawyer, or an international lawyer, which this author does not possess. Furthermore, the issue of the integration of customary laws and judicial mechanisms within a modern and statutory-based legal system will also not be discussed in depth, and neither will the question of how peacebuilders can contend with legal pluralism in a post-conflict context, for the reasons outlined below. Finally, the book will not address in any significant detail the grand questions of rule-of-law reform, such as whether it is true that there can be no peace without justice, whether amnesties granted through truth and reconciliation processes must indeed be shunned in favour of trials and prosecutions for past atrocities, and how broadly to attain *justice* in a post-conflict society.[54]

The book will touch upon a number of these topics, but there will be no substantive discussion of these issues; this is not because they are not interesting and relevant for justice sector reform, but simply because they are beyond the feasible scope of this study – each topic would warrant a lengthy study by itself. In essence, the main focus of the study will remain on an evaluation of the UN's legal and judicial reform efforts in its governance operations, particularly in Kosovo and East Timor, and on demonstrating that the UN's approach to such reforms was not well suited to its goal of establishing a sustainable legal system.

The book is divided into five chapters. Chapter 1 examines the UN's early legal and judicial reform efforts, focusing particularly on the first decade of post–Cold War operations; further, it investigates the assumptions which the UN formed about such reforms, and which eventually underpinned the UN's approach to these reforms in its governance operations. Chapter 2 briefly discusses the case-study selection – Kosovo and East Timor – and provides the rationale for that selection; it introduces the various criteria which are used in the case-study chapters for the assessment of the UN's approach, and briefly discusses the questions which are asked of each case study in the controlled comparison. Chapter 3 presents the Kosovo case study. After a brief introduction to the background of the conflict over Kosovo, and the UN Interim Administration Mission in Kosovo (UNMIK), the chapter goes on first to demonstrate how the five key elements of the UN's approach were implemented in practice, and then to discuss various legal and judicial developments in the territory which followed, in no small part as a result of that approach. The chapter moves on to analyse and discuss the developments as presented, and to evaluate the approach critically on the basis of the criteria introduced in Chapter 2. The concluding section summarizes the various ways in which the UN's approach was responsible for the problems and challenges which the mission had to face, and for the numerous violations of legal principles and judicial norms which resulted; it also suggests that it was the approach's failure to address adequately and balance the key tensions of a governance operation which led to these failures. Chapter 4 presents the East Timor case study, and follows a similar structure to Chapter 3. Chapter 5 highlights the issues raised by the UN's legal and judicial reform experience in Kosovo and East Timor, explores how these issues have been represented in the literature on the topic, contends with some of the main assumptions underlying the UN's approach and analyses and evaluates some of the proposed changes to key elements of that approach.

Notes

1. The two notable exceptions to this model were the UN's operations in the Belgian Congo (ONUC) and in Western New Guinea (UNTEA) in the early 1960s. For an overview of the UN's early peacekeeping operations see Ratner (1995).
2. Paris (2004: 15).
3. Ibid.
4. On this see Mayall (1996); Kaldor (1999).
5. Paris (2004: 16).
6. Any earlier moves towards dissolution of the Yugoslav federation would have been countered by the Soviet Union, and might also have met with military intervention by Soviet forces.
7. Paris (2004: 16).
8. UN General Assembly and Security Council (1992).
9. Ibid., para. 55.
10. Ibid.
11. Ibid., para. 21.
12. Ibid., para. 55.
13. For an overview of UNTAES and its challenges see Schoups (2001); Boothby (2004).
14. Caplan (2005: 2).
15. Richard Caplan (ibid.) draws this distinction between international administration and any "'expanded', 'complex', or 'multidimensional' peacekeeping" operations. Hansjoerg Strohmeyer (2001b: 46) argues regarding UNMIK and UNTAET that the "scope of the challenges and responsibilities deriving from these mandates was unprecedented in United Nations peacekeeping operations".
16. Mani (2002: 54).
17. See "Agreement on a Comprehensive Political Settlement of the Cambodia Conflict", Annex I: UNTAC Mandate, Section B: Civil Administration, para. 5.b – see Treaties list. For a discussion of UNTAC's civil mandate see Doyle (1995).
18. Mani (2002: 54).
19. Evans (1993: 56, 110). Gareth Evans was Australia's foreign minister from 1988 to 1996. He served as president and CEO of the International Crisis Group from 2000 until 2009 and is currently Honorary Professorial Fellow at the University of Melbourne. In his initial conception (ibid.: 56), the justice package contained four key elements: "the provision, as appropriate, of a body of criminal laws and procedures, drawing on universal principles; civil police, with training as well as law enforcement responsibilities; a panel of judges, prosecutors and defenders able to work with available local professionals during the transition period, again with an obligation to train their local successors; and adequate correctional facilities, and personnel to staff them while developing local replacements". On justice packages see also Plunkett (1998).
20. See UN Security Council (2004).
21. For a good overview of peacebuilding and police reform see Holm and Eide (2000).
22. UN General Assembly and Security Council (2000b) (Brahimi Report), para. 40.
23. The term "triad" is borrowed from Rama Mani (2002: 56), who refers to the judiciary, the prisons and the police as "the tripod or triad of the justice system".
24. Mani (ibid.). For a further discussion of police reform in Haiti see Neild (1995).
25. Caplan (2005: 60).
26. Mani (2002: 64–65). For an overview of judicial reform in Haiti see O'Neill (1995); see also MICIVIH (1994a). For a general overview of peacebuilding in Haiti see Kumar (1998).
27. Strohmeyer (2001b: 49).

28. Caplan (2005: 61).
29. Ibid.
30. Plunkett (1998: 69).
31. Plunkett (2003: 69).
32. See "Agreement on Provisional Arrangements in Afghanistan Pending the Re-establishment of Permanent Government Institutions", section II, 1(i) – see Treaties list.
33. Comments of UN Secretary-General Kofi Annan to the Security Council – see UN Security Council (2003).
34. Strohmeyer (2001b: 58).
35. See, for instance, Cohen (2002); see also the Brahimi Report (UN General Assembly and Security Council, 2000b), which attributes the difficulties with legal and judicial reform partly to the UN's attitude towards the allocation of resources.
36. Chesterman (2004); Caplan (2005); Zaum (2007); Fox (2008); Knoll (2008); Stahn (2008); Wilde (2008).
37. See, for instance, Chesterman (2001a, 2001b, 2002a, 2003, 2004); Kondoch (2001); Matheson (2001); Ruffert (2001); Stahn (2001); Wilde (2001a, 2003, 2004); Caplan (2002, 2004a, 2004b); Yannis (2004).
38. See, for instance, Linton (2001a, 2001b, 2001c, 2002); Stahn (2001); Cohen (2002); Dickinson (2003a, 2003b); Katzenstein (2003); Cockayne (2005a, 2005b); Nouwen (2006); Perriello and Wierda (2006).
39. Romano, Nollkamper and Kleffner (2004).
40. Rausch (2006).
41. Bull (2008).
42. Fairlie (2003); Oswald (2004); O'Connor (2005); O'Connor and Rausch (2005, 2007).
43. Wilde (2001b).
44. Baskin (2002); Carlson (2006); UN Department of Peacekeeping Operations (2006). Please note that Scott Carlson was the consultant with primary responsibility for developing the latter document for the UN's Department of Peacekeeping Operations.
45. Strohmeyer (2000, 2001a, 2001b, 2001c).
46. See, for instance, UN General Assembly and Security Council (2002), para. 98. For a further discussion of the *light-footprint* approach see Chesterman (2004: 88–92).
47. Bosnia was a case of international territorial administration since it was governed by the Peace Implementation Council, made up of "an *ad hoc* coalition of states and organizations operating with the backing of the UN Security Council" (Caplan, 2005: 34), but was not a case of UN governance, a point important for the discussion of the case-study selection in Chapter 2.
48. For instance, the World Bank, the UN Development Programme, the Office of the High Commissioner for Human Rights, the Inter-American Development Bank, the American Bar Association, the Organisation for Security and Co-operation in Europe and the US Agency for International Development.
49. See OHCHR (2006a, 2006b, 2006c, 2006d, 2006e).
50. Interview with UN official, April 2005.
51. See UNDP (2006).
52. Carlson (2006a), p. 14.
53. In his lessons-learned study, Scott Carlson calls for such a 'One UN Approach'; member states had also called for more coherent efforts since 2005.
54. On the latter question see Mani (2002).

1

Legal and judicial reform and the United Nations: Early practice and assumptions

This chapter has two main aims: firstly, it will introduce legal and judicial reform as an aspect of the UN's early peacebuilding efforts, and highlight that many of the initial reform decisions were taken largely *ad hoc*; and secondly, it aims to uncover the roots of the UN's assumptions about such reforms, especially as they were formed in the latter half of the 1990s. The chapter is thus divided into two sections. The first outlines the UN's legal and judicial reform efforts in Namibia, El Salvador, Cambodia, Somalia, Haiti, Rwanda and Bosnia. This discussion will demonstrate that the United Nations did indeed not have a particular approach when taking on such reforms. The second section goes on to show, however, how some aspects of this early experience, as well as some other factors, led to a crystallization of the organization's assumptions about the direction it should take when undertaking such reforms.

The UN's early legal and judicial reform efforts

As with many of its early post-conflict peacebuilding endeavours,[1] the UN's legal and judicial reform efforts were undertaken primarily *ad hoc*. The particular reform initiatives were not conceived as part of a legal and judicial reform strategy. Instead, the measures were taken on a case-by-case basis, they were not wide-reaching and, due to the UN's limited mandates and frequent local political opposition, they largely failed to

United Nations justice: Legal and judicial reform in governance operations
Trenkov-Wermuth, United Nations University Press, 2010, ISBN 978-92-808-1173-5

address adequately the wider legal and judicial needs of the particular society hosting the UN operation.

In Namibia the United Nations carried out what was the first, and one of the few moderately successful, legal reform endeavours of the early post–Cold War period. The UN Transitional Assistance Group (UNTAG) was heavily involved in the supervision of the abolition of various discriminatory laws: all in all, 56 distinct pieces of legislation, "some of the most egregious legal instruments of colonial repression and apartheid",[2] were either abolished or altered. Notwithstanding this significant alteration in the country's applicable law, however, the UN's limited mandate made it unable, despite persistent efforts, to overrule the administrator-general of the territory on the country's system of ethnic administration, which was entrenched through the country's AG-8 law; the law remained in place throughout Namibia's transitional period, on the grounds that repealing it early would not only demand a complete restructuring of local administration but would demand it at a time when Namibia was on the eve of elections, and had neither the time nor the resources to devote to such an endeavour.[3] The UN's other main legal reform efforts in Namibia were in the realm of drafting the electoral laws needed for the country's first elections; this drafting was a success, and became a model for the UN's similar task in its mission to Cambodia.

In El Salvador, one of the primary non-security objectives of the UN Observer Mission in El Salvador (ONUSAL) was the task of aiding the reform of the judicial system. However, the UN's role was relatively limited: ONUSAL was not given direct responsibility for judicial administration, and its mandate only called on it "to offer its support to the judicial authorities of El Salvador in order to help improve the judicial procedures for the protection of human rights and increase respect for the rules of due process of law".[4] Essentially, the mission was limited to "commenting on legislation; using good offices to solve problems at the local level; and advising authorities on judicial procedure and investigative techniques".[5] But it encountered "significant difficulties"[6] with its judicial reform efforts, in part as a result of local opposition to such reforms by politicians and senior members of the judiciary, and partly because it lacked an adequate mandate for institutional reform; thus the UN's own impact on judicial reforms was only "minimal".[7]

In order to fill the gaps on judicial reform left in the Mexico Agreement of 1991,[8] and make up for the deficiencies caused by its weak judicial reform mandate, the United Nations tried to influence the judicial reform process in El Salvador in several other ways. The first was through the Truth Commission, which it helped to establish and which was responsible for investigating and documenting human rights abuses committed by all parties involved in the conflict, and for making recommendations to the government.[9] The commission made various far-reaching recommendations, including the voluntary resignation of all Supreme Court justices and major Supreme Court reforms.[10] However, the Salvadoran government's response was "dismissive"[11] and few of the commission's recommendations were implemented: the Supreme Court justices declared their intention to stay in office,[12] and President Cristiani said that the report "[did] not respond to the wishes of the Salvadorans who [sought] to forgive and forget everything having to do with that very sorrowful past", arguing also that the commission had exceeded its powers in writing these recommendations.[13]

ONUSAL and the Salvadoran government also established another body, namely the Joint Group for the Investigation of Politically Motivated Illegal Armed Groups – that is, the so-called "death squads".[14] The joint group, which was composed of two candidates selected by President Cristiani, the human rights ombudsman of El Salvador and the director of ONUSAL's Human Rights Division, noted that such squads were still in existence after the 1991 peace process, and that the justice system "continued to provide a margin of impunity these structures require".[15] Essentially, though, no prosecutions or dismissals for involvement in these death squads resulted from the group's efforts.

There were several other efforts at judicial reform: ONUSAL organized judicial training seminars, and its Human Rights Division, along with the Truth Commission, made various recommendations on the judicial system's independence and effectiveness, as well as on judicial impartiality and competence; however, such efforts had "little impact".[16] Thus ONUSAL's attempts to reform the judiciary, through its mandated activities, its efforts as part of the Joint Group and its involvement with the Truth Commission, were on the whole unsuccessful. The UN's failed judicial reform efforts, and the "culture of impunity"[17] which neither the United Nations nor the Truth Commission was able to address, influenced some of the UN's later assumptions about how to conduct legal and judicial reform.[18]

The UN's legal and judicial reform efforts in Cambodia were equally unsuccessful. While the civil administration mandate of the UN Transitional Authority in Cambodia (UNTAC) included neither supervision nor control of the justice system, which remained firmly in the control of the Cambodian executive,[19] the mandate did include the task of assisting Cambodia's Supreme National Authority with judicial reform prior to the elections.[20] Furthermore, the Paris Agreement provided UNTAC with an unprecedented "intrusive and authoritative" mandate not only to implement universal human rights but also to oversee human rights, to investigate and engage in "corrective action" in regard to human rights violations and to prevent a return to "the policies and practices of the past" – that is, to genocide.[21]

This highly ambitious mandate was not matched with the resources which would have made its fulfilment possible: only 10 officers were assigned to the UNTAC human rights component in the initial planning of the mission, and eventually only one human rights officer was assigned to each of the 21 Cambodian provinces, with 10 additional officers sitting in Phnom Penh.[22] UNTAC completely failed to fulfil its role of fostering an environment in which human rights would be respected, and also in its "corrective" role.[23] To begin with, human rights violations continued largely unchecked; moreover, UNTAC decided to draft provisions relating to the judiciary, as well as to criminal law and criminal procedure, since the Vietnamese-drawn criminal code and criminal procedure code were deemed to be "woefully unworkable to achieve the UN's fundamental objectives".[24] But UNTAC's legal code was composed hastily, was not written by lawyers and ended up being in itself "seriously deficient":[25] for instance, assault was not punishable as an offence unless it led to an injury that either lasted six months or was permanent; furthermore, an absence of consent was not incorporated as an element of the crime of rape.[26]

Cambodia's Supreme National Council, which was designated in the Paris Peace Agreements as the body that would have domestic authority and sovereignty, did adopt the UN criminal law and criminal procedure code in 1992. However, the ruling Cambodian People's Party was upset with the adoption of this code, and decided quickly to approve its own criminal procedure code in 1993, which came to be known as the State of Cambodia Law on Criminal Procedure, or SOC Law.[27] Both codes applied throughout the 1990s, causing much confusion as to the applicable law, but the absence of a judicial framework, and the UN's failure to institute such a framework, meant that UNTAC was unable to carry out corrective actions.

UNTAC did take a "revolutionary step" in appointing its own special prosecutor[28] in response to mounting human rights violations and political violence, and the unwillingness of the local authorities to prosecute suspects.[29] But for reasons of neutrality and human rights, UNTAC was unable to rely on the State of Cambodia's (SOC) prison, court and police system. At the same time, however, UNTAC did not have its own prisons initially, and it lacked a court system. And even after UNTAC created the first UN detention centre, and the special prosecutor was able to issue warrants for arrest against those who committed atrocities and human rights violations, he had no way of prosecuting such individuals: the mission's civilian police component (CIVPOL) was unarmed, UNTAC's military force interpreted its mandate as lacking enforcement powers for this purpose and, more importantly, UNTAC lacked a functioning judiciary.[30]

Furthermore, after a few initial court appearances, Cambodian courts refused to hear the special prosecutor; thus the effort of establishing this UN special prosecutor position faltered.[31] So the United Nations found itself in a situation where it was expected to protect human rights and re-establish law and order, but it had no functioning court system which could help it to do so; the absence of a judicial framework was the "single largest cause of the failures UNTAC experienced in public security", and also resulted in the UN's holding of detainees in violation of their *habeas corpus* rights.[32] While the United Nations was able to create the first UN detention centre and the position of the first UN special prosecutor, it failed in establishing what was needed equally as much, namely a judiciary.

Gareth Evans, Australia's former foreign minister, who was involved in initiating the UN peace plan for Cambodia, summarized the UN's judicial failures in Cambodia quite aptly:

> The point is simply that if a peace keeping force is given a mandate to guard against human rights violations, but there is no functioning system to bring violators to justice – even those who violate others' right to life – then not only is the UN force's mandate to that extent unachievable, but its whole operation is likely to lose credibility.[33]

Thus UNTAC's experience in Cambodia identified the criminal justice system as one area where the United Nations needed to provide significantly more resources than it had, and that meant "a body of applicable law; an effective police force; an independent judiciary; prosecutors and defenders; correctional facilities; and gaolers".[34]

Even though on the whole the UN's legal and judicial reform efforts failed, UNTAC's human rights component did succeed in pushing the Supreme National Council to adopt the key human rights covenants, and the mission made a positive legal reform contribution with its efforts to draft an electoral law.[35] The UN's prior experience with drafting such a law in Namibia in 1989 and 1990 served as a model for UNTAC, which went on to devise procedures and regulations for electoral administration, outline requirements for voter and political party registration, establish guidelines for polling and the recoding of electoral results and stipulate a code of conduct for participants in the electoral process, all as part of this electoral law effort.[36]

While it was operating in Cambodia, the United Nations also became involved with legal and judicial reforms in Somalia. Security Council

Resolution 814 (1993) had empowered the special representative of the Secretary-General (SRSG) to assist in "the re-establishment of national and regional institutions and civil administration in the entire country ... [and the] restoration and maintenance of ... law and order".[37] When the Unified Task Force (UNITAF) handed over its responsibilities for Somalia to UNOSOM on 4 May 1993, the then SRSG, Admiral Howe, took this task seriously, and given that there was no Somali transitional government that he could *assist*, he decided to declare that UNOSOM II would enforce the Somali penal code of 1962.[38] UNOSOM II's Justice Division proceeded to draw up a detailed plan and budget for police and judicial reforms; the court structure that was to be established was modelled on Somalia's 1962 three-tiered judicial system, meaning that there were to be 21 district courts, seven regional courts and two courts of appeal – one in Mogadishu and one in Hargeisa.[39]

While the then Under-Secretary-General for Peacekeeping Operations, Kofi Annan, approved this plan, he felt that local, regional and district councils would first need to be set up, so that they could have supervisory authority over the police and the judiciary, before funding for justice sector reforms should be requested from donor countries; Annan failed to inform SRSG Howe of this decision, and Howe worked on the assumption that Annan and the Department of Peacekeeping Operations (DPKO) were in the process of implementing the funding and staffing requirements for the overall justice plan.[40] According to Ganzglass, "Annan's decision, which was not required by Resolution 814, was strategically flawed and fatal to the Justice Program."[41] Apart from the fact that Resolution 814 did not specifically say that regional councils must be formed prior to any police and judicial reforms, Ganzglass argues that it was up to the admiral to decide how and when to proceed on such reforms, and furthermore that the Security Council's intent was clearly to give priority to justice sector reforms.[42]

In June 1993 the conflict with Aided broke out, effectively preventing the efforts to establish councils in Mogadishu; however, Ganzglass believes that the door to justice sector reforms in other parts of the country still stood wide open, and accuses Annan and the DPKO of failing to make requests for any donations for such efforts.[43] Justice sector reforms were to be, in the words of Admiral Howe, UNOSOM's "ticket out of Somalia",[44] but as Ganzglass puts it, the "'ticket out' was never even purchased".[45] While the DPKO did eventually attempt to gather funds for this effort, it was the initial failure to seek funds for police and judicial reform which killed the UNOSOM justice programme.[46]

While the United Nations was trying to deal with Somalia, it also set up a joint mission with the Organization of American States (OAS) in Haiti in April 1993 – the UN/OAS International Civilian Mission in Haiti

(MICIVIH). In late 1993 MICIVIH became involved with legal and judicial reforms: it began with identification of the particular deficiencies in the judicial system,[47] and eventually expanded its work to a judicial assistance programme which provided technical assistance, advisory services and training, and assisted with the work to end impunity and also with mission activities regarding the police and prison authorities which had a judicial dimension.[48] Given that MICIVIH had limited resources for its judicial reform efforts, the mission did a "respectable job"; but the judiciary nevertheless remained relatively weak and inefficient, and impunity prevailed.[49]

The UN's judicial reform efforts in Rwanda were relatively minimal, and came primarily in the form of recommendations on areas for improvement. After the chaos that ensued with the flight of the Forces Armées Rwandaises and the Rwandan government, the judicial system was virtually destroyed.[50] The newly established government, set up by the Rwandese Patriotic Front, had no means in terms of human or physical resources to restore the rule of law to the country.[51] The UN Human Rights Field Operation in Rwanda (HRFOR) conducted an assessment of the tasks that needed to be completed,[52] but the UN's judicial reform efforts in Rwanda did not go much beyond the drafting of reports. Although international donors did respond to this crisis, provided materials for the rebuilding of courthouses and offered legal texts and basic supplies, as well as some legal training and advice to the Ministry of Justice, the judiciary's ethos was not restored.[53]

Despite some progress, such as the successful launch of the National Awareness Campaign on the Judicial System in October 1996, HRFOR noted its concern about the shortcomings in the administration of justice: "not only was there a serious shortage of judges, clerks and material resources for the courts, and a shortage of defence lawyers, but there had also been serious allegations that the military of Rwanda had acted in contravention of judicial orders".[54] By early 1997 it also emerged that some defendants had no access to legal counsel, and that most judicial officials had only had four months' training. But while its reports were helpful, the United Nations did not get seriously involved with judicial reforms in Rwanda, and failed to recognize publicly and address various other judicial problems, such as the trend of ethnic recruitment (i.e. largely Tutsi to the exclusion of Hutu) into the judiciary – a trend that significantly undermined judicial impartiality in Rwanda.[55]

The UN Mission in Bosnia and Herzegovina (UNMIBH) was the last instance prior to the UN's involvement in Kosovo where the organization had to undertake judicial reforms without being fully in charge of such reforms. Security Council Resolution 1184 (1998) mandated UNMIBH to create a programme to monitor and assess the Bosnian court system as part of an overall package of legal reforms coordinated by the Office of the High Representative.[56] The programme that was set up – the Judicial System Assessment Program (JSAP) – consisted of a number of teams of local and international lawyers, and carried out numerous assessments of the legal institutions in Bosnia.[57] Having successfully charted the key weaknesses in the legal system, the JSAP published a series of reports on the matter, making a number of recommendations.

Towards the end of 2000, however, the JSAP's responsibilities were transferred to an independent judicial commission within the Office of the High Representative, and thus the UN's judicial reform role was nearly terminated. In order to retain some judicial reform function, UNMIBH established a criminal justice advisory unit, which was to foster cooperation between the police and the criminal justice system. The unit monitored key court cases, acted as a liaison between the police and the judiciary, advised the International Police Task Force on procedural matters related to the legal process and helped train the local police in implementation of various criminal procedures. On the whole, UNMIBH had a relatively limited role in Bosnia, and the impact which the United Nations could have on the judicial reform process was therefore also limited.

The discussion above has demonstrated that while the United Nations did clearly undertake various legal and judicial reform endeavours, these early efforts were not part of a particular legal and judicial reform strategy, but were begun *ad hoc* and had at best a modest impact in the missions where they were carried out. As the following section will demonstrate, this negative experience, along with a few other factors, was responsible for the UN's development of certain key assumptions about how to undertake legal and judicial reform.

The assumptions about legal and judicial reform

Since the United Nations did not publish official reports on legal and judicial reform during the 1990s, and there is no public access to UN internal communications and documents,[58] the rationales behind the assumptions the United Nations made and the changes it implemented in regard to legal and judicial reform at the end of the 1990s are not documented. However, the UN's justice sector reform practice in its governance operations provides an indication of how the organization interpreted its early experience, and the lessons that it learned from it. This section attempts to explain the potential motivations and rationales behind five key assumptions the United Nations made, which led to the eventual adoption of a particular approach to legal and judicial reform.

Application of previously applicable laws

The failures of UNTAC's hastily drafted and enacted laws, which were unable to fulfil the UN's own basic standards,[59] did not push the United Nations in the direction of applying a pre-prepared *off-the-shelf* or *generic* criminal code and criminal procedure code in post-conflict societies, as Evans and Plunkett had recommended.[60] Instead, it adopted the principle that any applicable law chosen for a territory must be based on legal codes that have previously applied in that territory, and which are thus rooted in local legal and cultural customs, and potentially familiar to some in the local population. But why did the United Nations come to favour, and still favours,[61] selecting an applicable law that is based on prior legal codes?

A potential clue as to its reasoning is provided in a statement by an expert panel that was convened after the "Report of the Panel on United Nations Peace Operations" (the Brahimi Report) called on the Secretary-General on 21 August 2000 to:

> Evaluate the feasibility and utility of developing an interim criminal code, including any regional adaptations potentially required, for use by such operations pending the re-establishment of local rule of law and local law enforcement capacity.[62]

This panel of experts concluded in less than two months that it:

> Doubted whether it would be practical, or even desirable given the diversity of countries' specific legal traditions, for the Secretariat to try to elaborate a model criminal code, whether worldwide, regional or civil or common law based, for use by future transitional administration missions.[63]

This statement, which was made on 20 October 2000, less than two months after the Brahimi Report called on the Secretary-General to look into this matter, appears to have been a foregone conclusion, rather than a conclusion based on any serious research initiated after the report was published. Some of the members of this panel, which was to include "international legal experts, including individuals with experience in United Nations operations that have transitional administration mandates",[64] were some of the same individuals who advised the United Nations on the choices of the applicable law for prior UN operations; once it sets up a roster of experts in a particular field, the United Nations tends to seek their advice for many different missions and reports. The experts' statement shows that there was clearly a perception in 2000, and probably also much earlier, that the development of an interim legal code would be neither practicable nor desirable, for the stated reasons, but arguably also because the UN's failure to draft adequate laws in Cambodia meant that it should shun further law-drafting activities.

But apart from the fact that the "diversity of countries' specific legal traditions" and the failures in Cambodia suggested to some that a UN criminal law would be impracticable, the United Nations arguably also based its assumption about the need to use previously applicable laws on several other factors – historical precedents of legal and judicial reform in post-conflict societies, the law of belligerent occupation, practical considerations and the ideology of legitimacy. The assumption that legal and judicial reforms must be based on local legal traditions and customs has several precedents during the twentieth century. Notably, the Allies made such an assumption in Germany after the Second World War: they reinstated the penal code of 1871, the Court Organisation Act of 1877 and the Code of Criminal Procedure of 1877, as well as all later amendments, and chose to eliminate only the discriminatory laws of the Nazi regime and any sections of laws that reflected Nazi ideas.[65] Moreover, even though he himself clearly placed a significant stamp on the new Japanese constitution, General Douglas MacArthur nevertheless began legal reforms in Japan after the Second World War on the basis of the 1889 Meiji constitution.[66] Such precedents would leave few UN practitioners in two minds about the notion that even where significant justice sector reforms need to be undertaken, the basic legal framework must be rooted in a society's prior legal traditions and codes.

The assumption was also consistent with the requirements of the law on belligerent occupation regarding the choice of law for an occupied territory: the idea of continuity of the legal system is a fundamental principle of the law of occupation, as had been expressed in Article 43 of the Hague Regulations[67] and Article 64 of Geneva Convention IV (GC IV).[68] While the United Nations did not equate to an occupying power *de jure* in administering a territory internationally, selecting the path most consistent with international legal requirements on the administration of a post-conflict territory seemed sensible, particularly given the UN's previous and failed attempts to draft UN laws in Cambodia.

Also, there were some *practical* reasons behind the assumption: Hansjoerg Strohmeyer,[69] for instance, argues that the decision to apply the laws in Kosovo and East Timor that had applied immediately prior to the adoption of Security Council Resolutions 1244 (1999) and 1272 (1999),[70] respectively, was made "solely for practical reasons"[71] of avoiding a legal vacuum in the initial phase of the mission, and also to avoid the need for local lawyers, most of whom had obtained their qualifications at domestic universities, to be introduced to a new legal system. The discussion so far shows that *practical* reasons were not the only ones, even if they certainly affected the assumption. Finally, applying a previously applicable legal code was also consistent with the UN's ideology of legitimacy – that is, the notion that its actions must be perceived as legitimate if they are to be effective. Any legal reforms would seem less forced and more legitimate if they are rooted in prior legal traditions, since they would be perceived locally as less of an imposition from the outside; this would significantly increase the chances that they may be accepted, thereby making the UN's task of *selling* such a legal code much easier.

Implementation of human rights standards within the legal framework

The United Nations also made the assumption that it should incorporate international human rights standards and principles as part of the legal framework. This assumption followed naturally from the organization's broad obligations under the UN Charter regarding human rights. Article 1(3) states that one of the fundamental purposes of the United Nations is "To achieve international cooperation in ... promoting and encouraging respect for human rights and for fundamental freedoms ...";[72] similarly, Article 55 sets out the UN's obligation to promote "human rights" to help foster "stability and well-being".[73] Various other articles also hint at this key role for the United Nations in the area of promoting human rights, and since the early days of the organization it has worked to encourage states to adopt and adhere to the various conventions, covenants, treaties, charters, articles and other documents that make up the international human rights regime.

Thus it is not surprising that, in undertaking legal and judicial reforms, the United Nations would set out to promote human rights by arguing, for instance, for the adoption of international human rights instruments as part of a legal framework, and for the observance of human rights standards as part of the judicial process. However, the assumption that international human rights instruments must be incorporated into the local legal frameworks, and that the judiciary must uphold international human rights standards, only reflected the broad strategic objectives of the organization in promoting human rights, rather than a carefully devised strategy for legal and judicial reform.

Establishment of a regular court structure

In respect of the court structure, the United Nations assumed that the best course of action is either to allow the functioning of the regular courts to continue if they are still in existence or, if they have ceased to function, to re-establish the regular court structure of the territory. As with the choice of law, the law of belligerent occupation influenced the UN's choice of court system: GC IV requires that "the tribunals of the occupied territory shall continue to function in respect of all offences covered by the said laws",[74] and the UN's assumption was consistent with this requirement. Furthermore, the historical precedent for establishing post-conflict court structures was exactly that: once the Western Allies occupied Germany, they permitted German courts to function in the same configuration as they had done before and during the war. So there was a precedent that in governing territories, one does permit the courts to continue functioning as they have before, and this precedent did not escape the United Nations. The basic assumption about post-conflict judicial reconstruction was thus that in carrying out this function, the United Nations must indeed re-establish the regular court system rather than establish a new type of system.

Prosecution of past atrocities

The UN's stance in the latter half of the 1990s, that there is a need to end impunity for past atrocities, influenced its overall approach to judicial reform. The Nuremberg and Tokyo war crimes trials that followed the Second World War set a good precedent for addressing war crimes and genocide, but similar atrocities committed in the subsequent 50 years went largely unpunished. Various international legal instruments[75] were created in order to address such crimes, but until relatively recently "Nations ... honoured these obligations largely in the breach."[76]

As some states overthrew their dictators and authoritarian regimes in Southern Europe in the 1970s, Latin America in the 1980s and Eastern and Central Europe in the late 1980s and early 1990s, they entered a process of transition, and with this process came deliberations about the ways in which past atrocities could be addressed.[77] In particular, politicians and academics deliberated how best to balance the "legal and moral imperative of rendering justice for past atrocities"[78] with the various political constraints that a transition brings.[79] During the 1980s the order of the day was to grant amnesties for past human rights abuses,[80] and to establish truth commissions in order to address such abuses, deal with questions of the *disappeared*, help along the process of national reconciliation and healing, and set the historical record straight.[81] By and large, crimes went unpunished.

In the 1990s, however, this pattern began to change. Impunity did remain a major problem: even though various peace agreements made in the early 1990s, such as those for El Salvador and Guatemala, included provisions requiring individual accountability, amnesties were nevertheless granted; and quite commonly peace agreements did still include amnesty provisions, and amnesty laws were passed for the past crimes of various governments in Latin America and Africa.[82] However, the notion that prosecutions and punishment of atrocities are vital for a lasting peace in a post-conflict society, in that they hold the potential to end cycles of violence and strengthen democracy, began to dominate not only the debate over whether to have an amnesty-oriented or prosecutions-oriented transitional justice policy,[83] but also the debate on rule-of-law reform more broadly. Overall, the issue of accountability occupied the international community's time and resources more than any other matter related to justice sector reform.

While there was general agreement that amnesties should not be granted for either ongoing or future atrocities, the issue of how to address past atrocities was divisive. Various human rights groups,[84] victims' associations, some UN agencies and various observers came to believe that the punishment of criminal offences is the best insurance against any future repression.[85] Academics also became increasingly persuaded by the notion that atrocities must be prosecuted.[86] On the other hand, officials in states undergoing political transitions felt that holding the perpetrators of past atrocities liable for their crimes undermines and endangers the transition to democracy, and should therefore be either partially or completely limited.[87]

By the mid-1990s the attitudes towards the prosecution of past atrocities and the holding of war crimes trials had changed sufficiently in the international community to allow the establishment of the International Criminal Tribunal for the Former Yugoslavia (ICTY) and the International Criminal Tribunal for Rwanda (ICTR) for the atrocities committed during the break-up of Yugoslavia and the genocide committed in Rwanda, respectively. These *ad hoc* tribunals were the first serious attempt since the Nuremberg and Tokyo trials to bring war criminals to justice. The international community was apparently persuaded by the notion that some crimes must not go unpunished if there is to be a lasting peace. The United Nations itself became vocal about the need to end impunity, demanding accountability for past atrocities: on visiting the ICTY in 1997, UN Secretary-General Kofi Annan declared that "Impunity cannot be tolerated, and will not be. In an interdependent world, the rule of law must prevail."[88] Furthermore, he also hailed 17 July 1998, when the Rome Statute for the International Criminal Court (ICC) was adopted, as "the day the world finally united to bring an end to the culture of impunity" and said it sent "a message to those who would commit these heinous crimes that you have nowhere to hide; you will be made accountable".[89]

But if the respective positions of the UN Human Rights Committee, the UN General Assembly's resolution on Guatemala and the UN

Secretariat's policy on the 1996 Abidjan Agreement for Sierra Leone are any indication, the organization's stance on impunity and granting amnesties was not at all coherent in the early to mid-1990s. In the first instance, the Human Rights Committee had already condemned amnesties in 1992 by highlighting their negative impact on states' respect for the prohibition against torture;[90] by 1996 it expressed its disapproval of blanket amnesties more generally.[91] However, in 1996 the General Assembly failed to condemn amnesties for Guatemala, adopting instead a weak resolution which recognized "the commitment of the Government and civil society of Guatemala to advance in the fight against impunity and towards the consolidation of the rule of law".[92] Furthermore, the United Nations, which acted as the *moral guarantor* at the signing of the peace in Abidjan in 1996, made no comments about the amnesty granted to the Revolutionary United Front (RUF) under the agreement, which included the clause that "the Government of Sierra Leone shall ensure that no official or judicial action is taken against any member of the RUF ... "[93]

By the time of the Lome Agreement for Sierra Leone in 1999, however, the United Nations had changed its position: a similar clause in the agreement led a UN representative to comment on the document that "The United Nations holds the understanding that the amnesty provisions of the Agreement shall not apply to the international crimes of genocide, crimes against humanity, war crimes and other serious violations of international humanitarian law."[94] This statement clearly demonstrates the shift in the UN's position on impunity by the end of the 1990s; arguably, the position crystallized with the arrival of Kofi Annan and his administration in 1997.

By the end of the 1990s the acknowledgement of and pursuit of the truth about past atrocities were considered by many professionals and academics as key for a lasting peace. But the UN's preference was for some form of trials to take place wherever possible, and for truth commissions to be complementary to a trial mechanism, rather than for them to act as the only mechanism for addressing past atrocities along with the granting of amnesties. As the case-study chapters will amply demonstrate, the UN's assumption that an end to impunity and the prosecution of the perpetrators of atrocities are vital for a sustainable peace significantly influenced the organization's approach to judicial reform in its governance operations.

Local participation in the judicial reform process

The final assumption about legal and judicial reform made by the United Nations is that the local population of the host territory should actively participate in the judicial reform process. This was logical, given that a reformed legal system can be sustainable after the departure of the international community only if it can rely on the consent and prior involvement of local jurists. Furthermore, the perception was arguably that the involvement of local actors in the judicial process, despite potential problems, was a political necessity. Firstly, failing to involve local actors in a practice as significant to post-war reconstruction as the judicial process, a process from which such actors may well have been excluded, may be perceived as an attempt to impose outside justice, and may lose the vital trust of the local community. And secondly, especially in instances where ownership over judicial administration would rest with the United Nations, involving local actors in the judicial process would perhaps alleviate some concerns about the extent of the powers the international community wields in the territory: it would give some level of ownership over the judicial process to local actors for the time during which sovereignty rests not with the nation but with the international community.

Notes

1. For more on the UN's peacebuilding endeavours see De Soto and Del Castillo (1994); Ratner (1995); Mayall (1996); Doyle, Johnstone and Orr (1997); Pugh (2000); Cousens and Kumar (2001); Chesterman (2004); Paris (2004); Caplan (2005); Dobbins et al. (2005). For the peacebuilding efforts of the UN's agencies see Whitman (1999). For theoretical discussions on peacebuilding see, for instance, Galtung (1976); Lederach (1997); Doyle and Sambanis (2000); Jeong (2002).
2. Dobbins et al. (2005: 39).
3. Ibid., p. 40.
4. San José Agreement 1992, "The Path to Peace", para. 14(h), cited in Wilkins (1997: 272).
5. Wilkins, ibid.
6. Dobbins et al. (2005: 53).
7. Wilkins (1997: 272).
8. "Mexico Agreement" – see Treaties list.
9. Dobbins et al. (2005: 59).
10. See UN Security Council (1993b), a report discussed in Dobbins et al. (2005: 60); see also UN Security Council (1993c). Other reform proposals included that all members of the judiciary, armed forces and civil service named in their report were to be dismissed; all persons named in the report were also to be disqualified from public office for a period of 10 years; and new legislation was to be adopted so that due process was guaranteed in the criminal justice system and the effectiveness of *habeas corpus* could be improved.
11. Johnstone (1997: 321).
12. Ibid.
13. President Cristiani, quoted here in Johnstone, ibid.
14. Dobbins et al. (2005: 60).
15. "Report of the Joint Group for the Investigation of Politically Motivated Illegal Armed Groups", UN Doc S/1994/989, 22 October 1994, p. 29, cited here in Dobbins et al. (2005: 60–61).

16. Dobbins et al. (ibid.: 61); see also Johnstone (1997: 332–335).
17. Johnstone (ibid.: 335).
18. For a further discussion of judicial reform efforts in Central and Latin America see Domingo and Sieder (2001).
19. Dobbins et al. (2005: 77).
20. Mani (2002: 54); for more on UNTAC see Berdal and Leifer (1996); Heininger (1994).
21. Doyle (1997: 146).
22. Ibid.
23. Ibid., p. 147.
24. Plunkett (1998: 69).
25. Plunkett (1994: 71).
26. Plunkett (1998: 69); on this see also Amnesty International (2002a).
27. Human Rights Watch (2003); on this see also Linton (2002: 100–101).
28. The special prosecutor was Mark Plunkett, an Australian barrister.
29. Doyle (1997: 147).
30. Ibid., p. 148.
31. Plunkett (1994: 72).
32. Doyle (1997: 148); *habeas corpus* is a Latin legal term, literally meaning "[We command that] you have the body", and refers to a detainee's right to be seen by a judicial authority within a short amount of time after his or her detention, so that the authority can rule on the legality of the detention.
33. Evans (1993: 110).
34. Ibid.
35. Dobbins et al. (2005: 85).
36. Ibid.
37. See UN Security Council (1993a), paras 4(c) and (d).
38. Ganzglass (1997: 29). Mark Plunkett (1998: 69) refers to this code as the former Italian penal code.
39. Ganzglass, ibid., p. 30.
40. Ibid.
41. Ibid.
42. Ibid., p. 31.
43. Ibid., pp. 31–32.
44. Ibid., p. 31.
45. Ibid., p. 33.
46. Ibid.
47. See MICIVIH (1994b); document cited in Mani (2002: 65).
48. See "Le projet d'appui à la Justice de la MICIVIH" (MICIVIH's assistance to the judiciary report), July 1998, and "Summary of the Report on the Justice System (French/English)", May 1996, both available at www.un.org/rights/micivih/renforen.htm.
49. Mani (2002: 65); on this see also Maguire (1996); O'Neill (1995).
50. HRFOR (1996: 2), cited in Mani (2002: 64).
51. Mani, ibid.
52. The particular tasks were as follows: "Refurbishing material needs; transportation; basic supplies; legal texts; recruiting and training judicial personnel; technical assistance; prisons; judicial and legal reform." See Mani, ibid.; see also HRFOR (1996: 4–12).
53. Mani, ibid.
54. UN Commission on Human Rights (1997), paras 157–158; the reference made is to a HRFOR report of October 1996.
55. See Common Security Forum (1997).

56. UN Security Council (1998), section 1. The Office of the High Representative was directly responsible to the Peace Implementation Council and was not a UN-related body.
57. See "Background Information on UNMIBH", available at www.un.org/Depts/dpko/missions/unmibh/background.html.
58. There is no transparency when it comes to UN internal documents and communications; while the United Nations frequently pushes for greater transparency in the operations of certain governments, no Freedom of Information Act applies to the UN's non-classified documents, memoranda and other internal communications.
59. Plunkett (1998: 69).
60. See Evans (1993: 56, 100); Plunkett, ibid.
61. UN Security Council (2004); the report indicates that the United Nations has not changed its position on this matter.
62. UN General Assembly and Security Council (2000b) (Brahimi Report), para. 83.
63. UN General Assembly and Security Council (2000c), para. 31.
64. Brahimi Report (UN General Assembly and Security Council, 2000b), para. 83.
65. Friedlander (2002).
66. For a good discussion of American constitutional reforms in Japan see Shoichi (1997).
67. See Uhler et al. (1958), particularly the commentary on Article 64. The reference here is to "Convention (IV) Respecting the Laws and Customs of War on Land and Its Annex: Regulations Concerning the Laws and Customs of War on Land" – see Treaties list.
68. "Convention Relative to the Protection of Civilian Persons in Time of War" – see Treaties list. Henceforth, the convention will be referred to as Geneva Convention IV; Article 64 states that "The penal laws of the occupied territory shall remain in force, with the exception that they may be repealed or suspended by the Occupying Power in cases where they constitute a threat to its security or an obstacle to the application of the present Convention."
69. Hansjoerg Strohmeyer was a legal adviser to the SRSG in Kosovo and the UN's principal legal adviser in East Timor between October 1999 and June 2000. He is currently chief of the Policy Development and Studies branch at the UN Office for the Coordination of Humanitarian Affairs (OCHA) at UN headquarters.
70. See UN Security Council (1999a, 1999e).
71. Strohmeyer (2001b: 58).
72. "Charter of the United Nations" – see Treaties list; henceforth UN Charter.
73. UN Charter, Article 55.
74. See Geneva Convention IV, Article 64.
75. For instance, the Genocide Convention, 1948; the Universal Declaration of Human Rights, 1948; the Geneva Conventions on the Laws of Armed Conflict, 1949, and their two additional Protocols of 1977; the Convention against Racial Discrimination, 1966; the Convention against Torture and Degrading Punishment, 1984. For a good overview of these documents and some introductory commentary see Roberts and Guelff (1989); Brownlie (1992).
76. Neier (1998: 75); cited in Mani (2002: 88).
77. Mani (ibid.: 89).
78. Ibid.
79. On this issue see generally Kritz (1995); Huyse (1995); McAdams (1997); Robertson (1999); Bass (2000); Hayner (2001).
80. Mani (2002: 89).
81. For more on the early truth commissions see Hayner (1994).
82. On this see Chesterman (2004: 158–161); see also Chesterman (2001b). Among the Latin American countries granting amnesties for past atrocities in the 1990s were Chile,

Brazil, Uruguay, Argentina, Nicaragua, Honduras, El Salvador, Haiti, Peru and Guatemala. More recently this pattern has been repeated in African countries, such as Côte d'Ivoire, South Africa, Algeria, Sierra Leone and Liberia.

83. Chesterman (2004: 161).
84. For instance, the NGO No Peace Without Justice has been pushing for an end to impunity; Amnesty International has also come to favour prosecutions for past atrocities.
85. Chesterman (2004: 161); see also Mani (2002: 89); Bassiouni (1996).
86. See, for instance, Orentlicher (1991); Roht-Arriaza (1996); Scharf (1996); Ratner (1999); Popkin (2000); for an opposing view see Osiel (2000).
87. Chesterman (2004: 161).
88. The statement can be found on the ICTY's website at www.un.org/icty/cases-e/factsheets/achieve-e.htm.
89. OCHA (2006).
90. Chesterman (2001b: 160).
91. Ibid.; see also UN Human Rights Committee (1996), para. 9.
92. See UN General Assembly (1996), para. 8, cited here in Chesterman (2001b: 160).
93. See Article 14 of the Abidjan Agreement – see Treaties list.
94. UN official, cited here in OCHA (2006).

2

Introduction to the case studies: Assessment criteria, case study guidelines and case selection

The central question of this book is whether the five main elements of the UN's approach to legal and judicial reform in its governance operations were suited to the task of establishing a sustainable legal system. This chapter[1] introduces the ways in which the book will address this question. First, the elements of the UN's approach are outlined, and the rationale behind the particular focus and methodology of the work is clarified. The criteria by which the sustainability of a legal system can be assessed are then introduced, and the general questions which will be asked of each case study are discussed. And finally some relevant terminology is explained, and a justification for the case-study selection is offered.

In order to answer the central question, the case-study chapters investigate the relationship between the likelihood of establishing a sustainable legal system within the territory under UN administration and the five elements of the UN's approach, which derive from the five assumptions about legal and judicial reform discussed in Chapter 1 and their subsequent implementation into practice. The five elements of the UN's approach are concordance of the applicable laws with prior legal codes from the beginning of a mission; completeness of the human rights catalogue from the beginning of a mission; reinstitution of a regular court system from the beginning of a mission; pursuit of prosecutions for past atrocities from the beginning of a mission; and local participation in the judicial process from the beginning of a mission and to the fullest extent possible. Thus the overarching question that Chapters 3 and 4 focus on is whether these five practical steps enhanced or diminished

United Nations justice: Legal and judicial reform in governance operations
Trenkov-Wermuth, United Nations University Press, 2010, ISBN 978-92-808-1173-5

the likelihood of establishing a sustainable legal system in the two cases where the United Nations directly governed a territory.

There are two main reasons why the relationship between these five elements and the likelihood of establishing a sustainable legal system is the key focus of the investigation. In the first instance, the main goal of peacebuilding, according to the United Nations, is "the creation of structures for the institutionalization of peace",[2] or put differently, the consolidation of peace for the purposes of preventing the recurrence of armed conflict. Thus the *sustainability* of the peace has become a key goal of peacebuilding efforts. Since a sustainable legal system is integral to the rule of law, and the rule of law is integral to a sustainable peace, investigating whether the UN's legal and judicial reform efforts help to establish a sustainable legal system is in turn important for the question of whether or not the UN's efforts are in fact helping to establish a sustainable peace. And secondly, the reason why the *likelihood* of establishing a sustainable legal system is evaluated is because judging outright success in creating such a sustainable system is difficult without the passing of a significant amount of time. However, judging the likelihood of sustainability is a somewhat easier undertaking, even when only a relatively short period of time has elapsed since the beginning and/or end of an operation.

Certainly, judging what constitutes a *sustainable* legal system – that is, a sustainable legal framework and sustainable judicial institutions – is a difficult challenge in its own right: in the first instance, the criteria by which one judges whether a legal system is sustainable will determine the direction of the entire discussion, so the inclusion or exclusion of certain criteria will prejudice the conclusions to a certain extent. Secondly, what may be necessary in the views of some for a sustainable legal system may in the view of others lead to the downfall of that very system. Given that it will not be possible to satisfy all expectations, the least controversial set of criteria needs to be chosen.

Essentially, the criteria of sustainability selected for this book fall into five categories. The first of these looks at the credibility of the legal framework – that is, the system of rules which governs the respective territory – and the credibility of the official administration of these rules, and judges the sustainability of the legal system on whether or not the system of rules that has been put in place violates any principles fundamental for the existence of a legal system, and whether the rules are administered in accordance with such principles. The second category of criteria assesses the effectiveness and correctness of the delivery of justice, judging the sustainability of the system on whether or not the workings of the judicial institutions and judicial personnel violate a set of judicial norms. The third category assesses the quality of the legal framework, judging the sustainability of that framework on the inclusion of the most fundamental and basic human rights. The fourth category of criteria evaluates the acceptability of the legal framework and the judicial institutions in the local community, judging the sustainability of the system on whether it is tolerable locally and whether it has taken root in the society. And the fifth and final category evaluates the viability of the legal system, judging its sustainability on whether or not it has negative implications for the security situation on the ground.

Criteria for assessing the sustainability of a legal system

With regard to the assessment of the legal framework and its administration, the first category, it is possible to turn to legal theory and look for criteria that legal positivists and adherents to natural law agree upon as fundamental to a system of legal rules and legal administration. One such set of criteria was developed by Lon Fuller in his work *The Morality of Law*.[3] They comprise eight principles of legality, which a legal system must not fail on if it is to be considered a legal system at all and thus also if it is to be sustainable; these will be discussed in the first subsection. Legal theory does not, however, provide a similarly comprehensive set of criteria by which the related judicial institutions and their workings, the second category for assessment, can be judged, and consequently such a set of criteria will be devised in the second subsection. The third subsection sets out a number of fundamental human rights standards and principles which should be part of a legal system if that system is to be sustainable. The fourth subsection sets out a few simple indicators which are used to judge whether a legal system has taken root in a particular society. And the fifth and final subsection sets out some indicators which are used to establish whether the legal system has negative security-related consequences.

Fuller's principles of legality

Despite the age-old dichotomy in legal philosophy over the content of law,[4] when it comes to the procedural idea of law-making, the adherents of the natural law tradition and legal positivists agree that a legal system needs to adhere to certain principles. Lon Fuller expounded these principles in *The Morality of Law*. What renders his work particularly appropriate for an evaluation of the international community's effort at legal reform is that Fuller wrote specifically about the attempt to "create and maintain a system of legal rules" and the ways in which such an attempt may fail; he describes his eight principles of legality in terms of "eight distinct routes to disaster":[5]

- the first and most obvious lies in a failure to achieve rules at all, so that every issue must be decided on an *ad hoc* basis
- a failure to publicize, or at least to make available to the affected party, the rules he is expected to observe
- the abuse of retroactive legislation, which not only cannot itself guide action but undercuts the integrity of rules prospective in effect, since it puts them under the threat of retrospective change
- a failure to make rules understandable
- the enactment of contradictory rules
- the enactment of rules that require conduct beyond the powers of the affected party
- introducing such frequent changes in the rules that the subject cannot orient his action by them
- a failure of congruence between the rules as announced and their actual administration.[6]

Fuller's key contention about these principles is that "a sufficiently gross departure from [them] ... would result in something that was not simply bad law, but not law at all".[7] Even Fuller's harshest critics agreed that the eight principles are necessary if a legal system is to exist.[8]

Thus we can agree that, without some minimal compliance with Fuller's precepts, there can be no legal system at all, and that a high degree of compliance with them is necessary if the legal system is to deserve recognition as efficient and effective. The fact that his principles are widely accepted as a standard upon which the relative success or failure of a legal system can be measured, and that they provide a common ground among positivists and adherents of the natural law tradition, means that they can also be used as objective criteria to assess the success of the UN's efforts to establish legal regimes in its governance operations.

Fuller, however, was no utopian; he admitted that perfect compliance with the precepts of legality is neither feasible nor desirable: a system "in which all eight of the principles of legality are realized to perfection, is not actually a useful target for guiding the impulse toward legality ... ".[9] His reasoning was based on the distinction he made between the *morality of duty* and the *morality of aspiration*. Fuller explains that:

> Because of the affirmative and creative quality of its demands, the inner morality of law lends itself badly to realization through duties, whether they be moral or legal. No matter how desirable a direction of human effort may appear to be, if we assert there is a duty to pursue it, we shall confront the responsibility of defining at what point that duty has been violated. It is easy to assert that the legislator has a moral duty to make his laws clear and understandable. But this remains at best an exhortation unless we are prepared to define the degree of clarity he must attain in order to discharge his duty ... All this adds up to the conclusion that the inner morality of law is condemned to remain largely a

morality of aspiration and not of duty. Its primary appeal must be to a sense of trusteeship and to the pride of the craftsman. [The one important exception to these observations] relates to the desideratum of making the laws known, or at least making them available to those affected by them. Here we have a demand that lends itself with unusual readiness to formalization.[10]

Thus, following Fuller, when it comes to assessing the legal reforms which the United Nations has undertaken, we have to assess not the extent to which the laws are, but the extent to which they fail to be, for instance, clear, non-contradictory, constant, etc. The important exception, as the statement above indicates, is that we need to assess whether the laws *are* promulgated.

While it is evident that the United Nations is operating in complex political environments, and that therefore it cannot expect to achieve the highest levels of excellence in establishing legal regimes, Fuller's argument that "total failure"[11] or "sufficiently gross departure"[12] from any of his principles results in something that is not a legal system nonetheless stands, and an assessment about the relative success of the UN's legal reform efforts must be made in that respect. Certainly, what constitutes "total failure" or "sufficiently gross departure" from any of these principles is a matter of dispute; nevertheless, what we must assess in the UN's efforts is whether there is a failure to aspire to achieve these criteria.

The judicial norms

Fuller's theoretically agreed-upon principles do not extend to the principles or norms a judiciary must not fail on in order to be considered a sound judicial system, and thus cannot be used to judge the UN's institutional reform efforts. It is therefore necessary to devise such a set of criteria. Fuller wrote about the aim to "create and maintain a system of legal rules", and the ways in which such an effort may fail; this can also be adopted for the goal of establishing and maintaining a judiciary, and the ways in which such an effort may also fail. The proposed 10 distinct routes to judicial disaster are as follows:

- a failure to establish a hierarchical institutional structure
- a failure to provide access to justice
- a failure to provide access to effective counsel
- a failure to provide an appeals procedure
- a failure to reach judgments impartially
- a failure to reach judgments independently
- a failure to hear cases within a reasonable amount of time
- a failure to deliver judgments within a reasonable amount of time
- a failure to provide adequate translation during trial proceedings

- a failure to deliver justice across different judicial bodies in a consistent manner.

A total failure in any of these 10 routes does not simply result in a badly functioning judiciary, but in something which cannot legitimately be considered a sustainable judicial system or a judiciary which the United Nations should wish to create or be associated with.

A brief explanation of the rationale for the inclusion of these criteria may prove helpful. Firstly, perhaps the most obvious failure in the effort to establish a judiciary is the failure to create a hierarchical institutional structure. Without such a structure, a judicial system cannot exist, and the structure needs to be hierarchical, meaning that there needs to be at least a two-tier judicial system, so as to make the norm of providing an appeals procedure meaningful – an appeal can only be filed if such a two-tier judicial structure is in place since a higher judicial body is needed for the review of an appeal.

Even if such a structure exists, unless it is accessible to the population at large, the efforts at establishing and/or reforming a judicial system also fail; what is meant here is that members of society should be able to seek redress through the justice system, but also physical access in terms of the infrastructure, as well as economic access, meaning that the poorest members of a society should be able to access the justice system. What is also meant is access for all minorities and both gender groups.[13] The provision of access to *effective* counsel is a key principle that must also be observed.[14] The important point is that defence counsel must be *effective*. For instance, it is not sufficient to provide a detainee with a defence attorney who does not hold adequate qualifications. Any failure in this respect would clearly render the defence ineffective, and would thus violate a defendant's right to a fair trial.

The right to an appeal is one of the key provisions of a fair trial.[15] In order to uphold this right, it is not sufficient to provide a mechanism through which such an appeal can be launched, such as a higher tribunal; what is needed are the means to make an appeal possible and meaningful. For instance, "an unreasonably short time frame for lodging an appeal and long delays in the appeal court rendering a judgement" are potential obstacles to the realization of this right.[16] Similarly, the failure to provide transcripts of court proceedings upon which an appeal can be launched would also render this right meaningless, since an appeals judge would be unable to review a case adequately.

Furthermore, judicial impartiality is vital to the legitimacy of a judiciary, as is judicial independence.[17] A failure to deliver justice impartially would undermine the entire basis for the existence of a judicial institution, and a lack of independence would render parts or the whole of the judicial system obsolete. Detainees also have the right to a trial without undue delay,[18] which "includes the right to receive a reasoned judgment (at trial and appeal) within a reasonable time".[19] But the question as to what constitutes a *reasonable* amount of time for the preliminary hearings on a case, the opening of a trial and the delivery of a judgment is difficult. Amnesty International explains that:

> What is a reasonable time is judged on the circumstances of the individual case. Elements to be considered include: national legislation, whether the accused is in custody ... the complexity of the case, the conduct of the accused and the conduct of the authorities. Trials lasting as long as 10 years have been deemed reasonable, while others lasting less than one year have been found to be unreasonably delayed.[20]

The circumstances in a post-conflict society complicate matters slightly, and what is a *reasonable* amount of time will depend on the particular social and political circumstances. However, the end of a violent conflict arguably heightens the desire which a society has for the quick delivery of justice, given that it would frequently have been deprived of such justice for an extended period of time. Thus a public perception of *unreasonable* delays in justice holds the potential to lead to a return to violence as a way of dispute resolution, since any disaffected parties may seek justice by other means, which would undermine not only judicial reforms but also peace.

The right to an interpreter and to adequate translation of documents is also vital,[21] not only for a detainee's right to understand the proceedings of a trial, but importantly also for the determination of a party's guilt or innocence, and for the provision of an adequate transcript, which is, as we saw, indispensable for the right to an appeal. And finally, an inability to deliver justice across different judicial bodies in a consistent manner would render a judicial system unjust; the location of a trial, the jurists involved in the trial and the particular court in which a trial takes place should have no bearing on the potential outcome of a case. If similar cases result in different outcomes depending on such factors, the judicial system would be operating inconsistently and thus unjustly, and would fail in its existential purpose, which is to deliver justice.

The fundamental human rights standards and principles

The issue as to whether one can judge the sustainability of a legal system on the inclusion of human rights standards and principles is contentious. In the first instance, legal positivists, who unlike natural lawyers do not believe that law must have a moral content in order to be considered law,[22] would take the stance that judging the sustainability of a legal system on what are essentially moral principles is wrong, and would reject the need for such an element as a measure of sustainability. Furthermore, many would argue that even where such principles are part of a legal framework, they may not be observed, as has been the case in many nations under dictatorship; this fact, it could be argued, renders the inclusion of such principles as a measure of sustainability obsolete.

However, the reason why these principles will be considered as a measure of sustainability is because it can be demonstrated that few legal regimes which failed to incorporate the most basic human rights principles have been sustainable in the long run. Whether we consider the legal regime in place under successive apartheid governments in South Africa or in any number of other similar regimes, eventually they do come to an end. Thus the inclusion of fundamental human rights principles as part of a legal framework will be treated as an indicator of long-term sustainability.

Some basic human rights standards and principles are outlined below, and the inclusion as part of a legal framework of articles which reflect the spirit, if not directly the letter, of each of these principles is a key criterion on which the sustainability of the framework is judged. But their inclusion as sustainability criteria does not suggest that they must all be implemented from the beginning of a mission;[23] rather, the UN's overall efforts for the incorporation of these principles within the respective legal frameworks will be assessed.

The 10 basic human rights principles which must be part of a legal system if it is to be sustainable are as follows.

- Everyone has the inherent right to life, liberty and security of person. This right shall be protected by law. No one shall be arbitrarily deprived of his life.[24]
- Everyone shall have the right to recognition everywhere as a person before the law.[25]
- No one shall be held in slavery or servitude; slavery and the slave trade shall be prohibited in all their forms.[26]
- No one shall be subjected to torture or to cruel, inhuman or degrading treatment or punishment.[27]
- All are equal before the law and are entitled without any discrimination to equal protection of the law.[28]
- No one shall be subjected to arbitrary arrest, detention or exile.[29]
- Everyone is entitled in full equality to a fair and public hearing by an independent and impartial tribunal in the determination of his rights and obligations and of any criminal charge against him.[30]
- Everyone has the right to freedom of thought, conscience and religion; this right includes freedom to change his religion or belief, and freedom, either alone or in community with others and in public or private,

to manifest his religion or belief in teaching, practice, worship and observance.[31]

- Everyone has the right to freedom of opinion and expression; this right includes freedom to hold opinions without interference and to seek, receive and impart information and ideas through any media and regardless of frontiers.[32]
- Everyone has the right to freedom of peaceful assembly and association.[33]

Articles 1–5 and 8 are non-derogable rights; Articles 6–7 and 9–10 are rights from which the United Nations can derogate, especially during the emergency phase of a mission.

The acceptability of the legal system in the local community

A key measure by which one can judge the sustainability of a legal system is whether or not it is acceptable to the community that is meant to be bound by it, and whether it has taken root in that community. Even if a legal system is in line with Fuller's principles of legality, the judicial norms and the human rights principles, if it is not acceptable, and if it has not taken root, then the chances that it will be sustainable are slim. Below are four key indicators which can be used to judge whether or not a legal system set up by the United Nations is acceptable to the community it is meant to apply to, and the extent to which, if at all, such a system has taken root in that community.

A legal system cannot be deemed to be acceptable, or to have taken root, if either during or soon after the departure of the UN mission there is/are:
- substantial changes to the legal framework and/or the judicial structure
- major competing or parallel legal frameworks and/or judicial mechanisms operating
- major public opposition to the legal framework or judicial structure
- major opposition to the legal framework and judicial structure by local jurists.

A brief explanation of these indicators is warranted: while changes to specific laws and the creation or termination of particular judicial mechanisms, for instance, would not be considered as *substantial changes*, a wholesale change to the basic legal code or to the entire judicial structure either during the UN's mission or upon the departure of the United Nations will be interpreted as an indication that the legal system has been rejected. However, the coming into force of a new constitution, which the United Nations has helped to shape, will not be considered as a substantial change. Furthermore, customary dispute resolution mechanisms and laws, for instance those present in some societies at the village or tribal level, will not be deemed as competing or parallel judicial mechanisms so long as there is a mechanism whereby disputed cases can be referred to the UN-backed judiciary. However, should the legal system be wholly absent from a province or large district of a host territory, as a result of which a parallel court system functions and a parallel legal framework applies, this will indicate that the legal system has not taken root and/or is not acceptable.

The stipulation that there should be no *major* public opposition to the legal framework or the judicial structure allows for a healthy level of opposition or debate on proposed changes to laws or procedures, as can be found in any society. However, it would count as *major* public opposition if, for instance, there were rejection by a significant proportion of an ethnic or religious minority group, or by a major political party which plays an important role in a territory's political life, of the established legal system. Finally, even if a population at large does not find the legal system objectionable, if the jurists meant to operate within it are opposed to it, it cannot function. But only instances where a substantial number of local jurists register opposition to the legal system will be counted as *major* opposition; thus individual judges, prosecutors or other lawyers bent on spoiling the legal and judicial reform process would not count as *major* opposition.

The viability of the legal system in terms of its security-related implications

The final measure by which the sustainability of a legal system can be assessed is whether or not it is viable in terms of its implications for the security situation on the ground. It is conceivable that the United Nations establishes a legal system that aggravates the security situation; if this is the case, that system cannot be deemed to be sustainable by virtue of the fact that it endangers the very peace which is essential for its existence. Below are three key indicators which can be used to judge whether the legal system as set up has aggravated the security situation.

A legal system has negative implications for security if it can be shown that:
- it exacerbates pre-existing tensions which have previously led to overt violence
- it creates new tensions which have the potential to lead to overt violence
- it directly causes overt violence.

Case-study guidelines

Terminology

The central question of this book, identified above, is whether the five key elements of the UN's approach to legal and judicial reform in its governance operations are suited for the goal of establishing a sustainable legal system. As the previous section has indicated, a *sustainable legal system* for the purposes of this book is comprised of a system of legal rules and a framework of judicial institutions which fundamentally violate neither Fuller's principles of legality nor any of the judicial norms, and which, short of a duty of fulfilling these criteria, positively aspire to be in line with them. Furthermore, a sustainable legal system is one which incorporates and observes the 10 human rights principles and shows no indications that it is not acceptable locally, or that it aggravates the security situation. The word *reform* is used in the broadest sense possible, and includes, for instance, efforts to reform and/or establish a particular institution from the ground up. And a *governance*-type UN operation is a mission where the Security Council has vested all sovereign powers normally associated with a state, i.e. executive, legislative and judicial powers over a certain territory, in that particular mission.

But what is meant by *legal and judicial* reform? International institutions use a variety of names to refer to programmes that have a rule-of-law component, such as *administration of justice, judicial reform, legal reform*, etc.[34] When discussing the international community's rule-of-law reform efforts, however, much of the literature fails to analyse comprehensively the different components of such efforts, and is not precise in the use of terminology. Rama Mani, for instance, only discusses the reform of what she calls the "tripod" or "triad" of institutions of the rule of law – that is the police, judiciary and prison service – to the exclusion of legal reforms.[35] Yet reforming the content of the legal framework, the applicable law, is as vital to rule-of-law reform as any institutional reforms. Furthermore, her terminology lacks clarity and definition, because the chapter in which she fails to discuss legal reforms is entitled "*Legal Justice: Order or the Rule of Law?*"[36]

Moreover, while much of the literature distinguishes between, for instance, police reform and judicial reform,[37] the distinction between judicial reform and legal reform is not always made, and the two are frequently discussed under the common rubric of justice reform or the international administration of justice.[38] But while the two are indeed related, a distinction between them is analytically useful, since the skills required to undertake such reforms, and the principles these reforms must follow, are different. Thus the phrase *legal and judicial reform* seeks consciously to highlight the fact that the book is not just about legal reform or judicial reform, but is interested in investigating both.

Methodology

The methodological approach most appropriate for this study is known as a "controlled comparison".[39] The premise behind this research strategy is that the "intensive analysis of a few cases may be more rewarding than a mere superficial statistical analysis of many cases".[40] Furthermore, it is designed for instances in which the universe of cases of a particular phenomenon is smaller than would be required for a statistical analysis, or when scholars wish to study particular causal mechanisms in greater depth than would be possible simply by examining statistical correlations.[41] Both of these apply to a study that focuses on legal and judicial reform as an aspect of UN governance: firstly, the number of governance operations where legal and judicial reforms were attempted is very limited; and secondly, the complex nature of such reforms certainly warrants careful attention to the particulars of each case.

The emphasis of the methodology is on a *structured* and *focused* comparative approach. It is focused because "it deals selectively with only certain aspects of the historical case" – in this instance legal and judicial reform as an aspect of a governance operation; and it is structured because "it employs general questions to guide the data collection and analysis of that historical case".[42] Thus one of the key tasks in employing this methodology is to formulate adequately the general questions one must ask of each case, so that the information derived directly contributes to answering the question at hand.[43]

The analysis of each case will broadly consider the impact of the five elements of the UN's approach to legal and judicial reform on the mission's efforts to establish a sustainable legal system. The assumption will be that if the elements are suited to the task, then they should not detract from the essential goal of establishing such a sustainable system. What is meant by *detract* here is that these elements should lead neither to a violation of Fuller's principles nor to a violation of the judicial norms, but instead should aspire to be in line with them. Moreover, the UN's efforts should not have failed in incorporating human rights principles as part of the legal framework. Finally, the UN's approach should not have led to any of the circumstances which indicate that the legal system is not acceptable locally, and no aspect of the approach should have aggravated the security situation on the ground. Any of these outcomes would clearly call into question the suitability of the approach to the stated aim.

The "data requirements to be satisfied in the analysis of the cases",[44] that is the specific questions to be asked in each of the cases in the controlled comparison, will be as follows.

- Did any of the five elements of the UN's approach lead to a violation of any of Fuller's eight principles of legality? And did the five elements demonstrate the UN's aspiration to be in compliance with Fuller's principles?
- Did any of the five elements lead to a violation of any of the 10 judicial norms? And did the five elements demonstrate the UN's aspiration to be in compliance with the judicial norms?
- Did any of the five elements lead to a failure on the part of the United Nations or the local community to incorporate the 10 basic human rights principles in the legal framework, or to a rejection of them as part of that framework?
- Did any of the five elements lead to any of the factors which indicate that the legal system has been rejected locally or has not taken root in the society?
- Did any of the five elements lead to any of the factors which indicate that the legal system has aggravated the security situation?

In answering the above questions, the analysis of the case studies will give us an indication as to whether the UN's legal and judicial reform efforts aided or detracted from the goal of establishing a sustainable legal system, and thus whether they enhanced or diminished the likelihood that such a system would be established. If the key elements of the approach detracted from the goal, that approach would need to be reconsidered.

Case selection

The reasons why *UN* operations in particular are chosen for this investigation were expounded in the Introduction; but essentially, as the most active peacebuilding body in the world, and as the organization which has been recently involved in legal and judicial reform in war-torn territories to the greatest extent, its particular methods merit close scrutiny: firstly, because its past efforts are likely to influence any similar reforms undertaken by the United Nations and other bodies in the future, and secondly because any such future endeavours are more likely than not to be UN-led once again. The particular interest in studying legal and judicial reform in *governance* operations stems from the fact that, while international territorial administration has emerged again as a method applied by the international community for addressing the aftermath of a conflict in a particular territory, the efforts to reform the legal framework and judicial institutions in such operations have not been studied comprehensively or in any depth.

The *universe* from which the cases can be selected are instances where the United Nations undertook some form of legal and judicial reform as part of a governance operation. All in all, the United Nations has had four governance operations to date: the UN Temporary Executive Authority (UNTEA) in West New Guinea, or West Irian, from 1962 to 1963;[45] the UN Transitional Administration for Eastern Slavonia, Baranja and Western Sirmium (UNTAES) from 1996 to 1998; the UN Transitional Administration in East Timor (UNTAET) from 1999 to 2002; and the UN Interim Administration Mission in Kosovo (UNMIK), which began in 1999 and has not ended yet. UN governance missions were previously envisioned for Trieste (1947), Jerusalem (1947) and Namibia (1967), but were never created.[46] Even though the United Nations had "extensive administrative prerogatives"[47] in the Congo during its mission there between 1960 and 1964 (ONUC), it did not hold sovereign powers. And while the Paris Peace Agreement for Cambodia envisioned that the United Nations would exercise direct control over five key administrative responsibilities of each of the four warring factions,[48] the United Nations never did exercise such direct control as a result of a host of problems, and UNTAC's role was scaled down to the supervision and monitoring of the factions' activities.[49]

From the UN's four governance operations, it was only as part of UNMIK and UNTAET that the organization undertook legal and judicial reforms. The United Nations only briefly administered the territory of West Irian after the Netherlands withdrew in 1962, prior to handing over responsibility for the territory to Indonesia in 1963.[50] Other than its quiet acquiescence to an Indonesian-led and rigged popular consultation with representative councils, which unsurprisingly voted unanimously in favour of remaining with Indonesia after its occupation of the former Dutch colony, the United Nations had no undertakings of any major significance.[51] And in Eastern Slavonia the UN's primary responsibility was to govern the territory until it could be reintegrated into Croatia;[52] given that the ultimate aim of the mission was to administer the region until Croatia was in a position to extend its sovereign authority over the territory, no attempts were made to implement any justice sector reforms. The UN executive largely left the administration of the region to the Serbs, opting only occasionally to override certain decisions when it saw this as necessary.[53] Thus the two case studies at the centre of this work select themselves: they are UNMIK and UNTAET, two missions which saw the United Nations attempt to establish a new legal system virtually "from the ground up".[54]

What makes an investigation of the UN's approach to legal and judicial reform in these cases interesting is that both are quite different. While the East Timor mission was a case of UN governance in a territory which was designated to become a new state, and which was emerging from a two-decade-long illegal occupation, the Kosovo mission is a case of UN governance in a territory whose ultimate political status was uncertain. Looking at the reforms in cases which are politically different will demonstrate the relative feasibility of using a similar reform method in politically differing cases. Furthermore, looking at two cases rather than just one is useful not only because it helps to confirm that, despite some minor differences in the UN's approach to justice sector reforms in both of these missions, there was indeed a broad pattern to that approach, but also because it helps to draw analytical comparisons between the reasons for the relative successes and failures of that approach.

Notes

1. This chapter is modelled on Roland Paris's (2004: 55–62) similarly entitled chapter in his book *At War's End: Building Peace After Civil Conflict*.
2. UN General Assembly and Security Council (1995), para. 49; cited in Paris (ibid.: 56).
3. See Fuller (1969: 38–39).
4. While natural lawyers argue that law must necessarily have a moral element, and that what the law *is* cannot be separated from what the law *should be*, legal positivists argue that law and morality are two separate realms, focusing instead on what the law *is*.
5. Fuller (1969: 38).
6. Ibid.
7. Ibid., pp. 38–39.
8. Fuller (ibid.: 197–198) cites the responses of his most respected opponents.
9. Ibid., p. 41.
10. Ibid., pp. 42–43.
11. Ibid., p. 39.
12. Ibid.
13. For instance, "International Covenant on Civil and Political Rights" (ICCPR) – see Treaties list; Article 14(1) states that "In the determination of any criminal charge against him, or of his rights and obligations in a suit at law, everyone shall be entitled to a fair and public hearing by a competent, independent and impartial tribunal established by law." See also, for instance, Article 6.1 of the "European Convention on Human Rights" – see Treaties list.
14. See "Basic Principles on the Role of Lawyers" – see Treaties list; Principle 1 states that "All persons are entitled to call upon the assistance of a lawyer of their choice to protect and establish their rights and to defend them in all stages of criminal proceedings", thereby laying out the right to defence. Several other principles lay out the right that this defence must in fact be *effective*: Principle 2, for instance, states that "Governments shall ensure that efficient procedures and responsive mechanisms for effective and equal access to lawyers are provided for all persons" and Principle 9 states that "Governments, professional associations of lawyers and educational institutions shall

ensure that lawyers have appropriate education and training and be made aware of the ideals and ethical duties of the lawyer and of human rights and fundamental freedoms recognized by national and international law."

15. Article 14(5) of the ICCPR specifies that "Everyone convicted of a crime shall have the right to his conviction and sentence being reviewed by a higher tribunal according to law."

16. See Amnesty International (1998: Section B, Chapter 26.3).

17. See "Universal Declaration of Human Rights" (UDHR) – see Treaties list; Article 10 states that "Everyone is entitled in full equality to a fair and public hearing by an independent and impartial tribunal, in the determination of his rights and obligations and of any criminal charge against him." This article is similar to Article 14(1) of the ICCPR, which emphasizes that "In the determination of any criminal charge against him, or of his rights and obligations in a suit at law, everyone shall be entitled to a fair and public hearing by a competent, independent and impartial tribunal established by law."

18. Article 9(3) of the ICCPR stipulates that "Anyone arrested or detained on a criminal charge shall be brought promptly before a judge or other officer authorized by law to exercise judicial power and shall be entitled to trial within a reasonable time or to release", and Article 14(3)(c) of the ICCPR states that "everyone shall be entitled ... in full equality ... to be tried without undue delay".

19. Amnesty International (1998: Section B, Chapter 24.3).

20. Ibid., Chapter 19.2.

21. Article 14(3)(f) of the ICCPR states that "In the determination of any criminal charge against him, everyone shall be entitled to ... have the free assistance of an interpreter if he cannot understand or speak the language used in court." See also Amnesty International (ibid.: Chapter 23.3), which states that "the right to an interpreter has generally included the right of an accused to have relevant documents translated free of charge".

22. See, for instance, Hart (1961).

23. The issue of derogation from human rights principles is discussed in Chapter 5.

24. UDHR, Article 3; see also Article 6(1) of the ICCPR.

25. UDHR, Article 6.

26. Ibid., Article 4.

27. Ibid., Article 5.

28. Ibid., part of Article 7.

29. Ibid., Article 9.

30. Ibid., Article 10.

31. Ibid., Article 18.

32. Ibid., Article 19.

33. Ibid., Article 20(1).

34. Mani (2002: 55).

35. Ibid., p. 56; Mani does have a section entitled "Contending with Customary Law and Legal Pluralism", but a discussion of a reform of the legal framework is largely absent from her work.

36. Ibid.

37. See, for instance, Holm and Eide (2000).

38. See Chesterman (2002a).

39. See, for instance, George (1979).

40. Ibid., p. 50; on this see also Lijphart (1971: 685).

41. Paris (2004: 58).

42. George (1979: 62).

43. Ibid., p. 55; Paris (2004: 59).

44. George (ibid.).

45. For an overview of UNTEA see Higgins (1970: 101–106).
46. Caplan (2005: 18).
47. Ibid.
48. Foreign affairs, public security, finance, defence and information.
49. Caplan (2005: 18–19).
50. Ibid., p. 31.
51. Ibid.
52. Ibid., p. 19. See also "Basic Agreement on the Region of Eastern Slavonia, Baranja and Western Sirmium, or Erdut Agreement" – see Treaties list.
53. Caplan (2005: 19).
54. Ibid., p. 61.

3

The UN Interim Administration Mission in Kosovo

Background

The Kosovo conflict[1]

The hostilities over Kosovo, between Christian Orthodox Serbs and its predominantly Muslim Albanian population, go back to the defeat of the Serbs in the Battle of Kosovo on 28 June 1389. Until then, Kosovo was at the heart of the Serbian kingdom. However, when the Serb Prince Lazar lost against the invading Turks, Kosovo became a part of the Ottoman Empire for the following five centuries. Even though no longer under Serbian authority, Serbian folklore kept Kosovo firmly embedded in Serbian hearts and minds for six centuries after the territory was lost. With the disintegration of the Ottoman Empire and the first Balkan War in 1912, Serbia managed to reacquire Kosovo; since then, Kosovo has had a violent history.

Between the First and Second World Wars Serbia attempted to consolidate its power over Kosovo by expelling the territory's Albanian and Turkish population, and redistributing the land of those expelled and other non-Serb land-owners to Serb colonists. Once the German forces, which had occupied Yugoslavia during the Second World War, were driven from the territory in 1945, 10,000 Albanian troops fought 40,000 Serb forces for control of Kosovo. The Albanians lost, with heavy casualties being sustained on both sides; subsequently, the Serbs drove out many of

Kosovo's Albanian inhabitants, deporting thousands to Turkey. Throughout the 1950s violence against Albanians continued in sporadic outbursts, with some incidents claiming dozens of lives.[2]

In 1974 Tito's new Yugoslav constitution granted autonomous status to the province, which it enjoyed until 1989. After Tito's death in 1980, resentment against some of his policies began to crop up in the individual Yugoslav republics, and Serbia particularly felt that it had been treated unjustly under the 1974 constitution. On the 600th anniversary of the Battle of Kosovo in 1989, the then president of Serbia, Slobodan Milošević, travelled to the famous Kosovo Field where Prince Lazar had fought and lost the battle for Kosovo, and stripped the territory of its autonomy in an impassioned Serb nationalist speech.[3]

After Milošević's speech, the treatment of Albanians in Kosovo became increasingly worse: Albanians were barred from holding public office, and were effectively reduced to second-class citizens. In 1991 the Yugoslav federation fell apart, and Slovenia, Croatia and eventually Bosnia and Macedonia declared their independence; Kosovo followed suit in May 1992. Kosovo Albanians chose as the first president of the Republic of Kosovo Ibrahim Rugova, who at the time was the leader of the Kosovo Democratic League. Rugova requested that a UN protectorate be established in Kosovo until full independence, and set up a governing system to take charge of taxation, health and education. Rugova insisted that all anti-Serb protests remain non-violent; however, his campaign failed to achieve the international community's recognition of Kosovo's independence.

What followed were seven years marred by exchanges of violence between Serb authorities, police and paramilitary forces and Albanian separatists, a conflict which culminated in NATO's intervention in 1999. While the early 1990s were far from trouble-free, President Bush's Christmas warning of 1992 to Milošević that Serbia itself would be attacked if it used force in Kosovo had an impact on the Serbian leadership. Secretary of State Warren Christopher of the first Clinton administration reiterated the warning, and any indications of a potentially major Serb attack faded away initially.[4] While the situation in Kosovo remained relatively calm during the war in Bosnia, the province did not escape the violence which swept all of Yugoslavia. Even though Milošević had heeded Bush's warning, and did not instigate a major offensive throughout the early and mid-1990s, Serb violence against ethnic Albanian civilians, who made up 90 per cent of the population, became common. At the Dayton Peace Conference in 1995 the international community was unwilling to jeopardize the peace it had managed to secure for Bosnia by dragging further issues into the agreement; this led to its failure to address the Kosovo problem – a fact that came back to haunt it in 1998 and 1999.

As it became apparent that Rugova's non-violent political campaign had failed to place the Kosovo issue on the agenda at Dayton and prevent further Serb abuses against Albanians, the province's Albanians grew increasingly impatient with him. Their support for the Kosovo Liberation Army (KLA),[5] an organization which had been in existence in various forms throughout the twentieth century, but which surfaced once again in 1992, grew steadily. From 1997 onwards the KLA and the Serbian police and paramilitary forces fought each other, and the civilian population, on many occasions. KLA attacks on Serb forces would incite attacks by Serbs against Albanian villagers, which in turn would incite further KLA attacks. Strategically, the KLA wanted to draw the Serbs to commit many of the atrocities that they did commit, so as to attract the international community's attention to Kosovo; in the end, they succeeded in this. By the summer of 1998 Albanian civilian casualties were in the hundreds and approximately 300,000 Albanians had been displaced internally within Kosovo,[6] placing the Kosovo question firmly on the international agenda.

After several UN resolutions on the matter, and a near NATO intervention in October 1998, a staged attempt to resolve the crisis diplomatically through peace talks was convened in Rambouillet, France, in February 1999. The peace terms the United States offered to the Federal Republic of Yugoslavia (FRY) would have been unacceptable to any government, and Rambouillet was less of a peace conference and more the staging of a diplomatic effort to pacify those who would not go to war without such a last attempt at diplomacy.[7] After the conference failed, NATO launched the first air-strikes against Serbian military targets inside the FRY on 24 March 1999. Seventy-eight days later the war on Serbia, dubbed Operation Allied Force, came to an end after NATO and the FRY reached an agreement on Serbia's withdrawal from Kosovo on 9 June, and the deployment of an international security presence, the Kosovo Force (KFOR), among others.[8]

UNMIK

On 10 June 1999 the Security Council passed Resolution 1244, establishing the UN Interim Administration Mission in Kosovo (UNMIK).[9] The resolution mandated an international civilian presence "to provide an interim administration for Kosovo under which the people of Kosovo can enjoy substantial autonomy within the Federal Republic of Yugoslavia".[10] Resolution 1244 vested the UN mission with unprecedented sovereign powers: it provided the mission's head – the special representative of the Secretary-General (SRSG) – with full executive, legislative and judicial powers over Kosovo.[11] And indeed, the first *regulation* or law which the SRSG passed unequivocally stated that "all legislative and executive authority with respect to Kosovo, including the administration of the judiciary, is vested in UNMIK and is exercised by the Special Representative of the Secretary-General".[12] Unlike in Bosnia, however, the international community decided to place various actors under a single administrative umbrella, headed by the SRSG.[13] Four main *pillars* made up the original administrative structure of the mission, and each of these pillars had the lead responsibility in one specific area: the United Nations was in charge of civil administration (Pillar II), the Office of the UN High Commissioner for Refugees (UNHCR) was responsible for humanitarian assistance (Pillar I), the European Union (EU) was given economic reconstruction (Pillar IV) and the Organisation for Security and Co-operation in Europe (OSCE) was in charge of institution building (Pillar III). In June 2000, one year after the mission had begun, Pillar I for humanitarian assistance was phased out and transformed into the pillar for police and justice, which was placed under direct UN control.

UNMIK came to govern Kosovo in June 1999. While sovereignty over the territory effectively rested with the SRSG, who derived his powers from the Security Council and Resolution 1244, the United Nations nevertheless made the effort to involve local actors in the administration of the territory: UNMIK initially established the Kosovo Transitional Council (KTC), a body originally made up of 12 and later expanded to 35 members of key ethnic and political groups. While the KTC played an important role in the legitimization of UNMIK by virtue of its membership, the body was also meant to ensure that local actors had some input into the decisions that affected the running of the territory.[14] Furthermore, six months into the mission UNMIK also created the Joint Interim Administrative Structure (JIAS),[15] which saw various departments under the four different pillars co-headed by one local and one international official, the so-called *dual-desk* model,[16] thus again allowing for local input into the governing of the territory. Local input into policy-making was attempted through the establishment of the Interim Administrative Council (IAC), an advisory body made up of eight members – four international UNMIK officials, three Albanian officials and one Serb official.[17]

In May 2001 UNMIK created a constitutional framework which set out new Provisional Institutions of Self-Government (PISG),[18] replacing the JIAS and IAC. This framework saw the establishment of a new legislative assembly, made up of 120 local members, able to elect a president and propose laws; an executive branch, run by a prime minister who is nominated by the president; and also a judiciary, made up of minor offence courts, municipal courts, district courts and a supreme court. While this governance structure ensured that Kosovo continued to enjoy substantial autonomy from Serbia, it remained under the authority of the SRSG, and thus the territory was firmly in the grip of the international community.

The five elements in practice

As argued in the previous chapters, the UN's approach to legal and judicial reform consisted of five key elements. The aim of this section is to demonstrate the validity of this claim with regard to Kosovo: the first subsection focuses on the UN's choice of applicable law for Kosovo; the second considers the incorporation of human rights into the legal framework; the third discusses UNMIK's establishment of regular courts in Kosovo; the fourth subsection discusses the plans for a war and ethnic crimes court for the territory; and finally the fifth subsection specifies how the United Nations tried to involve local actors in the judicial process from the beginning of the mission.

Concordance of the applicable law with prior legal codes from mission's beginning

Given that Security Council Resolution 1244 (1999) vested the United Nations with legislative and executive powers, UNMIK had free rein in determining the applicable law; with this task, the United Nations found itself in uncharted territory. The mission could have, for instance, chosen to apply a generic *off-the-shelf* legal code, or martial law in combination with a basic legal code drawn from previously applicable laws. Guided by the assumption that the laws chosen from the beginning of a mission must conform to previously applicable legal codes, UNMIK's Regulation 1999/1 declared that "the laws applicable" in Kosovo immediately prior to the commencement of NATO's bombardments in the FRY in March 1999 would "continue to apply".[19] These laws were made up predominantly of the laws of Serbia,[20] which along with Montenegro was one of the two constituent territories of the FRY in 1999, and would continue to apply, *mutatis mutandis*,[21] as follows: firstly, only in so far as they did not conflict with internationally recognized human rights standards; secondly, as long as they did not conflict with the mission's mandate; and thirdly, they should not conflict with any UN regulations.[22] Thus the United Nations aimed to prevent contradictions in the legislation that could arise from its attempt to combine previously applicable laws with human rights standards and SRSG-issued laws.

While the decision to apply previously applicable laws was the UN's preferred option, it was supported by Russia, and possibly also China.

The UN's Office of Legal Affairs was involved in the process of drafting Regulation 1999/1,[23] and during that process UN lawyers consulted the member governments that had opposed NATO's intervention in Kosovo and supported the clause of Security Council Resolution 1244 (1999) which reaffirmed the FRY's territorial integrity.[24] Russia and China, in particular, had major political considerations regarding the future status of Kosovo: it was important for both states that NATO's intervention would not change the FRY's territorial boundaries. Any change in Kosovo's status would set a precedent which could have unwelcome legal, political and security implications in the two states, which were themselves struggling with secessionist movements at the time. Russia, historically an ally of the Serbs, would have insisted that the law in force in Kosovo should continue to be the law of the Federal Republic of Yugoslavia, as it had been throughout the 1990s, arguably believing that by applying the same law in Kosovo, a potential secession would be made legally and politically more difficult.

This would seem to contradict Strohmeyer's assessment that the decision to apply previously applicable laws in Kosovo was made "solely for practical reasons", such as "to avoid the need for local lawyers ... to be introduced to an entirely foreign legal system".[25] While the choice of law may indeed have had positive practical implications, there were clearly also political considerations at play. However, Russia's position did not force the United Nations into a position it did not already hold: Strohmeyer's point about the perceived practicality of adopting Serb and Yugoslav law, and the UN's assumption that laws must indeed be based on previously applicable laws, suggest that the United Nations was likely to have adopted such laws even without Russian pressure.

Completeness of human rights catalogue from mission's beginning

UNMIK aimed to establish a human rights regime within the legal framework: Regulation 1999/1 stipulated that the applicable laws would only apply to the extent that they were not inconsistent with "internationally recognized human rights standards", and made officials' observance of such standards binding.[26] This sweeping provision implied that human rights law would not only apply but would override any national legislation that came into conflict with it. The problem with this regulation, however, was that it failed to clarify which particular human rights instruments applied. As will be discussed later in this chapter, the question of whether or not human rights law applied in Kosovo's courts became a contentious issue, and it took five months to clarify the matter.

Reinstitution of a regular court system from mission's beginning

While the literature largely fails to pay attention to the type of courts UNMIK established, some articles term UNMIK's initial efforts to that end as the "Emergency Judicial System".[27] Referring to this system as an *emergency* system, however, is potentially misleading because it suggests that these courts were different from the courts as they used to function before NATO's intervention or after UNMIK officially created the court system with Regulation 2001/9.[28]

When UNMIK arrived in Kosovo, law and order had broken down: the Serbs' withdrawal left the territory in a legal vacuum since virtually all police officers and most jurists working in Kosovo during Milošević's reign chose to leave in fear for their safety. The majority of the population regarded the few jurists who remained as collaborators with the oppressive regime; thus such jurists were unacceptable as candidates for judicial posts, and the courts effectively ceased to function.[29] To address this problem, the SRSG first issued two emergency decrees – the first establishing an advisory council on judicial appointments, and the second appointing local and international officials to act as advisers on this council.[30] Subsequently the SRSG appointed 55 judges and prosecutors, and resurrected the district courts and prosecutors' offices in Pristina, Prizren, Mitrovica and Pec. Mobile units consisting of judges and prosecutors who travelled by helicopter to conduct hearings, primarily regarding bail for KFOR-arrested individuals, also began to operate out of Pristina District Court[31] and covered areas not included in the jurisdiction of the other district courts, such as the district of Gnjilane.[32]

The mobile courts were arguably an *emergency* measure designed to deal with the growing number of KFOR detainees. But while the restoration of the district courts was said to be only provisional, and therefore perceived as part of this *emergency judicial system*, very little about the system – apart from the few weeks in which the mobile courts operated – indicated that it was different from the regular court system existing in the territory prior to March 1999. Interesting to note in this respect is that the SRSG issued no emergency decree to establish an emergency judicial system: the first two emergency decrees related to the appointment of the council that was to select judges, and then these judges were simply appointed to some of the district courts as they had existed prior to NATO's intervention. The United Nations made the assumption that these district courts had not ceased to function, despite the fact that Belgrade's administrative ties with Kosovo were severed when Kosovo became an internationally administered territory. If UNMIK issued regulations on the applicable law and emergency decrees on judicial appointments, it is curious that no regulation or decree was issued regarding the courts.

The fact that UNMIK simply re-established the previously existing court structure is confirmed when considering that, apart from appointing criminal law judges within the judiciary, it also appointed five civil law judges, three of whom were said to be employed by the Pristina Municipal Court in 1999,[33] even though civil trials did not commence until 2000. The fact that this court was in existence in the first place, without a UN regulation or decree to create it, attests to the fact that rather than establishing a genuine emergency judicial system, UNMIK simply took on the regular court system which was in existence prior to the conflict, and gradually employed more and more judges throughout that system.

The mobile courts operating for a brief period throughout the territory were a potential indication that UNMIK may have been interested in a solution to the judicial problem other than the revival of regular courts; the other indication was UNMIK's establishment of the Ad Hoc Court of Final Appeal to hear appeals stemming from the district courts.[34] However, even those indications do not suffice to imply that UNMIK was interested in establishing anything but a regular court system: the Ad Hoc Court of Final Appeal was simply a replacement for the previously existing Kosovo Supreme Court, which used to function as the appeals court in Kosovo,[35] and the mobile courts were identical in their structure and procedures to the regular courts, the only difference being the lack of a physical court building for them.

The ultimate indication that UNMIK was set on simply establishing a regular court system early on, rather than an emergency court system, comes from the former chief of the OSCE Mission in Kosovo's Legal System Monitoring Section, and a legal adviser to that section, who noted that at the beginning of the mission:

> there was a consensus within UNMIK that it might be necessary to declare a state of emergency. Although such a declaration would have resulted in the derogation of certain human rights for a limited period of time, there was broad agreement among the human rights components that, given the circumstances, it was appropriate. Periods of detention could be extended (as they eventually were), international judges and prosecutors could be brought in for limited periods to preside over issues of arrest and detention, and an intensive legal educational training program could be instituted. UNMIK demurred and opted to forge ahead with plans to start the regular judicial system within a matter of months.[36]

When UNMIK did finally and officially establish the regular court system through the promulgation of Regulation 2001/9, many of the courts it created already existed. The regulation specifies that there shall be a Supreme Court of Kosovo, district courts, municipal courts and minor offence courts.[37] So the Supreme Court replaced the functions previously carried out by the Ad Hoc Court of Final Appeal, and the district courts had existed since the mission's beginning, as had many of the municipal and minor offence courts, even if they did not begin to hear cases until 2000. It should be noted that while a judicial structure may be referred to as an emergency judicial system, what determines whether it truly is an emergency framework is not the nomenclature used to describe it, but the extent to which it can be distinguished from the institutional structure, procedures and laws applied in courts which had previously operated in a particular territory.[38]

Pursuit of prosecutions for past atrocities from mission's beginning

UNMIK gave the issue of addressing past atrocities a high priority early on. The UN's position was that impunity cannot be tolerated, and addressing the war and ethnic crimes committed by Serbs and Albanians was vital for the reconciliation of the two communities. Due to the very hostile inter-ethnic relations and the highly unstable security situation, however, it became clear that such prosecutions would require special measures to ensure the fairness and effectiveness of the trials:[39] essentially, credible neutrality was indispensable.[40] However, it also became clear early on that the International Criminal Tribunal for the Former Yugoslavia (ICTY) would not be the primary organ for the investigation and prosecution of war crimes committed in Kosovo. In September 1999 Carla Del Ponte, the ICTY's chief prosecutor, stated that the "primary focus of the Office of the Prosecutor must be the investigation and prosecution of the five leaders of the Federal Republic of Yugoslavia, and the Republic of Serbia",[41] thus precluding any major involvement of the court in Kosovo-related cases. In addition, UNMIK rejected the notion of an international tribunal for Kosovo, believing initially that Kosovo's judges, many of whom had not practised law since being stripped of their positions by Milošević in the late 1980s, were capable of coping with a mounting caseload.[42]

But while the idea of an international tribunal was ruled out, a proposal for the creation of a special war and ethnic crimes court in Kosovo was circulating internally at UNMIK.[43] The presence of only local and predominantly Kosovo Albanian jurists within the judiciary had created a problem for accountability and impartiality, precipitating a justice crisis; and so support grew for the establishment of a special court which would have jurisdiction over ethnically motivated crimes and war crimes committed during the conflict itself.[44]

In December 1999 UNMIK's Technical Advisory Commission on Judiciary and Prosecution Service[45] proposed the creation of the Kosovo War and Ethnic Crimes Court (KWECC).[46] The idea was that the court would try individuals for genocide, war crimes and crimes against humanity, as well as other serious crimes committed on grounds of ethnicity, race, nationality, religion, political opinion or association with a minority in the territory of Kosovo since 1 January 1998.[47] Essentially, KWECC was to function within a broader system of adjudication between the domestic courts and those of the ICTY, and it was to have concurrent jurisdiction with the regular UNMIK courts. Importantly, it was to be separate from the regular court structure.[48] The chief prosecutor was to be given authority to decide whether to hear a case or send it to another court, and the court was to have primacy over other domestic courts and would be able to assume jurisdiction over any case at any given point. KWECC was to have concurrent jurisdiction with the ICTY but would defer to its competence, focusing primarily on the less high-profile criminals whom the ICTY did not have the capacity to try.[49] The court was to be composed of panels where local and international representatives would hear cases together, but its chief prosecutor, deputy chief prosecutor, registrar and staff, as well as its president and vice-president, would all be international.

The proposal for KWECC was initially supported by UNMIK's Department of Judicial Affairs, which also spent considerable time and resources in the development of operational plans for the court's establishment. Progress on the court's development was mentioned in two consecutive Secretary-General reports, and its creation appeared to be only a matter of time. However, despite the fact that according to one of those reports the local and international response to the establishment of the court was "favourable",[50] the court never became operational.[51]

While it is difficult to determine the precise reasons why the court did not come into being, there was local as well as international opposition, primarily on jurisdictional and budgetary grounds.[52] Albanians objected to the type of cases that the court would be allowed to try, feeling that international judges and prosecutors should be permitted to try war crimes, but that ethnic crimes should be left to the local judiciary; this essentially amounted to a sanctioning of trials of Serbs charged with committing war crimes, but an opposition to allowing internationals to get involved in trials where Albanians were the suspected perpetrators of violence.[53] Furthermore, Albanian legal experts claimed that KWECC would violate the legal system in Kosovo.[54] Their objection is likely to have been over the fact that the court was to have primacy over regular courts, meaning it would have had the right to request any case to be passed to it for trial. Finally, the Albanian community felt that the local judiciary was certainly capable of adjudicating these crimes in an impartial and competent manner.[55]

From the international perspective, international lawyers reported a general perception that the court would be "a mini-ICTY and very expensive", and several states also opposed it.[56] Some NATO member states in particular were concerned about KWECC's jurisdictional reach,[57] and arguably about the potential consequences its establishment might have for NATO troops and the organization itself. In the end, the court became the victim of the budgetary concerns of the UN's Advisory Committee on Administrative and Budgetary Questions in August 2000: one UN official is reported to have expressed the view that since the ICTY commands an enormous budget, "why pour money into a mini-ICTY that will cost a fortune?"[58] While the Albanians' objections are unlikely to have had a strong impact on the decision to do away with KWECC, the excessive costs associated with its creation,[59] along with the perception that the court's existence would interrupt the work of the ICTY and that a conflict of jurisdiction with the ICTY might exist,[60] tipped the scale against its creation.[61] Furthermore, the United Nations also came to believe that the presence of international judges and prosecutors, who had been introduced in small numbers into the regular court system from February 2000, made the establishment of KWECC obsolete anyway.[62]

Fernando Castanon, who was to be the chief of the court, defended its creation, arguing that the court would not violate the Kosovo legal system, claiming instead that it would strengthen Kosovo's legal capacities; Castanon also dismissed the apparent dilemma over the court's interruption of the Hague tribunal as entirely mistaken, but his defence was to no avail. Despite having put significant efforts into its creation, the United Nations at first repeatedly delayed the court's establishment,[63] then in September 2000 quietly discarded its efforts to form the court. Nevertheless, UNMIK considered the issue of past atrocities a key priority, and eventually chose to address war and ethnic crimes through the *hybrid* court system it set up within the UNMIK judiciary.

Local participation in the judicial process from mission's beginning

UNMIK's view that local judges were capable of staffing the judiciary, as discussed, initially prompted it to reject the creation of an international judiciary for Kosovo.[64] This approach was in stark contrast to the mission's police reform efforts: UNMIK gave international police officers, recruited from various UN member states, the prime responsibility for law enforcement, and aimed to transfer that responsibility only gradually to local authorities.[65] When it reopened the Pristina District Court, however, UNMIK appointed local judges and prosecutors. This initial group

of appointees included a number of Serbs, but they left their offices relatively quickly due to either threat of violence or actual aggression against
them.[66] While a UNMIK advance team had contemplated the option of
appointing international personnel as judges, it decided that "in view of
the knowledge required in the domestic judicial system, UNMIK [would]
continue to fill the judiciary and prosecution services with professionals
recruited from among local lawyers".[67] Furthermore, despite the Serb
judges' resignations and widespread concerns about intimidation,[68] as
well as ethnic bias among Albanian jurists, UN officials nevertheless did
not opt to admit international judges at that stage.[69] A high-ranking
UN official responded to such a proposal by stating that "This is not the
Congo, you know."[70]

Thus it is clear that the UN's initial position was that the challenges
of introducing international judges and prosecutors within the domestic
judicial system justified its position of appointing only local officials, and
outweighed the negative consequences which establishing a potentially
deficient justice system might bring.[71] This initial reliance on local jurists
was eventually reversed; however, during the early stages of judicial reform, UNMIK limited its involvement in the judicial process to the appointment of judges and prosecutors, and supporting the local jurists in
their administrative and organizational duties.[72] In July and August 1999
UNMIK appointed 55 judges and prosecutors on three-month short-term
contracts.[73]

In addition to employing Kosovan jurists, UNMIK created several
other mechanisms through which local actors became involved in the
judicial process from the beginning of the mission. The SRSG wanted to
involve locals in the process of appointments, and established the Joint
Advisory Council on Provisional Judicial Appointments (JAC/PJA) in the
first few weeks after his arrival;[74] he appointed two Albanians, one Serb,
one Bosniak and three internationals to this council.[75] In September 1999
came a few other initiatives: the SRSG established the Ad Hoc Court
of Final Appeal and also the Ad Hoc Office of the Public Prosecutor,
both of which were manned exclusively by local jurists.[76] Furthermore,
he created the Technical Advisory Commission on Judiciary and Prosecution Service, which he established with the purpose of advising "on the
structure and administration of the judiciary and the prosecution service
in Kosovo", and which was composed of "ten local and five international
members".[77]

Moreover, the SRSG turned the Joint Advisory Council into the Advisory Judicial Commission, which was to advise him "on matters related
to the appointment of judges and prosecutors ... as well as on complaints
... against any judge or prosecutor" and had the potential to advise on
"issues related to the judicial system"; once again, the composition of this

commission was mixed, but with a predominantly local element.[78] Important to note is that although the power to appoint judges and members of these commissions and administrative bodies remained in the hands of the SRSG, it is evident that the United Nations nevertheless wanted to involve local actors in the judicial reform process from the early stages of the mission, and to the greatest degree that it considered feasible.

Legal and judicial reform developments

The aim of this section is to discuss the developments that followed UNMIK's initial reform efforts, and set the stage for an analysis of these developments in the following section in terms of the set of questions to be asked of the case studies, as outlined in Chapter 2. The account is presented as a narrative about the legal and judicial reform developments from September 1999 onwards, and the specific challenges, obstacles and dilemmas which the United Nations faced. This account, however, is not comprehensive: it selectively discusses the major occurrences which are relevant to the arguments to be presented in the analysis section.

One of the first major obstacles confronting UNMIK was the Albanians' rejection of the choice of law. As we saw, the United Nations chose to use the laws applied prior to NATO's bombardments in March 1999, at which time mainly Serbian law was in force. Members of the Albanian legal community were particularly opposed to the application of any Serbian laws passed under Milošević's repressive rule.[79] While judges and prosecutors did not object to using the Federal Republic of Yugoslavia Criminal Code, and where necessary the Socialist Federal Republic of Yugoslavia Criminal Code for criminal proceedings, many of the same jurists disregarded Regulation 1999/1 and applied the Kosovo Criminal Code, which had been annulled and replaced by the Socialist Yugoslav Republic of Serbia Criminal Code when Kosovo was stripped of its autonomy.[80] Yugoslavia's criminal codes were in effect in Kosovo before the territory was stripped of its autonomy,[81] but the criminal code of Serbia in particular was considered the most potent instrument in Serbia's campaign of discrimination and repression against Kosovar Albanians.[82] Although the UN's formulation did clearly make provisions for the removal of discriminatory clauses from the law, the perception among jurists, and especially a few judges in the Prizren District Court, was that such a law signified the acceptance of the apartheid-like system of discrimination set up by Serbia in the 1990s.[83]

Kosovar Albanians were unhappy that Security Council Resolution 1244 (1999) left Kosovo as part of the territory of the FRY,[84] and their

views on the applicable law reflected this position. If outright independence could not be obtained, the general preference was for the Kosovo
transition to begin from the time just before the province lost its autonomous status in 1989.[85] But the views on how to deal with the newly established laws were split. A group of six judges and prosecutors from the
Prizren District Court decided to work with UNMIK in its attempts to
establish the new legal system, even though they were opposed to the
application of Serbian law.[86] This group of moderates decided that while
they would cooperate with the UNMIK authorities, they would not apply
any laws they interpreted as discriminatory and would seek a "constructive evolution" of the laws in the near future.[87] There was, however, another group of hard-liners who from the beginning insisted upon a formal
return to the law as it had been prior to 1989.[88] These hard-liners eventually persuaded others not to work, and found judges in Pristina who
supported their cause; they also succeeded in politicizing the issue in the
media, threatened other groups who opposed them and led a group of
politicians to threaten to break off their relations with UNMIK.[89]

On 12 December 1999, four-and-a-half months after it established the
initial legal framework, UNMIK responded to the political pressures
by passing Regulations 1999/24 and 1999/25, which made applicable the
law that was in force in Kosovo in March 1989.[90] While Kosovo's laws of
1989 did include both federal Yugoslav and Serbian law, after Milošević
stripped Kosovo of its autonomy Serbian law had completely replaced
Kosovan law; thus Regulation 1999/24 essentially replaced the Serbian
law which was applicable throughout the 1990s with the Kosovan legal
codes as they had been in 1989.[91] However, given that applying Kosovo's
old legal codes would have left many legal gaps, Regulation 1999/24
also made applicable other laws that had previously applied for cases not
covered by Kosovo's laws:

> If a court of competent jurisdiction or a body or person required to implement
> a provision of the law determines that a subject matter or situation is not cov-
> ered by the laws set out in section 1.1 of the present regulation but is covered
> by another law in force in Kosovo after 22 March 1989 which is not discrimina-
> tory and which complies with section 1.3 of the present regulation, the court,
> body or person shall, as an exception, apply that law.[92]

Importantly, the regulation also stipulated that the FRY's federal law
of criminal procedure would apply to defendants in criminal proceedings.[93] Shortly after Regulations 1999/24 and 1999/25 were promulgated,
the Secretary-General offered his interpretation of what the law actually
was according to these changes:

In essence, these regulations state that ... Federal law will continue to apply in any situation governed neither by UNMIK regulations nor the law in Kosovo as at 22 March 1989. This includes the law of criminal procedure. Serbian law will apply only in rare cases where the applicable law or Federal law fails to cover a given situation or subject matter. In no case will laws be applied that contravene, in any aspect, internationally recognized standards of human rights.[94]

Through Regulation 1999/24, UNMIK also specified the human rights instruments which would apply. Even though international criminal law already applied in Kosovo through domestic legislation,[95] and the FRY's constitution stipulated that international law is an integral part of the state's legal order,[96] UNMIK wanted to ensure that international human rights law applied expressly. As we saw, Regulation 1999/1 only stipulated that human rights standards must be observed by those holding public office or undertaking public duties. Regulation 1999/24 took this statement further by listing the specific instruments which applied.[97] Notably, the list in this regulation included a number of instruments to which the FRY was not a party,[98] and there was no mechanism in place for the ratification of these treaties by a local assembly; they essentially became applicable law by UN decree.

Initially, there was disagreement within UNMIK and in Kosovo's legal community as to whether or not international human rights law applied in Kosovo, and also on whether the United Nations had the authority to incorporate it into the legal framework.[99] The OSCE held that "most of the international treaties which apply directly in Kosovo are statements of standards which may be very difficult to apply to individual cases";[100] it also argued that applying in domestic courts, for instance, the case law of the European Court of Human Rights "creates problems across the continent",[101] and that this problem pertains to Kosovo "in particular as most of the judiciary and lawyers are familiar with a judicial system where human rights law had never been applied, and where the use of case law is unknown".[102] Furthermore, the president of Mitrovica District Court announced in October 2000 that international human rights standards are not part of the applicable law and would not be applied by his judges.[103] Indeed, the fact that such standards were not part of the legal framework until UNMIK's arrival, and that local jurists were not previously exposed to such human rights laws and procedures, initially caused a problem with their acceptance.

However, the view of those who argued that UNMIK's mandate to "protect ... and promot[e] human rights"[104] meant that such human rights standards must be observed and the Secretary-General's position that persons holding public office and undertaking public duties are required to observe such standards[105] gave strength to the argument that human rights law must apply in Kosovo, and this applicability was eventually accepted.[106] By 2001 any remaining doubts about the applicability of international human rights law were resolved: the Constitutional Framework for Provisional Self-Government[107] incorporated the majority of the international and European human rights instruments, and made them directly applicable in the territory.[108]

The applicability of international criminal law was less controversial, since it was already applicable through the FRY's federal criminal code, which makes various war crimes and the crime of genocide punishable.[109] But while the federal criminal code frequently went beyond the definitions of the Geneva Convention on Genocide[110] on some matters,[111] the fact that it makes no mention of *crimes against humanity* or any punishment for such crimes, as international law has come to define them, was problematic.[112] The United Nations wanted to punish such crimes and was prepared to prosecute them under international law, even though such crimes were not mentioned in the federal criminal code:[113] UNMIK passed Regulation 2001/1, which specifies that international humanitarian law will be interpreted as defined in Chapter XVI of the federal criminal code *or* in the Rome Statute of the International Criminal Code.[114] The term *or* here allows room for including trials of violations of international humanitarian law under the definition of the Rome Statute, which includes crimes against humanity as part of that definition.

Cerone and Baldwin offer a precise and succinct summary of the status of the applicability of international law in Kosovo:

> Kosovo courts may apply international law in a number of ways. First, certain international norms were fully incorporated into pre-existing domestic legislation, rendered applicable by UNMIK Regulation. In such cases, what is applied is essentially domestic law, although the norms, as the domestic incorporation of international norms, retain an international character. Secondly, the Yugoslav law on war crimes refers back to international law for its application. In such cases, what is applied is a combination of international and domestic law. Finally, the incorporation of human rights law into the applicable law by Regulation 1999/24 and Chapter 3 of the Constitutional Framework enables the direct application of this branch of international law by the Kosovo courts.[115]

While the judiciary welcomed UNMIK's reversion to the 1989 legal codes, this decision did not prove to be popular over time.[116] In 2004 the deputy SRSG for the police and justice pillar, Jean-Christian Cady, reported that:

> There is still widespread dissatisfaction among certain politicians, judges, and prosecutors and sections of the public with Kosovo's continued reliance on the

law of the former Yugoslavia, which for Kosovo Albanians in particular is associated with a repressive socialist regime which is out of step with Kosovo's aspirations for its future.[117]

With the exception of some minor changes to the applicable law,[118] and despite this popular dissatisfaction, the FRY's criminal procedure code and the FRY, Serbian and Kosovar criminal codes continued to apply for nearly four years.[119] It was not until July 2003, after many efforts to create a modern criminal and criminal procedure code for Kosovo which would not only be in line with international human rights standards but would also reflect the legal and penal developments of the 1990s and the early twenty-first century, that such codes were promulgated;[120] they entered into effect in April 2004.[121]

Apart from UNMIK's substantive policy reversal on its choice of law, the mission similarly had to reverse its position on the appointment of only local jurists to judicial posts. Early in 2000 there was a serious outbreak of ethnic violence in Mitrovica, a northern Kosovo city, triggered by a grenade attack on a bus carrying Serb villagers and the bombing of a local café;[122] the violence resulted not only in a number of deaths on both sides of the ethnic divide, but also in significant clashes with KFOR. Such outbreaks of violence were in no small part attributed to local frustration with the failure of the judicial process.[123] More specifically, the violence in Mitrovica made it clear to UNMIK that there were serious concerns about the judiciary's impartiality, competence and sensitivity to human rights.[124] Thus, eight months after UNMIK opted for hiring only Kosovans for judicial posts, the mission found itself in a position where the failures of the judicial reform process were directly linked to some of the ensuing violence in the province, and consequently it had to alter its approach.

On 15 February 2000 UNMIK passed Regulation 2000/6,[125] which enabled the SRSG to appoint international judges and prosecutors to work in the Mitrovica District Court, as well as the Mitrovica municipal and minor offences courts.[126] Within two days an international judge and prosecutor had been sworn in,[127] with the power to take on any case pending in the district.[128] While one academic attributes the change in UNMIK's position more to a rebellion of Albanian judges and a number of attacks against Serb judges,[129] it is clear that the violence in Mitrovica, sparked in part by the UN's failed judicial reform efforts, played a key role in the UN's revised policy.

The introduction of international judges and prosecutors (IJPs) in Mitrovica soon led to their introduction throughout the whole province. Two months after the violent clashes in Mitrovica led to the appointment of IJPs there, Serb and Roma detainees in Kosovo staged a hunger strike in complaint about their lengthy pre-trial detention periods, and about alleged bias in how the judiciary treated them in comparison to how it treated Albanians.[130] Soon after the protest began, the SRSG promised this group that either Serb or international judges would hear their cases; this development led to the amendment of Regulation 2000/6 through Regulation 2000/34 in May 2000, expanding the IJPs' reach to the entire Kosovan territory.[131] Thus the SRSG was able to send international appointees to any court or prosecutor's office in Kosovo.

The passing of these regulations, however, had not completed the UN's policy reversal. It was not until December 2000, when UNMIK promulgated Regulation 2000/64,[132] that the judicial process was transformed from one controlled by local jurists, as was originally intended, to one dominated by the international community. The regulation essentially gave the accused, the defence counsel and the prosecution the right to petition UNMIK to intervene and assign a panel of three judges,[133] at least two of whom would be international, including the presiding judge, the right to change the location of a trial and the right to request an international prosecutor to be assigned to a particular case.[134] With the promulgation of Regulation 2000/64, Kosovo's justice system gained for the first time in more than a year a semblance of credible neutrality.[135]

Apart from UNMIK's policy reversals on the applicable law and the employment of international jurists, some aspects of its method of addressing the security situation are of particular relevance for the analysis in the next section: the permission to carry out preventive detentions, the issue of executive detentions and the problem of lengthy pre-trial detention periods. In the first two months after the conflict ended there were a number of violent incidents; as the SRSG's legal adviser, Hansjoerg Strohmeyer, put it: "Looting, arson, forced expropriation of apartments belonging to Serbs and other non-Albanian minorities, and, in some cases, killing and abduction of non-Albanians became daily phenomena."[136] In response to this surge in violence, and the consequent threat to the security situation, KFOR carried out a number of large-scale arrests to restore order; in two weeks, KFOR detained 200 individuals, some of whom were held for violent crimes and some for serious violations of international humanitarian and human rights law.[137] While these efforts helped to stabilize the security situation, UNMIK felt it necessary to go one step further and issued Regulation 1999/2, which gave the law-enforcement authorities the right to carry out preventive detentions for security purposes,[138] a controversial right from the perspective of international human rights law.

What was arguably more controversial than the law on preventive detentions was UNMIK's issuing of executive detention orders on a number of occasions. One of the more prominent cases was that of Afram Zeqiri, a former KLA fighter. The authorities arrested Zeqiri for the murder of three Serbs, but the Albanian judge presiding over his case ordered his release for lack of evidence, which raised suspicions of judicial bias.[139] When an international judge upheld this decision, however, the then SRSG, Bernard Kouchner, ordered that Zeqiri be held with an executive order of detention, citing security reasons for this decision and arguing that such a move was possible through the powers vested in him by Security Council Resolution 1244 (1999).[140] Kouchner's successor, Hans Haekkerup, also issued executive detention orders. For instance, four Albanians had been arrested on suspicion of having bombed in February 2001 a KFOR-escorted bus carrying Serbs from the Serb town of Nis into Kosovo; the bombing had resulted in the death of 10 Serbs and had wounded over 40 others.[141] While a panel of international judges ordered the suspects' release, this order was overridden by successive SRSG orders of executive detention.[142]

Various human rights groups, including Amnesty International and Human Rights Watch, as well as other bodies, such as the OSCE Ombudsperson Institution in Kosovo, criticized these *executive orders*, and similar *special holds* issued by KFOR, for lacking a clear legal basis in the Security Council mandates, and also for breaching human rights standards which guarantee individuals the right against arbitrary arrests.[143] UNMIK responded to such criticism by stating that Kosovo:

> Still ranks as an internationally-recognised emergency ... [and that] international human rights standards accept the need for special measures that, in the wider interests of security, and under prescribed legal conditions, allow authorities to respond to the findings of intelligence that are not able to be presented to the court system.[144]

Nevertheless, UNMIK established a detention review commission, comprised of three international judges, who were to judge the legality of such executive detentions.[145] The Ombudsperson Institution questioned the legitimacy of this commission, but the commission upheld the SRSG's continued detention of several suspects, who were only released when the commission's three-month term had ended by an order from Kosovo's Supreme Court.[146] Eventually, the issuing of extra-judicial detention orders subsided significantly, and several measures aiming to protect the rights of detainees were introduced;[147] but the precedent of executive interference with the judiciary was set.

The basic legal and judicial framework remained largely unchanged thereafter. There were a few minor changes in judicial administration and the institutions,[148] and many new laws were introduced, mostly by the United Nations in the early stages but more recently also by Kosovo's assembly;[149] fundamentally, however, the 2001 Constitutional Framework for Provisional Self-Government maintained the legal and judicial framework as it had been for UNMIK's first two years. The Regulation 64 courts remained in operation, and the SRSG maintained the ability to approve or deny petitions for the introduction of IJPs or the change of location for trials. The overall aim of UNMIK's legal and judicial reform efforts was the establishment of a multi-ethnic judiciary which is impartial and independent; the question is whether the UN's approach, and some of the developments it led to, aided or detracted from the establishment of a sustainable legal system, and thus the achievement of this goal.

Analysis and discussion

The analysis of this case study will broadly consider the impact of the five elements[150] of the UN's approach on the likelihood that the mission would succeed in its effort to establish a sustainable legal system. Five sets of decisive questions[151] are asked of the case study in judging whether or not the UN's approach enhanced or diminished the likelihood of establishing a sustainable system. The analysis and discussion presented here answer each of the five questions in separate subsections, with the ultimate aim of discovering whether or not the UN's approach was suited to the challenges and complexities of the mission's task.

Adherence to Fuller's principles of legality

This subsection focuses on the question whether the UN's approach led to a violation of any of Fuller's eight principles of legality,[152] and also whether the adoption of the particular approach demonstrated the UN peacebuilders' aspiration to be in compliance with these principles. Fuller argued that a complete failure in any one of his eight principles amounts to something that cannot be legitimately called a legal system. Thus the aim here will be firstly to assess the extent to which the UN's approach led to any such failures, and secondly whether the UN's approach indicates an aspiration to be in line with these principles. If a *total failure* or *gross departure* from any of them has occurred, or if it can be shown that the UN's efforts do not demonstrate an attempt to be in line with these principles, the approach cannot be the appropriate method for building a lasting legal system. The discussion begins first with an exposition of the various ways in which Fuller's principles were breached, and then links these breaches to the UN's approach.

Fuller believed that "*clarity* represents one of the most essential ingredients of legality";[153] indeed, the "failure to make rules understandable" is one of the eight routes to disaster.[154] However, this principle of clarity not only refers to the need for laws to be formulated in clear language, but also to the need for clarity on the applicability of laws; rules are just as difficult to understand if they are not worded clearly as if there is a lack of clarity on when, how and in what circumstances they should apply, and this was one of the very early and significant problems with the UN's system of rules in Kosovo.[155] The essence of the problem was that various bodies of law operated within the legal framework, creating a lack of clarity on what the law actually is, and particularly how it should be applied. As discussed, after UNMIK was forced to reverse its policy on the applicable law, the legal framework was made up of UNMIK regulations and the law of Kosovo as of 22 March 1989; in cases not covered by either of these laws, federal law was to be applied, and if federal law did not cover a particular case, Serbian law would apply. In addition, the federal law of criminal procedure would apply to defendants in criminal proceedings. However, all judges, prosecutors and defence counsellors also had to take human rights legislation into account.

Clearly, such a system would be confusing for even the best lawyers. With the multitude of applicable laws, it would be up to the judges, prosecutors and defence lawyers to dispute what laws should apply in specific circumstances. This inevitably created an unfair system: defendants were not treated equally under the law, since different judges and prosecutors applied different laws to similar cases. Kosovar lawyers from Prizren stated that while some laws were applied, others were not; furthermore, OSCE lawyers complained that there were "too many laws – from Kosovo, Serbia, FRY, UNMIK, European Convention", and UN lawyers also stated that it was not possible to establish what body of law, or which specific law, to use in a particular case.[156]

The OSCE's first report on the criminal justice system summarizes the problem succinctly:

> The myriad of sources of law in Kosovo created by UNMIK mean that understandable confusion continues to exist amongst the judiciary and lawyers as to which law applies in specific cases. This confusion is most noticeable when it comes to applying human rights standards. The major problems found by LSMS relate to: first, a lack of clarity over which laws take precedence in the case of conflict; second, the problems of directly applying human rights law, including the lack of knowledge of such law and how to implement it; and third, the problems of ensuring that all authorities are bound by the law – which is a basic principle for all democratic countries ... With so many potential sources of law, it is very important for clarity to exist as to which takes precedence. This is not, however, the case in the current law in Kosovo. Although regulations take precedence over the 1989 law, the hierarchy between the other sources of law is not made clear ... The major problem remains that the supremacy of

international human rights laws over domestic laws is not expressly stated in *Regulation 1999/24.*[157]

Furthermore, the OSCE also highlighted another problem with the clarity of the laws, namely that the UNMIK regulations "frequently add further confusion to the applicable law, either through their lack of contextualisation or due to the fact that some regulations are themselves in breach of human rights provisions".[158] And finally, the OSCE was concerned about the "quality of the official translations of regulations".[159] Some of the translators lacked the required standards of knowledge of legal terminology, adding a further problem of clarity for the rules.

Fuller wrote that "obscure and incoherent legislation can make legality unattainable by anyone".[160] While Kosovo's legislation was not necessarily incoherent, it was certainly obscure: the individual paragraphs of the various codes applied were in themselves expressed clearly, but obscurity resulted from the multitude of applicable legal codes. The suggestion here is that creating a legal framework made up of so many different legal codes that it becomes difficult to know which to apply in what circumstances is the logical equivalent of writing a law that is not clearly expressed and cannot be understood; thus if there is so much competing legislation in a legal framework that it becomes difficult or impossible for legal experts to determine what laws should apply, there is a situation of obscurity in the law. Fuller also wrote that "it is a serious mistake – and a mistake made constantly – to assume that, though the busy legislative draftsman can find no way of converting his objective into clearly stated rules, he can always safely delegate this task to the courts or to special administrative tribunals".[161] UNMIK committed a similar mistake: it created a confusing system of rules, and relied on courts and lawyers to identify the appropriate laws to apply to the given circumstances.

The contentious question is whether UNMIK's creation of an obscure legal regime amounts to a *total failure* to establish understandable rules. On the one hand, it can be argued that it does not, because the rules as written are understandable; on the other hand, creating an obscure legal regime is certainly a violation of the spirit of Fuller's principle of clarity. All in all, it can be concluded on the issue of clarity that in establishing a legal regime for a war-torn society where local and international interests may not overlap fully, yet a legal system agreeable to both is needed, Fuller's desideratum that rules must be understandable needs to be expanded to apply to the entire regime.

Thus creating an understandable legal regime must be an essential requirement for the establishment of a sustainable legal system. Fuller wrote that "there can be no rational ground for asserting that a man can have [an] ... obligation to obey a legal rule that ... was unintelligible".[162]

In a similar vein, the public cannot be expected to know what rules to follow in a legal regime that is confusing; and jurists cannot be expected to operate within a system made up of many and potentially competing legal codes, where it is impossible to judge what laws to apply. While some of the problems of clarity about the applicable law, the hierarchy of the laws, etc., did eventually subside,[163] it will be argued below that it was the UN's approach which led to these problems of clarity.

Apart from creating a confusing system of rules, UNMIK also enacted contradictory legislation. While Regulation 1999/1 determined that human rights standards have to be observed, Regulation 1999/2 contradicted this rule: with Regulation 1999/2, UNMIK granted powers to the authorities to detain individuals temporarily if they need to prevent access to certain locations or prevent interference with public duties of emergency services or any other emergency activities.[164] However, this regulation was a violation of human rights standards, in that it permitted preventive detention for security purposes, which is "a form of detention clearly forbidden by Article 5(1) of the European Convention on Human Rights (ECHR) and its case law".[165] Even though Regulation 1999/1 did not specify that the ECHR in particular would apply, Regulation 1999/24 made the ECHR applicable in Kosovo.[166] And thus, in making applicable a human rights convention under which preventive detentions are not permitted, yet also allowing a law to stand which calls for such preventive detentions, the United Nations clearly violated the principle that rules must not be contradictory.

Furthermore, in passing Regulation 1999/26 "On the Extension of Periods of Pre-trial Detention",[167] UNMIK enacted a further piece of legislation which stood in direct contradiction to Regulation 1999/24 and the applicable human rights standards. Various organizations deemed Regulation 1999/26 to be unlawful: an OSCE report, for instance, argued that it "fails ... to strike a proper balance between the imperative duty to safeguard the right to liberty and the need to detain those charged with serious criminal offences, pending the establishment of a fair and adequately functioning criminal justice system"; more specifically, it deemed the regulation to be in violation of Articles 5(3)–(4) of the ECHR and Articles 9(3)–(4) of the ICCPR, which also became applicable law through Regulation 1999/24, in that it fails to "make adequate provision for the periodic review of the extension of custody time limits" and to "provide the detainees the right to initiate a review of an order for detention throughout the period of detention".[168] Furthermore, it considered three months to be an excessive extension of the period which UNMIK allows before an application for renewal of extension is required.[169]

Amnesty International also noted that the detention of certain individuals went six months beyond the pre-trial detention period provided for in the FRY Code of Criminal Procedure, which was applicable. It was particularly "concerned that the extension of pre-trial detention permitted by *Regulation 1999/26* should not result in violations of the rights to which all those held in pre-trial detention are entitled under international human rights law".[170] Also citing Articles 9(3)–(4) of the ICCPR, Amnesty urged that "UNMIK promptly amend *Regulation 1999/26* so that it conforms with internationally recognized human rights standards".[171] Finally, Amnesty highlighted that detainees had no ability to challenge decisions by the Ad Hoc Court of Final Appeal,[172] and that it was unclear "whether the procedure involving the Ad Hoc Court of Final Appeal provides a comprehensive review of the legality of continued detention, as envisaged in international standards".[173]

UNMIK regarded Regulation 1999/26 as necessary "in order to ensure the proper administration of justice", and wanted to allow for the extension of the pre-trial detention period in order to ensure that justice was carried out.[174] Its concern was that detainees who had not been brought to trial for the lack of a well-functioning judiciary should not be released, so as to limit impunity for serious crimes. Releasing serious crimes suspects without a trial into communities where they could be recognized as offenders had the potential to undermine UNMIK's effort to establish local trust in the justice system and destabilize the security situation, since these individuals had the potential to inflame the unstable peace.

While the regulation was conceived with good intentions, it clearly constituted the enactment of contradictory legislation; however, whether this amounts to a *gross departure* from the principle of non-contradiction is a different matter. There are indeed many legal systems where individual pieces of legislation are contradictory, and thus the enactment in Kosovo of some laws which are contradictory to the applicable human rights instruments may not in itself amount to a *total failure* of the principle of contradiction: overall, the legal regime in Kosovo was non-contradictory. But it could be argued that the enactment of such laws demonstrates that UNMIK did not aspire to be in line with a fundamental legal principle. It also created further legal confusions: although Regulation 1999/1 required that the previously applicable laws apply only as long as they are not inconsistent with human rights standards and any UN regulations, it was not clear whether the UN's own laws also applied only so long as they were not inconsistent with such standards.

While the passing of Regulations 1999/2 and 1999/26 amounted to the enactment of contradictory rules, the SRSG's *executive detentions* violated Fuller's principle on the need for congruence between the rules as announced and as administered. As discussed, several SRSGs issued extra-judicial detention orders for suspects whose release had been ordered by UNMIK-appointed international judges due to a lack of evidence. The Ombudsperson Institution in Kosovo called on the SRSG to stop using such executive orders on the grounds that "no law ... in force in Kosovo provides for deprivations of liberty grounded solely on the discretion of the SRSG",[175] arguing that even if such a law existed, it would be incompatible with the ECHR's Article 5.[176]

The Ombudsperson Institution further argued that the executive detention orders violated the ECHR's Article 5 in that no court was involved in the order of detention, they provided no grounds for the detention to the detainees, failed to provide a mechanism for detainees to challenge the lawfulness of the detention, thereby violating the detainees' *habeas corpus* right, and finally failed to provide a mechanism through which detainees could receive compensation for an unlawful detention.[177] Especially the failure to provide a mechanism for *habeas corpus* review violated Fuller's principle of congruence: Fuller considered *habeas corpus* to be one of the key procedural devices designed to maintain the desired congruence between the laws as announced and their actual administration,[178] but the extra-judicial detention orders, and the SRSGs' failure to establish a detention review mechanism for such orders until 2001, clearly violated this principle.

Finally, the Ombudsperson Institution stressed that the ECHR case law confirms that the list of reasons for detention is exhaustive, and any expansion of this list by an executive or a legislature would violate the convention's Article 5(1). Thus, in accordance with the convention, citing national security or public order as grounds for detention is not a legitimate reason for the deprivation of liberty.[179] The UN's response to this criticism, as we saw, was to pass Regulation 2001/18, establishing a detention review commission for executive orders;[180] however, in a further report the Ombudsperson Institution rejected the notion that this commission would constitute a court in the sense of Article 5(4) of the ECHR, and recommended that the SRSG end the practice of issuing executive orders.[181]

The executive detentions clearly violated Fuller's principle that there must be no failure of congruence between the rules as announced and their actual administration: UNMIK made the ECHR and ICCPR applicable law in Kosovo, but the executive detentions were in direct contravention of these conventions, and thus UNMIK was acting outside the legal parameters it itself established. While Regulation 1999/1 did indeed give the SRSG full executive, legislative and judicial powers, UNMIK's mandate neither permitted the SRSG to act outside the law nor placed the SRSG above the law. Security Council Resolution 1244 (1999) certainly mandated UNMIK to maintain law and order.[182] But while the executive detentions were arguably important for the maintenance of law and order, and while it is conceivable that international judges could not have been given crucial evidence against the detainees for security reasons, the orders not only violated Fuller's principle of congruence but also undermined UNMIK's judicial reform efforts.

One of the greatest challenges in reforming judiciaries is to eliminate the executive's influence over the judiciary.[183] In 2001 US President George W. Bush received widespread criticism for issuing executive detention orders for foreign nationals,[184] criticism which alleged that these executive orders were a breach of the ICCPR. At the same time, the organization which has allegedly stood for the protection of human rights for over 50 years – the United Nations – was encroaching on judicial independence in Kosovo, also issuing executive detention orders for security reasons. While Kosovo's security situation may indeed have required that such executive orders be issued, in demonstrating a model of governance where the executive interferes with the judiciary and acts extra-judicially, the United Nations failed to lead by example. It cannot be argued that the executive detention orders represent a total violation of Fuller's principle of congruence – on the whole, UNMIK administered the laws as they had been conceived; however, they show that UNMIK placed more importance on containing the security situation than on aspiring to be in line with this legal principle.

UNMIK's final failure, in this case of aspiration to be in line with one of the principles of legality, relates to Fuller's principle that one should not introduce such frequent changes in the rules that the subjects cannot orient their action by them. In *The Morality of Law*, Fuller tells the story of King Rex, a hypothetical and benevolent king who passes legal codes, withdraws them for revision, passes them again, amends them, withdraws them again and passes them in new form, time and time again. Fuller uses his story as a starting point to his discussion of the ways in which "the attempt to create and maintain a system of legal rules may miscarry".[185] While the story is clearly hyperbole, UNMIK's experience was not wholly dissimilar. This particularly refers to the complete change of the applicable law – from the law as it had been in March 1999 to the revival of Kosovo's 1989 legal code less than six months after the initial promulgation of the applicable law.

It also refers to the frequency with which UNMIK regulations were amended in the first six months of the operation: out of the 27 UN laws passed from June to December 1999, five were amended. While not all of these regulations were important in guiding a citizen's actions, it remains true that one in five laws passed during that period was altered, an indication of the *ad hoc* manner in which they were promulgated. And even though the change in the applicable law enacted by Regulation 1999/24 does not by itself amount to what Fuller refers to as "frequent changes", since it was only one substantial change, it is possible to argue that this change, along with the other amendments, shows that the UN's approach did not demonstrate an aspiration to be in line with Fuller's principle.

We have seen thus far that there were problems with the clarity of the applicable laws and their application in practice, that UNMIK's activities were frequently not in congruence with the law as UNMIK itself had established it, that UNMIK enacted some contradictory legislation and that there were some important changes in the legal code not too long after it had been promulgated. The question is whether any of these violations of Fuller's principles of legality, or the failure to aspire to be in line with them, can be attributed to the UN's approach to legal and judicial reform. The following few paragraphs will demonstrate that particularly the UN's approach of basing the applicable laws on prior legal codes and its pursuit of a complete human rights catalogue within the legal framework from the beginning of the mission are the two elements most responsible for these violations.

First, it can be shown that the problems of clarity and of having to introduce a major change to the legal code are directly related to the UN's notion of the need to base the transitional legal framework on a previously applicable legal code. In 2000 the Brahimi Report attributed the problem of finding a suitable applicable law to the fact that "the law and legal systems prevailing prior to the conflict were questioned or rejected by key groups considered to be the victims of the conflicts".[186] The UN's early strategy to base the legal framework on previously applicable laws led to the hasty decision to implement the law as it had been just before NATO's intervention, and to the failure to realize that while previously applicable legal codes may be acceptable, not just any such code will in fact be accepted. Essentially, UNMIK's legal advisers did not recognize the potential legal and political fall-out that would follow the adoption of the FRY's laws. Some UN officials at first regarded the Albanian judges' rejection of the legal framework as "total nonsense", but later recognized that this was a "politically uninformed position" and that they had "blinders and did not understand the political problems".[187] An approach which allowed for consultations with local jurists on the applicable law early on might indeed have prevented the eventual change of the legal code six months into the mission.

Furthermore, basing the law on previously applicable laws, in combination with the UN's perceived need to implement a complete human rights catalogue from the beginning of the mission, led to the problems of clarity. As we saw, the eventual need to return to Kosovo's 1989 legal code left many gaps in the law, which had to be filled with FRY and Serbian laws, and the courts also had to adhere to international human rights standards; however, for the first six months it was unclear which international standards were meant. Even when this matter was clarified through Regulation 1999/24, the question of the hierarchy of the laws remained unclear until UNMIK created the new constitutional framework in 2001. The adoption of a number of legal codes and human rights instruments, and the consequent inability of jurists to be clear on the applicable law, demonstrates a failure to achieve understandable rules. Had the United Nations implemented, for instance, a generic criminal and criminal procedure code which could have incorporated human rights legislation, this problem might have been averted, as the Brahimi Report suggested.[188]

UNMIK's enactment of contradictory legislation and its failure to administer the rules as announced can be attributed directly to its approach of implementing a complete catalogue of human rights early on. When KFOR and UNMIK arrived in Kosovo they faced an unstable security situation which constituted a public emergency; some academics later suggested that the implementation of martial law at the beginning of the mission might have been an appropriate course of action.[189] Through Regulation 1999/24 UNMIK enacted the ICCPR, which permits derogation from certain rights in times of public emergencies.[190] But in pushing for the implementation of a full catalogue of human rights, and in particular through the inclusion as part of the legal framework of the ECHR, which does not have similarly liberal clauses permitting derogation from key rights in times of public emergency, the United Nations closed the legal door on the possibility of derogating from such rights without violating the enacted standards or creating contradictory legislation.

Importantly, the ICCPR lists the articles from which no derogation can be made, even in times of public emergency: Article 9, which deals with the matters of arbitrary arrests and detentions, *habeas corpus* provisions and the matter of pre-trial detention, is not one of them.[191] Had the United Nations enacted only the ICCPR, and made it clear that the security situation in Kosovo did constitute a national emergency and therefore certain rights provided under the convention had to be derogated, then the matter of preventive or executive detentions, as well as the problem of the extension of the pre-trial detention periods, would not have constituted a violation of the principle of congruence between rules as announced and as administered, or the requirement for legislation to be non-contradictory, since such activities and regulations would have fitted within the legal parameters of permissible derogation. However, the UN's approach of enacting as complete a catalogue of human rights as possible, and especially its enactment of the ECHR, led to the violations discussed above.

Compliance with basic judicial norms

The focus of this subsection is the question of whether any violation of the 10 judicial norms[192] can be attributed to any of the five elements of the UN's approach. It will first outline how some of these norms were breached in Kosovo, and will then argue that it was particularly the UN's strategy of involving local actors in the judicial process from the beginning of the mission, and its insistence on pursuing prosecutions for past atrocities, which can be linked to many of the violations.

Perhaps the biggest problem for UNMIK's fledgling judiciary before the introduction of international judges and prosecutors was a lack of judicial independence and impartiality. Most of the Albanian judges and prosecutors who were initially employed within the judiciary had not practised law since 1989, a time when judicial independence was not respected in Yugoslavia.[193] The SRSG's legal adviser, Hansjoerg Strohmeyer, saw the problem as follows:

> In a society that had never before experienced respect for the rule of law, and in which the law was widely perceived as yet another instrument for wielding authority and control over the individual, the meaning of independence and impartiality of the individual had to be imparted gradually.[194]

Furthermore, the security situation was such that it was easy for rogue elements within the society to exert great pressure on the judiciary, as reported by Amnesty International early in 2000:

> unacceptable pressure, in the form of threat, intimidation and even violent attacks, is being exerted on some members of the judiciary by extremist elements of ethnic Albanian society. This pressure may be affecting the ability of some judges to take decisions impartially and independently based on legal, rather than political, considerations.[195]

By December 1999 UNMIK had recognized that it would need to introduce IJPs in order to restore some semblance of judicial independence and impartiality. However, despite the introduction of IJPs, UNMIK failed to achieve this goal: the majority voting system in the judicial system, where panels of either three or five judges presided over a case, allowed for the possibility that the local judges would be able to outvote an international judge.[196] Thus the influence of the international judges over cases was fairly restricted.[197] The OSCE's assessment of this initiative was essentially that "the distribution and role of international judges and public prosecutors [were] still insufficient to properly address concerns relating to objective impartiality, or to remedy cases involving actual bias".[198]

Furthermore, this intended remedy for the problem of judicial bias and independence triggered a further violation of a judicial norm, namely the requirement that justice be delivered in the same manner across different judicial bodies: essentially, "the manner and timing of appointment and the *ad hoc* composition of the judging panels ... resulted in the unequal treatment of defendants before the courts in cases of a similar nature of seriousness".[199] The problem was that the panels before which such defendants stood had a varying composition – some with IJPs and others without.[200] Inevitably, the "limited and sporadic"[201] allocation of IJPs to such cases led to situations where they were dealt with unequally. Moreover, while the Ombudsperson Institution was in a position to and did issue guidance on the relative compatibility of laws with international standards, such guidance could not be treated as binding and could not be applied uniformly by all courts. The lack of adequate institutional support made the task of judges unfamiliar with human rights law more difficult, and also created a judicial system whereby human rights law was not applied uniformly, which made it consequently unfair.[202]

It was not until UNMIK passed Regulation 2000/64 in December 2000, and the SRSG acquired the ability to introduce a majority of international judges to any case, to assign an international prosecutor to a trial or to move the location of a trial, that the problems of judicial bias and impartiality, as well as the consistent delivery of justice, were alleviated. It is thus not difficult to see how the UN's initial approach of choosing to employ only local jurists directly led to the violation of three key judicial principles for the first year and a half of the mission. While it should have been fairly easy to foresee that the tense security situation, ethnic bias and outside pressures influencing the decisions of a majority Albanian judiciary might lead to these problems, the UN's approach, and the initial attempt to fix the resulting judicial problems, led not only to the establishment of a dysfunctional judiciary, but also to a loss of UNMIK's confidence in local jurists,[203] which was detrimental for the UN's overall judicial reform efforts.

The decision to employ only local jurists also led to the breach of a further judicial norm, namely the need to hear cases within a reasonable amount of time. As the initial task of establishing order and security on the ground was left to the military, KFOR detained many suspected criminals soon after its arrival; this inevitably created a large number of cases. However, as the judicial system was not fully operational in UNMIK's first few weeks, this resulted in a substantial backlog of cases awaiting trial.[204] But the task of clearing this backlog was complicated by the lack of professionalism of the jurists hired and the pressure under which they were put, leading to the aforementioned judicial bias and lack of independence; this was the case because any convictions obtained under these conditions had to be regarded as questionable.[205] When IJPs were eventually introduced, this was not only done in order to remedy the problems of judicial bias and lack of independence, but, importantly, to help clear the accumulated backlog of cases.[206] Thus it is evident that the strategy of pushing for extensive local participation in the judicial process early on was partly responsible for this backlog; the implication was not only that courts would be unable to hear cases within a reasonable amount of time, but that ordinary citizens would be unable to seek redress for crimes committed against their property or person through the judiciary within a reasonable amount of time, thereby increasing the likelihood of reprisal violence.

The problem of the large backlog of cases was further exacerbated by UNMIK's decision to pursue war and ethnic crimes from the early stages of the mission. When UNMIK realized that in permitting trials for war crimes, genocide and various other serious breaches of human rights to continue within a biased judicial system, it would be facilitating and complicit in serious breaches of justice, it decided to establish the Kosovo War and Ethnic Crimes Court. Once it became clear that KWECC would not be created, and UNMIK dropped the proposal for its establishment in August 2000, it chose instead to pursue such high-profile trials within the regular court system. UNMIK persuaded itself that the presence of IJPs made the establishment of KWECC obsolete,[207] as mentioned, and that IJPs working in regular courts were in a position to do the same work that KWECC would have done.

But the decision to try war and ethnic crimes within the regular courts ensured a continuing backlog of a large number of highly complex cases, and also meant that many resources had to be devoted to them, to the detriment of other criminal cases. By August 2003 there was a backlog of 11,000 criminal cases in Kosovo, and, as one official put it, removing war and ethnic crimes from UNMIK courts "would [have] allow[ed] the system to get on with its work", since so many resources were used on such trials "to the exclusion of anything else that [Kosovo] need[ed] to move forward".[208] Thus UNMIK's wish to end impunity exacerbated the backlog of criminal cases and came at the expense of the justice system's efficiency, and particularly the ability of courts to hear more low-profile criminal cases within a reasonable amount of time.

The approach of addressing past atrocities from a mission's beginning was in itself not the problem: had KWECC been established, these difficulties would not have arisen. The problem resulted from UNMIK's view that addressing war and ethnic crimes early on was so important as to burden with this task a fledgling judicial system which clearly did not have the capacity to take on such cases.[209] While it is indeed true that impunity for past atrocities has the potential to undermine the peace process, in that the different ethnic groups may find it more difficult to come to terms with their past and thus focus on their common future,[210] the prosecution of such crimes should not come at the expense of the effective delivery of justice for regular crimes within a new judiciary. If trying such crimes within the regular judiciary presents a threat to effective delivery of justice, then alternative methods for addressing past atrocities have to be considered.

The final violation of a judicial norm to result from UNMIK's decision to pursue local participation in the judicial process early on was the failure to provide access to effective counsel. The applicable law clearly made such access mandatory; however, access to effective counsel, particularly for Serb detainees in Mitrovica, was hampered by the inability of their Serbian defence counsel to access relevant police files, even after indictments had been issued.[211] Failing to provide access to such files "render[ed] entirely devoid of meaning the detainees' right to *effective* counsel and to ensure that the decision to continue detention is properly reached".[212] The detainees' ethnicity and that of their defence counsel was clearly the reason for the failure of the Albanian judges presiding over the hearings to ensure access to files; thus the employment of Albanian judges early on, without adequate training in procedural standards that are in accordance with human rights, was the principal reason why access to effective counsel was denied.

The incorporation of human rights principles as part of the legal framework

Given that one of the five elements of the UN's approach to legal and judicial reform was its effort to include in the legal framework as complete a catalogue of human rights as possible, the question of whether any of these five elements led to a failure of UNMIK to incorporate human rights principles as part of the legal codes may appear odd. However, it is important to make the distinction between the UN's pursuit of this goal as part of its overall strategy in legal and judicial reform and its actual success in achieving the goal. It is possible to conceive of a scenario where the pursuit of this goal was in itself responsible for the failure of its achievement. And thus the question is not irrelevant. However, none of the five elements led to UNMIK's failure to incorporate the 10 basic human rights principles.[213] UNMIK's establishment of the Constitutional Framework for Provisional Self-Government did eventually solidify the place that human rights have in Kosovo's legal framework. But the incorporation of a full catalogue of human rights as part of the legal framework early on did in itself lead to a host of violations of legal principles and judicial norms, as discussed in the two preceding sections.

The legal and judicial framework and its acceptability within the community

A legal system cannot be deemed to be acceptable within a society if there is either major public opposition or major opposition from within the legal community to that system, if such opposition leads to substantial changes to the legal framework or judicial structure, or if there is a major competing parallel legal or judicial framework.[214] This subsection answers the question of whether any of the five elements of the UN's approach led to any of the factors which indicate that the legal system was not acceptable. In essence, it can be shown that virtually all these factors did in fact occur, and were in part triggered by some elements of the UN's approach.

First, UNMIK's decision to apply previously applicable laws resulted in the general population's unhappiness with and jurists' rejection of the legal framework. UNMIK's assumption about the timing and content of legal reforms led it to adopt the prior legal codes without allowing time for consultations on the matter, and it failed to foresee the problems this decision would create. Basing the legal framework on prior legal codes was in and of itself not the problem; the failure to allow sufficient time for consultations on an acceptable legal framework, perhaps filling the legal vacuum with a temporary measure in the meantime, created a situation which not only led to opposition to the UN's choice of law, but also to a substantial change of that law.

Furthermore, UNMIK's decision to insist on local participation in the judicial process from the beginning of the mission was partly responsible for the extent of the utilization of the parallel court structure operating in the territory. It should be firstly stressed that the UN's approach to legal and judicial reform cannot be blamed for the establishment of these parallel courts. Soon after the conflict ended, Kosovo Serbs established and ran, with substantial support from Belgrade, a parallel court system in northern Kosovo.[215] The existence of these courts was part of the political struggle between Belgrade and the United Nations regarding the territory of Kosovo,[216] and can also be attributed to the unwillingness of Kosovo Serbs to cooperate with and recognize the UNMIK structures. However, in 2004 "a direct correlation was discovered between access to justice and the functioning of the parallel courts. In the absence of access to justice people simply used whatever was available to them."[217] The problem of access related to physical access to a functioning court, but also to the fact that minorities felt the courts were not accessible to them due to the perceived judicial bias against them. In a hostile environment, and with structures that were not impartial, minority groups felt that their interests would be served better by parallel structures, and this included parallel courts. Some Serbs would have used the parallel courts out of principle and loyalty to Serbia; however, the extent of the early use of such parallel courts was certainly affected by the employment of primarily Albanian judges and prosecutors within the judicial system.

The examples above indicate that instead of devising a method which made the legal system appealing and acceptable in the society, the UN's approach initially prevented the legal system from taking root in that society.

Legal and judicial reform and its security-related implications

The final set of questions to be answered in relation to the UN's reform efforts is whether any aspect of its approach caused fighting to resume, whether it exacerbated any pre-existing tensions which previously led to violence and whether it created new conditions which had the potential to spark a resurgence of fighting.

Various practitioners and academics attribute the violence in Mitrovica in 2000 to the failures of the judicial reform efforts, one observer noting that "local frustration with the failure of the judicial process contributed to increasing ethnic violence".[218] The failures referred to are the lack of fairness, competence and sensitivity to human rights and the long pre-trial detention periods. All of these can indeed be linked to the UN's strategy on local participation in the judicial process. In the immediate post-conflict environment, where most of the Serbs who had served in the judiciary had fled, UNMIK's decision to rely on local judges and prosecutors who had not practised law for over a decade, and who were predominantly Albanian, introduced an element of judicial bias into the system, created a judiciary lacking independence as a result of intimidation and corruption, and established a system unable to handle the mounting caseload, resulting in long detention periods. The fact that violence ensued as a consequence of these failings is unsurprising.

Conclusion

Rather than aiding the goal of establishing a sustainable legal system, the UN's approach to legal and judicial reform essentially detracted from it. Basing the law on a previously applicable legal code from the beginning of the mission led to the eventual need to change the legal framework, since this decision created no opportunity to consult with local actors on the choice of law. The subsequent change to the legal code applicable in Kosovo in 1989 and the consequent need to fill legal gaps with laws from other legal codes, i.e. from the FRY and Serbia, led to the establishment of a confusing legal regime.

The decision to make human rights standards broadly applicable from the very beginning of the mission also exacerbated the problem of clarity: it was not clear for the first six months what instruments applied. But even once the applicable instruments were specified, the relationship between them and the other legal codes was still unclear, particularly in terms of the legal hierarchy. Thus the problem was not that human rights instruments applied, but that they applied in a manner which resulted in an obscure system of rules, and at a time when there was no institution or mechanism in place which could determine how such laws would apply or their relationship to other laws.

What detracted perhaps even more from the goal of establishing a sustainable legal system was the decision to apply a full catalogue of human rights at a time when the security situation was still unstable. Given the tensions between the ethnic groups and the sporadic outbreaks of violence, UNMIK felt forced to issue regulations which would allow it to address any situation that had the potential to destabilize the fragile peace. However, some of these regulations contravened the human rights legislation UNMIK had enacted, and their promulgation thus amounted to the enactment of contradictory legislation. Similarly, in order to address security threats and curb continuing impunity for past atrocities, the SRSG chose to detain certain individuals under executive orders. But since there was no UNMIK law that legalized such orders, they amounted to official deviations from the law.

Human rights should certainly apply in a post-conflict environment, and the United Nations needs to work towards the implementation of a full catalogue of human rights. However, the case of Kosovo demonstrates that the decision to implement an extensive human rights catalogue from the beginning of the mission led UNMIK to violate fundamental legal principles. The initial implementation of a more limited catalogue of human rights, which would have allowed for derogation from certain human rights principles, would have prevented such violations from occurring.

The UN's approach of involving local actors in the judicial process from the beginning of the mission led to the establishment of a judiciary that was initially neither impartial nor independent. Some Albanian judges were biased; but even when judges wanted to remain impartial, the situation was such that external actors could easily influence them through threats and intimidation. This bias and lack of independence led to many other problems: firstly, a large backlog of cases could not be heard within a reasonable amount of time, in part because judgments from such trials could not be regarded as fair. Judicial bias prevented defence counsel in some cases from accessing police files, thereby violating defendants' right to effective counsel, and led to a more extensive utilization of the parallel court structure than might otherwise have occurred. The problems also led to frustrations with the system, which boiled over into violence. Far from resolving the problem of judicial bias and lack of independence, UNMIK's introduction of international judges and prosecutors to some trials resulted initially in a failure to deliver justice consistently across different judicial bodies.

Finally, the UN's decision to pursue war and ethnic crimes through the regular courts, in the belief that the initial introduction of some IJPs would be sufficient to provide the required neutrality, not only exacerbated the problem of the backlog of cases, many of which could consequently not be heard within a reasonable amount of time, but also slowed down access to the courts for more low-profile criminal cases. Pursuing an end to impunity from the beginning of the mission meant that high-profile crimes were tried within a system that was unable to handle such cases, to the detriment of the overall judicial process and the credibility of the judicial system.

But why did the UN's approach lead to the violations of legal principles and judicial norms, to local rejection of the legal framework and to violence in some cases? The answer lies in the fact that rather than helping to ease two of the key tensions at the heart of the UN's mission, the approach actually either aggravated these tensions or failed to strike the right balance between them: the first set of tensions related to UNMIK's need to balance demands for order and security on the one hand and justice on the other hand; and the second set of tensions required UNMIK to balance its mandate to govern the territory to a high standard with its need to empower the local community through local participation in or ownership of institutional processes, thereby creating locally sustainable institutions.[219]

The lessons the United Nations learned from its experience in its missions in the early 1990s, and academics' critiques of the UN's approach to peacebuilding, led the United Nations to strive for a more coherent and integrated approach to peacebuilding. However, the UN's interpretation of how such a coherent and integrated approach translates into practice when it comes to legal and judicial reform was unsuited to easing some of the tensions that complicate such a challenging mission as Kosovo. The United Nations took the view that not only would human rights apply in the territory, but a full catalogue of human rights and all possible human rights instruments would apply. Local jurists would not only be involved in the judicial process as advisers, but they would be judges and prosecutors. Previously applicable legal codes would not only serve as the inspiration for the drafting of a new criminal and criminal procedure code, but they would be the applicable law. And not only would the perpetrators of past atrocities be pursued and impunity for their crimes ended, but in the absence of a feasible international judicial mechanism, they would be tried in local courts.

This approach not only confused ends with means, but also failed to ease the tensions of the mission. The tension that exists between the need on the one hand to establish security, and on the other to do so within a framework of international standards, while aiming to instil human rights values in the local community and seek justice for past atrocities, is familiar to officials working in post-conflict operations and is discussed in the literature.[220] A key challenge for a peacebuilding mission is to resolve or ease this tension as best as possible. However, rather than easing the tension, the decision to introduce a full catalogue of human rights from the very beginning of the mission, while the security situation on the ground was still unstable, aggravated it significantly. The implementation of a full human rights catalogue made the task of establishing security, while not deviating from such rights, that much more difficult. This decision failed to strike the right balance between the need for order and the need for justice and rights, and led to many of the legal and judicial reform failures. The initial introduction of a more limited human rights catalogue, with the option gradually to accumulate more rights from which this initial catalogue has derogated as the security situation improves, would have been a better way to address the tension and would have prevented many of the problems that occurred.

Furthermore, rather than easing the tension between the demand for high international standards on the one hand and locally sustainable institutions on the other, the decision to pursue war and ethnic crimes through the regular justice system failed to address it adequately. In a UN-governed war-torn territory, there is an expectation that the duty of governance will be fulfilled to the highest standard, whether in relation to healthcare, education, elections[221] or the holding of war crimes trials. However, carrying out such responsibilities should not hinder the establishment of sustainable institutions. The United Nations did consider the establishment of a special court for war and ethnic crimes, which would have allowed high-profile trials to be staged to the required standard, and for the regular justice system to carry on with its work without the burden of highly complex cases. But the decision to pursue war and ethnic crimes through the local judicial system ensured that such trials were initially not held under conditions that fulfilled the expected international standards; this practice also hindered access for more low-profile criminal trials to the courts, significantly impeding the judicial process and thereby also the establishment of a sustainable judicial system. Instead of pursuing war and ethnic crimes, as well as other complex trials, through the regular courts, the United Nations would need to consider alternative mechanisms which would better balance the needs for high standards and sustainable institutions.

Moreover, the UN's decision to rely on local jurists to fill judicial posts did not ease the tension between the need for international governance and the need for local empowerment. Simon Chesterman writes of this tension inherent to post-conflict operations: "Local control of political power is appropriately seen as the end of a transitional administration, but if an international actor has assumed some or all governmental power then local ownership is surely not the means."[222] While this reference is about political power, it also applies to ownership of various other institutional processes. The United Nations has understood that, regarding police reform, the international community would not only need to be in control of the process, but would also have to staff the police service with international police recruits and fill the higher ranks with international officers, who would then be able to train and gradually take on more local recruits.

However, while the United Nations held judicial powers in Kosovo and was in charge of judicial administration, its decision to staff the judiciary with local jurists from the beginning of the mission only aggravated the tension, especially once it became clear that international judges and prosecutors would have to be introduced into the system: empowering locals first and then removing their powers is certainly a wrong-headed approach if one is to establish a sustainable judiciary. An approach more similar to that adopted in reforming the police service, meaning the early introduction of IJPs with a gradual increase in the number of local jurists operating within the judicial system, would have prevented many of the problems that did occur. Such an approach would also have created enough time to retrain jurists and introduce them to the human rights laws which they were unfamiliar with but had to apply, and would thus have created a more solid foundation for a sustainable legal system.

Finally, UNMIK's decision to designate the previously applicable laws as the initial legal code also failed to strike the right balance between international governance and local empowerment: in this instance, UNMIK needed to empower local actors by including them in the process of selection of the applicable law. While it was indeed UNMIK's prerogative to select the laws, in doing so without allowing for consultations it overstepped its call of duty, and rather than helping to resolve a key tension of its mission, its approach aggravated that tension. Local jurists eventually had to confront UNMIK and boycott the chosen legal regime so as to obtain the legal framework they desired, a change which in itself led to many legal problems. The initial application of a basic legal framework which could be rooted in previously applicable legal codes, and which along with martial law would have filled the legal vacuum, would have created an opportunity for UNMIK to hold consultations with the local legal community on an acceptable legal framework.[223]

Notes

1. Parts of the factual information on Kosovo presented in this section derive from my prior research for my MPhil thesis; see Trenkov-Wermuth (2001).
2. For more on the history of Kosovo see Malcolm (1998); O'Neill (2002).

3. For a comprehensive review of Slobodan Milošević's rise to power and the role which Kosovo politics played in this see Silber and Little (1997).
4. Gompert (1996: 137).
5. Kosovo Liberation Army (KLA) is the translation of the group's official name – Ushtria Clirimtare E Kosoves (UCK).
6. AFSOUTH NATO Regional Headquarters Allied Forces Southern Europe (2003).
7. For a good overview of the Rambouillet Conference on Kosovo see Weller (1999).
8. "Military Technical Agreement Between the International Security Force ('KFOR') and the Governments of the Federal Republic of Yugoslavia and the Republic of Serbia" – see Treaties list.
9. For an introduction to UNMIK see Matheson (2001); Stahn (2001); Wilde (2001a, 2004); Yannis (2004).
10. UN Security Council (1999a), Article 10.
11. Ibid., Articles 10 and 11 authorize the UN's SRSG to provide a transitional administration, which will perform "basic civilian administrative functions where and as long as required" (11.b) and maintain "law and order" (11.i).
12. UNMIK (1999c), section 1, para. 1.1 states that "All legislative and executive authority with respect to Kosovo, including the administration of the judiciary, is vested in UNMIK and is exercised by the Special Representative of the Secretary-General."
13. Caplan (2005: 37) argues that this was the result of the various difficulties the international community had in Bosnia, especially those emanating from the failure to have various actors under one single administrative hierarchy.
14. Ibid., p. 94.
15. UNMIK (2000a).
16. Caplan (2005: 99).
17. Ibid.
18. UNMIK (2001c).
19. UNMIK (1999c), section 3.
20. Cerone and Baldwin (2004: 43 n. 9.)
21. Latin phrase meaning "that having been changed which had to be changed", or more commonly, "with the necessary changes".
22. The exact wording of section 3 on the "Applicable Law in Kosovo" of UNMIK (1999c) reads as follows: "The laws applicable in the territory of Kosovo prior to 24 March 1999 shall continue to apply in Kosovo insofar as they do not conflict with [international human rights] standards ... the fulfilment of the mandate given to UNMIK under the United Nations Security Council Resolution 1244 (1999), or the present or any other regulation issued by UNMIK."
23. Interview with UN official, April 2005.
24. Baskin (2002: 15); the relevant clause of Security Council Resolution 1244 (1999) states that the Security Council is "*Reaffirming* the commitment of all Member States to the sovereignty and territorial integrity of the Federal Republic of Yugoslavia and the other States of the region, as set out in the Helsinki Final Act and annex 2"; emphasis added.
25. Strohmeyer (2001b: 58).
26. UNMIK (1999c); section 2 reads: "In exercising their functions, all persons undertaking public duties or holding public office in Kosovo shall observe internationally recognized human rights standards and shall not discriminate against any person on any ground such as sex, race, colour, language, religion, political or other opinion, national, ethnic, or social origin, association with a national community, property, birth or other status."
27. See, for instance, Marshall and Inglis (2003); see also OSCE Mission in Kosovo (1999a).
28. UNMIK (2001c); see Chapter 9, section 4 on "The Judicial System."

29. OSCE Mission in Kosovo (1999a: 10).
30. UNMIK (1999a, 1999b). See also OSCE Mission in Kosovo (1999b).
31. Marshall and Inglis (2003: 101).
32. The accounts of this differ in the literature: while some claim that only three district courts were initially established and the mobile units covered the remaining two areas (Marshall and Inglis, ibid.), other accounts state that four district courts were initially established (OSCE Mission in Kosovo, 1999a: 10).
33. See OSCE Mission in Kosovo (1999b: 2); the other two civil law judges were working within the Pristina District Court.
34. UNMIK (1999e).
35. Ibid., section 1.1, which states that the "Court of Final Appeal ... shall have the powers of the Supreme Court which exercised jurisdiction in Kosovo, as regards appeals against decisions of District Courts."
36. Marshall and Inglis (2003: 101).
37. See UNMIK (2001c), section 9.4.4; the American Bar Association's Central and East European Law Initiative (ABA/CEELI, 2002: 2) specifies that there are 23 municipal courts, five district courts, a commercial district court and the Supreme Court; it also clarifies that there are 24 municipal courts of minor offences and the High Court for Minor Offences; a special chamber operates within the Supreme Court and hears cases on constitutional framework matters.
38. One good example of an emergency judicial mechanism is the Detainee Management Unit (DMU) set up by INTERFET upon its arrival in East Timor; the DMU will be discussed further in Chapter 4.
39. Cerone and Baldwin (2004: 48).
40. Betts, Carlson and Gisvold (2001: 375).
41. ICTY (1999).
42. Cerone and Baldwin (2004: 48–49).
43. Ibid., p. 49.
44. Dickinson (2003b: 1062).
45. This body was created by UNMIK (1999f), section 1, in order "to advise the Special-Representative of the Secretary-General on the structure and administration of the judiciary and the prosecution service in Kosovo".
46. "The Justice System of Kosovo 2000", UNMIK Administrative Department of Justice, para. 36.
47. Conflict Security and Development Group (2003a: para. 156); on this see also Cerone and Baldwin (2004: 49), who explain in a footnote that "Initial proposals for KWECC envisioned granting the court subject matter jurisdiction over crimes under international law, as well as serious inter-ethnic offences under domestic law."
48. Cady and Booth (2004: 60).
49. Betts, Carlson and Grisvold (2001: 381).
50. UN Security Council (2000c: para. 60); see also UN Security Council (2000b: para. 111).
51. Baskin (2002: 19).
52. Interview with UNMIK official, August 2003.
53. Conflict Security and Development Group (2003a: para. 200).
54. UNMIK (2000e).
55. Cerone and Baldwin (2004: 49).
56. Baskin (2002: 19).
57. Cerone and Baldwin (2004: 49).
58. Baskin (2002: 20).
59. International Crisis Group (2002: 20); the introduction of international judges and prosecutors is discussed later in this chapter.

60. Interview with UNMIK official, August 2003.
61. See UNMIK (2000e).
62. International Crisis Group (2002: 20); for a good introduction to the model of using international judges and prosecutors in Kosovo see Hartmann (2003).
63. Strohmeyer (2001a: 119).
64. Cerone and Baldwin (2004: 48–49).
65. Ibid., p. 48.
66. Conflict Security and Development Group (2003a: para. 159).
67. UN Security Council (1999b: para. 68); cited here in Conflict Security and Development Group (ibid.: para. 178).
68. Strohmeyer (2001b: 50).
69. Chesterman (2002a: 5).
70. UN official, cited here in Chesterman (ibid.).
71. On this see Conflict Security and Development Group (2003a: para. 193); Chesterman (2004: 166).
72. Conflict Security and Development Group (ibid.: para. 195).
73. Ibid., para. 183.
74. UNMIK (1999a).
75. UNMIK (1999b); see Chesterman (2004: 167 n. 46).
76. UNMIK (1999e).
77. UNMIK (1999f); see sections 1 and 2.
78. Eight local and three international experts were appointed; see UNMIK (1999g). This regulation was eventually repealed by UNMIK Regulation No. 2001/8 (6 April 2001), which established a similar body, the Kosovo Judicial and Prosecutorial Council; this in turn was repealed by UNMIK (2005), which established the third-generation council of this type – the Kosovo Judicial Council.
79. OSCE Mission in Kosovo (2000c: 12); see also Cady and Booth (2004: 69).
80. OSCE Mission in Kosovo (ibid.).
81. Ibid.
82. Kaminski (1999: A12).
83. Baskin (2002: 14).
84. Ibid.
85. Ibid.
86. Ibid.
87. Ibid.
88. Ibid.
89. Ibid., pp. 14–15.
90. UNMIK (1999h); section 1.1(b) establishes the law in force in Kosovo on 22 March 1989 as the applicable law; UNMIK (1999i) repealed section 3 of UNMIK (1999c), which had established the laws applicable immediately before 24 March 1999 as the applicable law for Kosovo.
91. Cerone and Baldwin (2004: 43 n. 10.)
92. UNMIK (1999h), section 1.2; section 1.3 lists various international human rights instruments which must be observed.
93. Ibid., section 1.4 stipulates that "In criminal proceedings, the defendant shall have the benefit of the most favourable provision in the criminal laws which were in force in Kosovo between 22 March 1989 and the date of the present regulation."
94. UN Security Council (1999d: para. 56).
95. Cerone and Baldwin (2004: 44) explain the applicability of international criminal law: "The Yugoslav Federal Criminal Code, which remained applicable through the promulgation of Regulation 1999/24, prescribes punishment for the crime of genocide, as

well as various war crimes. However, crimes against humanity, as that category of crimes has come to be understood in international law, are not proscribed as such."

96. Cerone and Baldwin (ibid.: 46) note that federal Yugoslav law was made applicable through Regulation 1999/1, and remained applicable through Regulation 1999/24.

97. UNMIK (1999h), section 1.3; the specific human rights instruments are the Universal Declaration of Human Rights, 10 December 1948; the European Convention for the Protection of Human Rights and Fundamental Freedoms, 4 November 1950, and its Protocols; the Convention on the Elimination of All Forms of Racial Discrimination, 21 December 1965; the International Covenant on Civil and Political Rights, 16 December 1966; the International Covenant on Economic, Social and Cultural Rights, 16 December 1966; the Convention on Elimination of All Forms of Discrimination against Women, 17 December 1979; the Convention against Torture and Other Cruel, Inhumane or Degrading Treatment or Punishment, 17 December 1984; and the International Convention on the Rights of the Child, 20 December 1989.

98. Cerone and Baldwin (2004: 46).

99. Ibid.

100. OSCE Mission In Kosovo (2000c: 16).

101. Ibid.

102. Ibid.

103. Cerone and Baldwin (2004: 46 n. 34). The announcement is mentioned in a report from the OSCE Legal System Monitoring Section.

104. UN Security Council (1999a: para. 11).

105. UN Security Council (1999b: para. 38).

106. Cerone and Baldwin (2004: 47).

107. See UNMIK (2001c), Chapter 3.

108. Cerone and Baldwin (2004: 47).

109. Ibid., p. 44; note, however, that the Yugoslav Federal Criminal Code remained applicable through UNMIK (1999c, 1999h).

110. "Convention on the Prevention and Punishment of the Crime of Genocide" – see Treaties list.

111. For instance, it includes "forcible dislocation of the population" in its list of genocidal acts; see Cerone and Baldwin (2004: 44).

112. Ibid.

113. Ibid., see n. 14.

114. See UNMIK (2001a), section 1.

115. Cerone and Balwin (2004: 47).

116. Cady and Booth (2004: 69).

117. Ibid., pp. 69–70.

118. The promulgation of UNMIK (2001f) brought the rights of arrested persons in line with international human rights standards. Also, section 1.5 of UNMIK (1999h) abolished the death penalty, and a few other regulations brought the criminal laws more in line with legal developments since the late 1980s: for instance, UNMIK (2001b) prohibited the trafficking of persons in Kosovo, and UNMIK (2003a) amended the law on criminal offences involving sexual violence.

119. Cady and Booth (2004: 70).

120. UNMIK (2003b, 2003c).

121. Cady and Booth (2004: 70).

122. Ibid., p. 60.

123. Dickinson (2003a: 297).

124. Cerone and Baldwin (2004: 49).

125. UNMIK (2000b).

126. Cerone and Baldwin (2004: 49).
127. See UNMIK (2000c).
128. Cady and Booth (2004: 61).
129. Chesterman (2004: 167).
130. UN Security Council (2000c: para. 47).
131. Cady and Booth (2004: 60); see UNMIK (2000d).
132. UNMIK (2000f).
133. The applicable law on criminal procedure prescribed that in trials of serious offences, a case would have to be heard by five judges – two professional and three lay judges; see Cady and Booth (2004: 61).
134. UNMIK (2000f), sections 1 and 2.
135. UNMIK (2000b, 2000d) allowed the assignment of (an) international judge(s) to a panel, but the composition of that panel was still such that the international judge(s) could be outvoted.
136. Strohmeyer (2001b: 48); Hansjoerg Strohmeyer served as the SRSG's legal adviser in Kosovo between June and August 1999. On this see also generally Human Rights Watch (1999).
137. Strohmeyer (ibid.: 49).
138. UNMIK (1999d); section 1.1 states that the authorities have the right to "temporarily remove a person from a location, or prevent access by a person to a location ... to prevent a threat to public peace and order"; section 2.1 gave the authorities the right to "temporarily detain a person, if this is necessary ... in light of the prevailing circumstances on the scene, to remove a person from a location, or to prevent access to a location".
139. Chesterman (2004: 167).
140. Ibid.; see also O'Neill (2002: 86).
141. Caplan (2005: 64).
142. Ibid.
143. Friman (2004: 336); on this issue see Ombudsperson Institution in Kosovo (2001a); OSCE Mission in Kosovo (2002); Amnesty International (2002c); Human Rights Watch (2002a: 386); Caplan (2005: 65); Chesterman (2004: 168).
144. UNMIK (2001d), cited here in Caplan (ibid.: 64–65).
145. See UNMIK (2001e); see also Chesterman (2004: 168).
146. Caplan (2005: 65).
147. In addition to the establishment of the Detention Review Commission in August 2001, Friman (2004: 336) highlights that KFOR issued a directive setting out some key policies and procedures aimed at improving the rights of detainees (COMKFOR Detention Directive 42, 9 October 2001). Amnesty International (2004: section 2.1.1), however, rejected this directive as still failing to live up to international standards.
148. For instance, the replacement of the Advisory Judicial Commission first with the Kosovo Judicial and Prosecutorial Council in 2001, which was then transformed into the Kosovo Judicial Council in 2005. Also, a Kosovo Special Prosecutor's Office was established in 2006.
149. However, the SRSG was in a position to veto such law.
150. See Chapter 2, p. 33.
151. See Chapter 2, p. 45.
152. See Chapter 2, pp. 35–37.
153. Fuller (1969: 63); emphasis added.
154. Ibid., p. 38.
155. OSCE Mission in Kosovo (2000c: 15).
156. Baskin (2002: 15).
157. OSCE Mission in Kosovo (2000c: 15–16).

158. OSCE Mission in Kosovo (2001a: 12).

159. Ibid.

160. Fuller (1969: 63).

161. Ibid., p. 64.

162. Ibid., p. 39.

163. See OSCE Mission in Kosovo (2001b: 15); the OSCE reported in October 2001 that "any confusion over the application of [human rights] standards should finally be over. The Constitutional Framework states (Article 3.1) that ... human rights laws ... are directly applicable in Kosovo ... Consequently, it is now clear that every institution, administrative body, organisation or 'presence' in Kosovo ... is bound by the requirements of international human rights law."

164. See UNMIK (1999d), sections 1 and 2.

165. OSCE Mission in Kosovo (2000c: 17).

166. See UNMIK (1999h), section 1.3(b).

167. UNMIK (1999j).

168. OSCE Mission in Kosovo (2000a: 2–3).

169. Ibid.

170. Amnesty International (2000a: 8); emphasis added.

171. Ibid., emphasis added.

172. This court was established under UNMIK (1999e).

173. Amnesty International (2000a: 8).

174. UNMIK (1999j).

175. Ombudsperson Institution in Kosovo (2001a: para. 13).

176. Amnesty International (2002c) made similar calls for the SRSG to stop the practice of executive detentions.

177. Ombudsperson Institution in Kosovo (2001a: paras 17–25).

178. Fuller (1969: 81).

179. Ombudsperson Institution in Kosovo (2001a: para. 9).

180. UNMIK (2001e).

181. Ombudsperson Institution in Kosovo (2001b); Article 5(4) of the ECHR states that "Everyone who is deprived of his liberty by arrest or detention shall be entitled to take proceedings by which the lawfulness of his detention shall be decided speedily by a court and his release ordered if the detention is not lawful."

182. See UN Security Council (1999a), section 11(i).

183. Mani (2002: 65).

184. See White House (2001).

185. Fuller (1969: 38–39).

186. UN General Assembly and Security Council (2000b: para. 79) (Brahimi Report).

187. UN legal officials, quoted here in Baskin (2002: 15).

188. UN General Assembly and Security Council (2000b: para. 81) (Brahimi Report).

189. See, for instance, Chesterman (2004: 168); on this point see also O'Neill (2002: 75); Caplan (2005: 64).

190. Article 4.1, Part II of the ICCPR reads: "In time of public emergency which threatens the life of the nation and the existence of which is officially proclaimed, the States Parties to the present Covenant may take measures derogating from their obligations under the present Covenant to the extent strictly required by the exigencies of the situation, provided that such measures are not inconsistent with their other obligations under international law and do not involve discrimination solely on the ground of race, colour, sex, language, religion or social origin."

191. See Article 4(2) of the ICCPR.

192. See Chapter 2, pp. 37–38.

193. International Crisis Group (2002: 5).

194. See Strohmeyer (2001b:. 55); cited here in International Crisis Group (ibid.).
195. See Amnesty International (2000a: 5), cited here in International Crisis Group (ibid.); on this see also OSCE Mission in Kosovo (1999a).
196. International Crisis Group (ibid.).
197. OSCE Mission in Kosovo (2000b: 2).
198. Ibid., p. 71.
199. Ibid.
200. OSCE Mission in Kosovo (2001a: 76).
201. Ibid.
202. OSCE Mission in Kosovo (2000c: 16).
203. International Crisis Group (2002: 5).
204. Ibid., p. 3
205. Ibid., p. 5.
206. Ibid.
207. Ibid., p. 20.
208. Interview with former judge working as an international official in Kosovo, August 2003.
209. It should be noted, however, that while there clearly was a failure to hear cases within a reasonable amount of time, no automatic failure to deliver judgments within a reasonable time follows from this. Once a case did go to trial, the period between the commencement of that trial and the delivery of a verdict was not unreasonable, especially given the complex nature of the cases.
210. International Crisis Group (2002: 27).
211. OSCE Mission in Kosovo (2000c: 8); internationally accepted standards require that such access be given before an indictment hearing.
212. OSCE Mission in Kosovo (ibid.).
213. See Chapter 2, pp. 39–41.
214. See Chapter 2, pp. 41–42.
215. ABA/CEELI (2002).
216. OSCE Mission in Kosovo (2003: 16–23).
217. Vicovac (2004); Vicovac was the acting coordinator of the Judicial Integration Section of UNMIK's Department of Justice.
218. Dickinson (2003: 297); on this see also Cerone and Baldwin (2004: 49).
219. These tensions are frequently discussed in the literature: on the first tension see, for instance, Mani (2002) Chapter 4; on the second see, for instance, Chesterman (2004: 5–6).
220. See, for instance, Mani (ibid.).
221. Chesterman (2004: 5).
222. Ibid.
223. As will be discussed in Chapter 4, the Australian-led security forces operating in East Timor (INTERFET) implemented exactly such a code.

4

The UN Transitional Administration in East Timor

Background

The conflict in East Timor

The Democratic Republic of Timor-Leste, or East Timor as the territory was previously known, became an independent state for the first time in 2002. In the sixteenth century Portugal established outposts on the island, which comprised a number of small chiefdoms and princedoms. During the Habsburg rule over Portugal, the Portuguese lost all these outposts to the Dutch; however, by 1702 the Portuguese had colonized the whole island and ruled it until the Dutch were officially given the western part of the island through the Treaty of Lisbon in 1859. The eastern part of the island remained under Portuguese rule until Indonesia, the successor state to much of the Dutch East Indies, invaded the territory in 1975.[1]

In July 1975 the UN's decolonization movement finally caught up with East Timor: the Portuguese government passed a new law which provided for the establishment of a transitional government in East Timor, and which envisaged Portugal's complete withdrawal from the territory by October 1978.[2] However, Timorese parties held different views on the political future of the colony – while some, such as the UDT, held that the territory should continue its association with Portugal, others, such as Fretilin, held that it ought to become independent immediately; importantly, one of the smaller parties, Apodeti, held that the territory should be integrated into Indonesia and become an autonomous province of

United Nations justice: Legal and judicial reform in governance operations
Trenkov-Wermuth, United Nations University Press, 2010, ISBN 978-92-808-1173-5

that country.[3] From mid-1975 the disagreements between the parties over the future political status of the territory gradually evolved into a civil war, and on 28 November Fretilin, which reportedly controlled most of the territory, declared independence and the establishment of the Democratic Republic of East Timor; two days later a coalition of the UDT and Apodeti and a few other pro-Indonesian parties also declared the independence of the territory, but its integration with Indonesia.[4]

Even though Indonesia held that it had no territorial claims on East Timor, the territory never having been part of the Dutch East Indies, it launched an invasion of East Timor in December 1975 and engaged Fretilin in battles which led to increasing Indonesian control over the territory. Meanwhile the pro-Indonesian parties established what they claimed was East Timor's provisional government, as well as a regional popular assembly.[5] In late May 1976 this assembly invited Indonesia to integrate East Timor into its territory, and in July Indonesian President Suharto formally integrated the territory as Indonesia's twenty-seventh province, arguing that by the act of that assembly the East Timorese had exercised their right to self-determination and had gained their independence in joining Indonesia.[6] Between 1975 and 1982 the UN General Assembly and Security Council passed various resolutions reaffirming the right of the East Timorese to self-determination, and called upon Indonesia to withdraw from East Timor;[7] however, neither the General Assembly nor the Security Council condemned the invasion as an act of aggression, nor did the Security Council take any further steps in an effort to resolve this matter until the late 1990s.[8]

The time of Indonesia's occupation, between 1976 and 1999, when the United Nations took over the administration of the territory, can be divided into three periods: the first of these, 1975–1979, saw the death of over 200,000 East Timorese, or about one-third of the population, as a direct result of Indonesia's occupation; the period between 1980 and 1989 saw both large-scale Indonesian military operations and the strengthening of East Timor's resistance to Indonesia's rule; and finally the period between 1989 and 1999 saw the relaxation of various restrictions regarding the accessibility of the territory to foreigners and increased international media coverage of the conflict; however, the repression continued.[9]

The collapse of Suharto's regime in 1998 was a turning point for East Timor's struggle for independence. The newly appointed President B. J. Habibie stated in June 1998 that he was prepared to grant East Timor a special status, potentially substantial autonomy within Indonesia, but excluded the option of full independence at that stage.[10] By January 1999 Habibie responded to international pressure and announced his intentions to hold a referendum which would allow the East Timorese to choose between autonomy within Indonesia or a transition to self-rule.[11]

And after nearly a quarter-century of negotiations, Portugal and Indonesia finally agreed in May 1999, under UN auspices, to ask the UN Secretary-General to hold a *popular consultation* of the East Timorese to determine which of the two options was preferred.[12] While the agreement provided for the UN's organization of the referendum, and the UN Mission in East Timor (UNAMET) arrived in East Timor later that month to prepare for the consultations, Indonesia managed to remain in control of the responsibility for security arrangements. But although Indonesia did agree that its police rather than its army would be in charge of providing security for the referendum, the army and the various pro-Indonesian militias it supported went on numerous violent rampages against pro-independence supporters prior to the elections, in an effort to intimidate the population.[13]

Despite this Indonesian-sponsored campaign of violence, and the fact that many people were internally displaced within East Timor, the United Nations managed to register 450,000 voters, which far exceeded its expectations.[14] The eventual election turnout at the end of August equally exceeded expectations, at 98.5 per cent, 78.5 per cent of whom voted to reject Habibie's offer of special autonomy in favour of outright independence.[15] When the results of the consultation were announced, violence erupted almost immediately, and what was an already violent situation escalated to new heights, with "widespread murders, kidnappings, rape, property destruction, theft of homes and property and the burning and destruction of military installations, offices and civilian residences".[16] The withdrawing Indonesian army and pro-Indonesian militia essentially carried out a *scorched earth* campaign which saw the murder of over 1,000 civilians, the destruction of over 70 per cent of East Timorese infrastructure and the displacement of over three-quarters of the population, or circa 600,000 people.[17] Only the arrival of the International Force for East Timor (INTERFET) on 20 September 1999, a UN-mandated and Australian-led security force, saw the beginning of the end of this campaign of violence, the return of some of the UNAMET staff, who had been evacuated during the worst violence, and the start of a restoration of law and order.[18]

UNTAET[19]

On 25 October 1999 the UN Security Council passed Resolution 1272, establishing UNTAET.[20] In essence, the resolution mandated the mission with the administration of the territory, the provision of assistance for "the development of civil and social services" and the support for "capacity-building for self-government".[21] UNTAET was to have a similar type of authority as UNMIK: it was given the power to "exercise all legislative and executive authority, including the administration of justice".[22] The mission's initial attention focused on addressing the humanitarian disaster and facilitating the return of refugees, as well as on the provision of vital services, the restoration of law and order through the reconstruction of the judiciary and law-enforcement mechanisms, the recruitment of civil servants, the revival of the economy and the reconstruction of key infrastructure in the hope that local governance and administration could be restored.[23]

While there were many similarities between UNMIK and UNTAET, the United Nations did not implement the same governance structure for its mission in East Timor as it had done in Kosovo. As with UNMIK, the SRSG or transitional administrator (TA) was "responsible for all aspects of the United Nations work in East Timor and [had] the power to enact new laws and regulations and to amend, suspend or repeal existing ones".[24] However, unlike in Kosovo, where the SRSG was the head of an operation but working alongside the OSCE, the UNHCR and the European Union, in East Timor the TA was solely in charge of all administrative responsibilities and there were no other lead agencies involved in the management of the territory. UNTAET also had a pillar structure, with three main pillars at the beginning of the mission: governance and public administration, humanitarian assistance and emergency rehabilitation, and the military. But while in Kosovo KFOR was not under the UN's command structure, in East Timor the military component was under the direct authority of the TA.

UNTAET decided early on to involve local actors in the decision-making process, as UNMIK had done with the Kosovo Transitional Council. With Regulation 1999/2 the TA set up the National Consultative Council (NCC), which was initially composed of 15 members, four of whom were representing UNTAET.[25] While this council was established to provide advice to the TA, who was serving as its chairman, the body was also meant to confer legitimacy upon the rule of the TA.[26] In August 2000 the United Nations transformed its governance and public administration pillar into the East Timor Transitional Administration, to involve more local actors in the governance of the territory and enable these individuals eventually to replace the international staff working in East Timor.[27] In the first instance a transitional cabinet was established, which was initially composed of four international and four local officials, but which was later expanded to five local actors when the foreign affairs portfolio was handed to a local.[28] This co-administration model was somewhat similar to the dual-desk model in Kosovo, in that it gave local individuals in both Kosovo and East Timor the opportunity to gain professional experience under the supervision of internationals.[29] Importantly, a national council was also established; this was exclusively Timorese, and included representatives of all the different interest groups in the territory.[30] This structure, while not necessarily as well functioning and effective as may have been initially hoped, remained in place until East Timor became an independent nation in 2002.[31]

After UNTAET came to an end on 20 May 2002, the Security Council immediately replaced it with the UN Mission of Support in East Timor (UNMISET), mandated to assist all administrative structures which are essential to the stability and viability of a new state.[32]

The five elements in practice

As in the previous chapter on Kosovo, it is important to demonstrate the validity of the claim that there were five key elements at the heart of the UN's approach to legal and judicial reform, and to show how they affected UN practice in East Timor. To this end, this section is divided into five subsections: the first discusses the UN's choice of applicable law for East Timor; the second considers the incorporation of human rights into the legal framework; the third subsection discusses the establishment of a regular court structure; the fourth discusses the establishment of the special panels for serious crimes; and finally the fifth subsection describes how the United Nations tried to involve local actors in the judicial process from the beginning of the mission.

Concordance of the applicable law with prior legal codes from mission's beginning

As we saw, SC Resolution 1272 gave UNTAET the mandate for the administration of justice, as well as full executive and legislative powers in the territory; thus the SRSG was at liberty to select the applicable law for East Timor. UNTAET's chosen solution was very similar to the course of action adopted a few months earlier in Kosovo: UNTAET's Regulation 1999/1 codified the previously applicable law as the legal framework. However, this regulation was different to UNMIK's first regulation in one important respect: while UNMIK Regulation 1999/1 had stated that "the laws applicable" in Kosovo immediately prior to the commencement of the NATO bombardments would "continue to apply", UNTAET's Regulation 1999/1 stated that the "laws applied" immediately prior to the establishment of UNTAET "shall apply".[33] Stating that the "laws applied" rather than the "applicable laws" would apply was an attempt to address the political sensitivities of the population vis-à-vis the Indonesians, whom many locals and the majority of the international community regarded as occupiers and not as the lawful rulers of the territory,[34] and thus avoid the retroactive legitimization of Indonesia's occupation of East Timor.[35]

The Indonesian laws were to apply *mutatis mutandis*[36] as follows. They would apply firstly only in so far as they did not conflict with internationally recognized human rights standards; secondly, as long as they did not conflict with the mandate given to the missions under the respective Security Council resolutions; and thirdly, they were not to conflict with any UN regulations or directives issued by the TA.[37] The wording of the regulation does show that the United Nations aimed to prevent any possible contradictions in the legislation that could arise from its attempt to combine previously applicable laws with internationally accepted human rights standards and directives issued from its own administrators. However, as will become clear in this chapter, the UN's failure to specify the Indonesian legal code as applicable caused not only a problem of clarity in the law but also a political crisis in the territory.

In this respect, Simon Chesterman's assessment that the choice of law was "uncontroversial"[38] is inaccurate: while there may not have been the same type of popular and vocal opposition to Indonesian law as there was to Serb law in Kosovo, the question of whether or not Indonesian law actually ever applied or should apply in East Timor became a point of contention. There was disagreement as to whether the laws of Indonesia legally applied prior to 25 October 1999, or those of the old colonial power – Portugal. As the discussion below will demonstrate, this point ended up pitting one court against another, thus temporarily splitting the judiciary, and precipitated one of the first major political and judicial crises in Timor-Leste. Importantly, it was the UN's failure to give an opportunity to local actors to debate this contentious matter prior to deciding upon an applicable law which precipitated this political crisis.

Completeness of human rights catalogue from mission's beginning

The United Nations incorporated a human rights regime into the Timorese legal framework in much the same way as it had done in Kosovo. The laws used previously would apply only to the extent that they did not conflict with any UN regulations or directives, or with international human rights standards and principles. However, unlike in Kosovo, in East Timor UNTAET Regulation 1999/1 specified which particular human rights instruments would need to be observed in the territory.[39] It should be noted, however, that the regulation did not in fact make international treaties directly applicable in the territory;[40] it just provided that all persons holding public office must adhere to these instruments in carrying out their official duties,[41] and that the existing laws needed to be subject to certain human rights instruments.[42] Interestingly, even though such instruments were not directly applicable in East Timor, they would still determine the relative applicability of the Indonesian legal codes. Furthermore, Regulation 1999/1 also abolished capital punishment[43] and a set of specific laws from the Indonesian legal code, and their amendments and administrative regulations, which were clearly in conflict with international human right standards.[44]

Reinstitution of a regular court system from mission's beginning

As in Kosovo, the United Nations opted to establish a regular structure in East Timor from the early stages of the mission. On 6 March 2000 the TA promulgated Regulation 2000/11, establishing a judiciary that was composed of eight district courts[45] and one Court of Appeal.[46] It is important to note that UNTAET was left for several months without a functioning court structure; the mission opted to operate without such a structure instead of introducing an emergency judicial system until such time as a transitional court structure could be established. This decision clearly indicates that the United Nations was intent on establishing a regular court structure from the early stages of its mission, rather than another type of institutional arrangement that could address crimes in the territory.

Pursuit of prosecutions for past atrocities from mission's beginning

In mid-December 1999 the UN Secretary-General told the General Assembly that "Accounting for the violations of human rights which occurred in the aftermath of the consultation process is vital to ensure a lasting resolution of the conflict and the establishment of the rule of law in East Timor."[47] Three months after UNTAET was established, the United Nations published the report of its International Commission of Inquiry on East Timor, which assesses the atrocities committed in the territory in 1999.[48] Based on the determination that the nature of the terror and violence was *widespread* and *systematic*, two of the key requirements for deciding whether or not the violence constitutes a crime against humanity, the commission recommended that an international tribunal be established under UN auspices.[49] This recommendation fitted in well with the UN's desire to address such atrocities promptly and through prosecutions. However, having had the opportunity to observe the developments with the ICTY and the ICTR for several years, Indonesia decided to investigate the violence itself and hold trials in domestic tribunals, thereby deferring the establishment of an international tribunal.[50]

As Kofi Annan's statement above indicates, what was important for the United Nations was that perpetrators would be pursued. However, it appears that the United Nations was not prepared politically or financially to establish another *ad hoc* tribunal for East Timor. Kofi Annan made clear that:

> The main thing is to send a message that crimes against humanity and such gross violations against human rights will not be allowed to stand and that those responsible will be held accountable ... [And thus] there will be no need for the Council or the UN to set up another tribunal to compete with one set up by the Indonesian government that is going to do exactly the same thing.[51]

Essentially, the unstable political situation in Indonesia meant the international community was reluctant to push the country on the issue of atrocities committed by its own forces, and declare officially that Indonesia was either unwilling or unable to provide justice using its own judicial system; moreover, in terms of both international law and UN policy, domestic Indonesian trials remained the preferred course of action.[52] Thus, while Indonesia's decision to hold trials initially appeared to defer the establishment of an international tribunal, the international community's reluctance to push for its creation essentially meant that Indonesian war criminals would either not be held accountable or would be given very light sentences by a domestic judiciary influenced by the country's political leadership.

But while the United Nations was unwilling to push for an end to impunity in Indonesia, it nevertheless opted to hold trials for serious crimes locally in East Timor. Interestingly, justice by national means was never explicitly mentioned as part of the UNTAET mandate.[53] However, even before the Secretary-General's above-mentioned comments, the United Nations and the international community had made the broad decision to pursue the perpetrators of atrocities. Arguably, this *moral imperative* for the mission to pursue such individuals was already ingrained in Security Council Resolution 1272 (1999), which stressed the need for reconciliation and demanded that the perpetrators of atrocities be held accountable.[54]

In March 2000 UNTAET passed Regulation 2000/11, which gave Dili District Court exclusive jurisdiction over genocide, war crimes, crimes against humanity, torture, murder and sexual offences, altogether known as *serious crimes*.[55] The regulation furthermore empowered the TA to establish panels composed of both East Timorese and international judges for trials of such serious offences. Three months later the TA passed Regulation 2000/15, establishing several panels of judges to operate within the district court in Dili with exclusive jurisdiction to deal with these serious criminal offences, and several panels within the Court of Appeal in Dili to hear and decide on appeals stemming from the district court panels.[56] This approach stands in contrast to the one the United Nations took in Kosovo, where the *internationalized panels* did not have exclusive jurisdiction over serious crimes, and were also not specifically appointed to adjudicate them.[57] Two international judges and one East Timorese judge would sit on the respective panels, but for graver crimes three international and two East Timorese judges would hear the cases.[58] These panels were essentially modelled on the UN's draft plans for the establishment of extraordinary chambers for Cambodia, and represented an entirely new international justice mechanism, operating at the domestic level under UN administration.[59]

Finally, Regulation 2000/16 completed the mechanism for the prosecution of serious crimes: it set out the organization of the public prosecution service, and in particular the establishment of the Office of the Deputy General Prosecutor for Serious Crimes, which was granted exclusive responsibility for all serious crimes cases.[60] Both East Timorese and international prosecutors were to be appointed to this office.[61]

The establishment of an international tribunal for the crimes committed in East Timor in 1999 was technically only deferred, and the trial of serious crimes in this *hybrid* court system with special panels was not meant to prejudice the eventual jurisdiction of such an international tribunal over these crimes. However, in the meantime, in the absence of such an expensive tribunal, the United Nations considered the prosecution of such crimes to be significant enough as to wish to address them within the regular justice system, and to begin this process as early as possible. As one barrister who worked in East Timor put it, a "state-of-the-art system for prosecuting international crimes [was] grafted onto the fledgling criminal justice system of East Timor".[62] The types of problems these special panels experienced, as well as the negative repercussions which their creation had for the justice system, will be discussed in detail in the following sections. What is clear, though, is that as with Kosovo, the United Nations was bent on addressing serious crimes early on in its mission, and through a justice system that it was rebuilding at the same time from the ground up.

Local participation in the judicial process from mission's beginning

When the Indonesian army and its paramilitary supporters withdrew from East Timor, the territory's judicial infrastructure collapsed completely. The former principal legal adviser to UNTAET, Hansjoerg Strohmeyer, wrote that "Most court buildings had been torched and looted, and all court equipment, furniture, registers, records, archives, and – indispensable to legal practice – law books, case files, and other legal resources dislocated or burned."[63] The Secretary-General observed in his report on East Timor that "local institutions, including the court system, have for all practical purposes ceased to function, with ... judges, prosecutors, and other members of the legal profession having left the territory...".[64] The problem for these jurists and clerical support staff was that they were either "perceived as being members de facto of the administrative and intellectual privileged classes" or seen as having "been publicly sympathetic to the Indonesian regime".[65] As such, they felt that there was not going to be any place for them in a new East Timor; fearing reprisal violence, many of them fled East Timor after the results of the popular consultation were announced.

The lack of qualified lawyers who could serve within a rebuilt judiciary presented a very difficult problem for the UNTAET administrators. The Secretary-General had stated his desire that any members of the newly created judiciary be "professionals recruited from among the East Timorese, to the largest extent possible".[66] However, the exodus of qualified legal personnel left the territory virtually without any individuals who would be sufficiently competent to undertake a task which was already very challenging given the level of physical destruction. Under Indonesia's occupation, no East Timorese had been appointed to either judicial or prosecutorial office, and thus even if there were any East Timorese with law degrees to be found, they would not have had any practical legal experience.[67]

Nevertheless, the United Nations and its mission felt that the appointment of East Timorese to judicial positions was politically important, and practically the only feasible solution. In the first instance, in a post-conflict environment, and especially one where a local population has been oppressed, employing local individuals in judicial posts that would not have previously been accessible to them was considered to be of tremendous symbolic and political significance.[68] According to Strohmeyer, the local expectation that went along with the euphoria after the international intervention was that the international community would involve East Timorese in the process of democratic institution building, and particularly in the legal sector; appointing local judges, which had not occurred under either Indonesia's occupation or Portugal's colonial rule, was thus symbolically important as well as necessary if the United Nations was to act in a politically sensitive manner.[69]

A more practical consideration was the fact that INTERFET-detained prisoners were awaiting trial, and neither the United Nations nor any other body in the international community had the capacity to deploy an adequate number of international jurists who would be able to commit for a long period of time, were proficient in English, had enough practical experience in a civil-law-based justice system and would have sufficient knowledge of the local legal traditions to try these suspects immediately.[70] Evidently, the United Nations perceived that this imminent problem would need to be overcome through the appointment of individuals familiar with the local civil law system. Furthermore, Strohmeyer noted that:

> the experience of other United Nations missions [had] shown that the appointment of international lawyers leads to a myriad of practical concerns that would have overburdened the [mission] in [its] set-up phase, such as the costly requirements of translating laws, files, transcripts, and even the daily conversations between local and international lawyers, as well as the enormous time and expense of familiarizing international lawyers with the local and regional legal systems.[71]

Moreover, it appeared to UN officials that international judges would only be a temporary measure and could not be sustained in the long run, and that would itself cause further dislocation when the funds began to run out.[72] All these perceptions would seem to support the argument presented in this book that as a result of its prior mission experience, as well as political considerations, the United Nations did indeed come to lean towards the appointment of local officials to judicial posts as a matter of priority.

Since UNTAET did not know how many individuals with a legal background still lived in East Timor, the mission staff went out to search for any remaining qualified lawyers, as well as law students and graduates, by word of mouth.[73] INTERFET aided in this difficult undertaking by dropping leaflets from its planes throughout the territory, calling upon any such individuals to get in touch with any of the UN mission offices or its own outposts; within a week 17 individuals came forward as a result of this effort, and within two months over 60 local jurists had applied for judicial positions, either as judges or prosecutors.[74] While all these applicants had law degrees, mostly from Indonesian but in some cases from foreign law schools, none of them had the practical experience normally needed to apply for such positions: some had gained legal experience in Indonesian law firms and legal organizations, others had worked as paralegals with either Timor's resistance groups or human rights organizations, but none had ever held the position of judge or prosecutor.[75]

But despite the candidates' lack of adequate qualifications, the United Nations proceeded to make appointments to judicial posts. In doing so, the organization wanted to contrast its actions with those of the territory's prior political masters, who had flagrantly politicized judicial appointments: the mission aimed to make such appointments as transparent as possible so as to ensure that the process would be viewed as legitimate, thereby also legitimizing the new judiciary.[76] UNTAET's method was the creation of the Transitional Judicial Service Commission, which was mandated with the task of selecting the territory's first East Timorese judges

and prosecutors.[77] The commission was not only the main vehicle for selecting new jurists, but attested to the fact that in addition to wanting to
involve locals in the newly established judiciary, the United Nations was
committed to involving local actors in all stages of the judicial process,
including the selection stage. Three of the five commission members, including the chairman, were East Timorese. Strohmeyer explains that:

> in order to build a strong sense of ownership over their new judiciary, and
> to inject as much domestic expertise as possible in the process, it was deemed
> essential that the majority of the Commission members be recruited from
> among local experts and that they be empowered to overrule the international
> members.[78]

While the commission was not in a position to appoint jurists – it could
only recommend able candidates to the TA, who would then be able to
appoint them – it nevertheless fulfilled the crucial task of pre-selecting
the best East Timorese law-degree-holding candidates. On 7 January 2000
the TA appointed the first eight judges and two prosecutors to office
from those who had been pre-selected by the commission. Due to the
relatively low level of qualifications of the candidates, UNTAET devised
a training programme composed of three elements: a one-week *quick impact* course before the actual appointment, continued training while in
office and the provision of a mentor.[79] However, Strohmeyer decided in
January to transfer complete control of the judiciary, and complete jurisdiction over ordinary crimes, to local East Timorese jurists.[80]

The merits of appointing underqualified individuals to key posts will
be discussed in more detail later in this chapter. Important to note, however, is that the UN leadership did put a great emphasis on involving
local actors in the judicial process to the greatest extent possible, and
from the beginning of the mission. What is also interesting to note is the
fact that UNTAET was much more aggressive in the *Timorization* of the
rule-of-law institutions, and the judiciary in particular, in comparison to
its approach to the involvement of local actors in the civil administration
of the territory or its political institutions.[81] The evidence to this effect
clearly demonstrates that the involvement of local actors in the judicial
process was treated early on as a matter of priority over and above other
sectors important for sustainable and democratic governance.

Legal and judicial reform developments

This section discusses some of the developments which resulted from
the UN's approach to legal and judicial reform, focusing particularly on
those occurrences which are most relevant for the analysis and discus-

sion section to follow. As mentioned earlier, Simon Chesterman's assessment that the UN's choice of law was "uncontroversial"[82] is inaccurate. The UN's choice not only proved to be controversial, but also led to one of the first major political crises in Timor-Leste. As one of the first prosecutors for the special panels, Suzannah Linton, argues, "the decision to apply Indonesian law was a controversial one and remains so to this day".[83] While initially there was not the same type of uproar about the choice of law as there was in Kosovo, the crisis over the law did come eventually – in 2003, one year after the country became independent. Strohmeyer explains that when the United Nations chose Indonesian law, "various parts of the East Timorese community objected to the very idea of continuing the application of the same laws that had been used for more than two decades by the Indonesian regime, and which were, therefore, widely perceived as being tools of the Indonesian occupation of East Timor".[84] Linton further explains that "Part of the objection stems from a lack of appreciation that UNTAET is simply a transitional administration and the choice of law that will eventually be applied in the independent East Timor is a decision to be made by the new state and its officials."[85] However, despite 25 years of Indonesian oppression, pragmatism caused East Timor's local leadership to accept the application of Indonesian law as the most practicable solution to the rule-of-law vacuum.[86]

Until July 2003 it was commonly understood that the applicable law was Indonesian law. However, on 15 July 2003 a legal crisis ensued that precipitated a political crisis, and created much doubt and confusion about the applicable law. The whole issue began when the Court of Appeal delivered a ruling in the *Dos Santos* case, which sentenced the defendant on three counts of murder and "a crime against humanity in the form of genocide".[87] This would have been impossible under the Indonesian penal code. While the public prosecutor had charged Dos Santos with crimes against humanity, the special panel for serious crimes had convicted him of murder as a standard crime under the Indonesian penal code, and the defendant was sentenced to 20 years' imprisonment.[88] The public prosecutor, however, had decided to appeal this decision by arguing that Dos Santos should have been convicted of murder as a crime against humanity, which carries a minimum 22-year sentence under the Portuguese penal code, two years longer than the sentence which Dos Santos had received. The Court of Appeal's decision to sentence Dos Santos for crimes against humanity created much confusion and uncertainty within East Timor's legal community, and eventually divided the courts and the legal establishment regarding the source of the East Timorese laws.[89]

The Court of Appeal ruled by a two to one majority that since the Indonesian occupation of East Timor between 1974 and 1999 was illegal under international law, the *valid* applicable law prior to 25 October 1999 was that of Portugal, the former colonial power. The court concluded that since:

> Portugal continued to be recognised by the international community, by the United Nations Security Council and by the Timorese People as the Administering Power of East Timor during the period between December 1975 and 25 October 1999, the "laws applied in East Timor prior to 25 October 1999" could only be the Portuguese laws.[90]

But in relation to a further case where the Court of Appeal applied Portuguese law, the dissenting judge in the *Dos Santos* case stated that she disagreed with the interpretation of Article 3.1 of Regulation 1999/1, and that in her view "what is meant by the law applicable before 25 October 1999 refers more to Indonesian law".[91] She made her case on the basis that clauses 2 and 3 of Article 3 unambiguously refer to laws to be repealed that are part of the Indonesian legal code.

After its majority decision, the Court of Appeal applied Portuguese law in a few more cases, but the Dili District Court and the special panel for serious crimes refused to apply Portuguese law and continued applying Indonesian law.[92] Thus for a while a dual system of laws operated in the territory. But the implications for legal reform of having such a dual system were serious: in the first instance, if Portuguese law was applied in the long term, all legal transactions of the period between 1974 and 1999 would have been potentially rendered invalid since they would have been made under Indonesian and not Portuguese law. This in turn would have caused a significant disruption to the functioning of the legal system, and also a disruption of the economy.[93] Furthermore, the uncertainty as to the applicable law for the duration of UNTAET between 1999 and 2002 would also cast doubt on the validity of the decisions of the special panels taken over the course of those years.[94]

The issue became highly political, and nine parliamentary deputies took it upon themselves to propose a law in the National Parliament which would determine that the applicable law was Indonesian law.[95] Timorese lawyers, most of whom had graduated from Indonesian law schools, threatened to resign from their positions as judges, public defenders or prosecutors unless parliament voted in favour of the proposal. After a series of parliamentary debates, with frequent negative references to the four centuries of Portuguese colonial rule, the proposed law passed overwhelmingly with 62 votes to three and 12 abstentions on 30 September 2003, and the dispute was resolved.[96] It is clear, though, that this episode undermined public trust in the new judiciary. Between 2003 and 2006 the legal framework remained based on Indonesian law. However, in 2006 this framework was replaced by civil and penal codes based on Portuguese law.[97] This important change in the legal system appears to indicate that while the local jurists and the population at large may have initially accepted the Indonesian legal codes for pragmatic reasons, the general sentiment was in favour of the more progressive Portuguese legal codes.

Apart from being unpopular, and eventually leading to a legal and political crisis, the UN's initial choice of law was problematic in a further key respect. Strohmeyer explained that:

> It is difficult for any lawyer, for example, to interpret the Indonesian Penal Code and Criminal Procedure Code through the lens of those international human rights instruments which are now part of East Timorese domestic law. Moreover, only a few East Timorese lawyers are familiar with the application of international human rights norms in practice.[98]

The decision to require the interpretation of the Indonesian laws through the lens of a complex international legal regime not only placed a heavy burden on inexperienced lawyers, but also created an unnecessary lack of clarity within the legal framework.

Furthermore, the legal regime which the United Nations chose to establish for the special panels created various difficulties. Linton explains that legally, Regulation 2000/15 "Incorporates, almost verbatim, the substantive legal provisions dealing with subject matter jurisdiction and the general principles of law contained in the proposed *Rome Statute of the International Criminal Court*."[99] The problem with this regime, as Linton puts it, is that:

> This highly ambitious document has imported a regime created for a radically different setting, the International Criminal Court ... into a district court of one of the world's poorest nations. The Rome Statute ... is premised upon the assumption that an international body will be created receiving maximum international support, able to administer and uphold the highest international standards that set an example for all ... By adopting provisions meant for the ICC, UNTAET may have "bitten off more than it can chew". As it is slowly discovering, Regulation 2000/15 has created a tremendous legal and financial burden.[100]

So the mission adopted a highly complex legal regime for the prosecution of serious crimes while it was trying at the same time to build from the ground up, and with very few resources, the judicial system within which this complex framework was to apply. As will be discussed further below, the application of such a complex legal regime by inexperienced lawyers led to many problems.

One of the curious developments of the UN's judicial reform efforts was the appointment of judges and prosecutors at a time when no court system was in existence. As we saw, the TA appointed the first jurists in early January 2000; however, Resolution 2000/11 "On the Organization of Courts in East Timor" was not promulgated until 6 March, nearly two months after the judges began their work, issuing arrest warrants, etc. A further curiosity was that in the first few months of 2000 only a handful of individuals had copies of the Indonesian Criminal Code and the Indonesian Code of Criminal Procedure in a language they understood.[101] While this failure to distribute the applicable law quickly and widely in a language that was commonly understood was eventually rectified, the problem of the failure to publicize laws nevertheless kept reappearing at various stages of the mission. Regulation 1999/4 had established the official *Gazette* which was intended as the formal mechanism for publishing UNTAET laws and relevant legislation.[102] However, the publication of the *Gazette* was initially irregular and then lapsed altogether in 2001.[103]

With the establishment of the courts in March 2000 and the serious crimes panels in June 2000, the wheels of justice started to turn, although not without difficulties and serious flaws. In the first instance, the United Nations had established eight district courts and one Court of Appeal; however, as a result of the lack of trained judges and resources, the number of district courts had to be reduced to four two months later.[104] Furthermore, East Timorese judges, prosecutors and public defenders met the establishment of the special panels and the adoption of the relevant legal regime for those panels with great resentment and hostility; Linton explains that these jurists:

> Publicly voiced anger and disappointment that they were not included in any meaningful way in the consultation process that led to its adoption. The East Timorese jurists perceived that, as in previous times, they were being denied the right of meaningful participation in momentous decisions affecting them. The Presidency of the District Court of Dili was particularly outraged that, despite the provisions of s. 10.3 of *Regulation 2000/11*, it had not been consulted about the establishment of Special Panels. There was a strong feeling that the international community was taking the cases away from the East Timorese; there was a loss of ownership and involvement in this crucial process.[105]

The jurists' vocal protests about the lack of consultation and inclusion in the process that led to the establishment of the special panels arguably cancelled out the intended benefit of the UN's approach of including local actors from the early stages of the mission.[106] On the one hand the United Nations wanted to give locals a sense of ownership over the judicial process; but when it came to a crucial task for the judiciary – the prosecution of serious crimes – the United Nations failed even to consult the local jurists.

When the first serious crimes trials began, it became clear that the judicial system was marred by many procedural and institutional deficiencies and political problems which undermined the entire judicial reform effort. For instance, some of the defendants had not only been held in pre-trial detention for a period longer than that normally acceptable under international standards, but had been kept in such detention illegally: the orders of arrest and detention were issued or sanctioned by individuals not in a position to do so, since they were appointed to a legal entity which was not yet in existence.[107] However, irrespective of the unlawfulness of these detentions, UNTAET retroactively validated all of them: Regulation 2000/14 included Article 12a.10, which legalized "all warrants for detention issued by the Investigating Judge or Public Prosecutor prior to the coming into force of the present Regulation".[108]

One of the political problems stemmed from the conflicting objectives of UNTAET's mandate: the first of these was to ensure the return and resettlement of refugees;[109] the second objective was the need to bring the perpetrators of atrocities to justice. The conflict arose from the fact that many of the refugees were ex-militia who did not want to return to East Timor for fear of prosecution; thus a vigorous prosecution policy would clearly discourage such refugees from returning, and would therefore make it very difficult for the United Nations to fulfil a key aspect of its mandate.[110] Furthermore, some of the militia leaders who fled to West Timor were influential in their communities, and many of the key suspects were therefore politically vital in the matter of refugee returns; thus the political objective of wishing to bring back refugees did compromise the justice process. As one report described the situation:

> Militia leaders and other prominent opponents of East Timor's independence ensconced in Indonesian West Timor are feted and treated like state visitors on UN sponsored "look see" visits to East Timor, supposedly designed to encourage the return of refugees held captive by the militias in West Timor ... In the name of reconciliation the UNTAET Chief of Staff spends much of his time courting militia leaders such as the Carvalho brothers whose militias razed Ainaro town to the ground.[111]

The problem was that the Serious Crimes Unit (SCU), which was charged with UN prosecutions, became involved in negotiations with these ex-militia leaders, and there was a legitimate concern that their will to prosecute some of these leaders objectively had diminished due to this interaction.[112]

In addition to being unfair, the UN's approach to prosecutions was also incoherent. UNTAET was mandated to prosecute "those responsible" for the atrocities in 1999,[113] but the lack of a prosecution strategy led to a situation where "whether a person is prosecuted or not appear[ed] to be the result of an accident of geography": while many of the high-ranking officials remained at large, small-time members of the militia were indicted simply because they were "in the wrong place, at the wrong time".[114] The UN's desire to prosecute atrocities from the early stages of the mission led to the adoption of an early indictment policy. However, it is evident that this policy, along with the fact that Indonesia was intent on protecting its own war criminals, meant that virtually all serious crimes trials in East Timor involved only small-time perpetrators; unsurprisingly, this led to the development of a perception among the local population that the decisions about who would be tried were not based on any fair or objective criteria.[115]

What was arguably the worst blow to the prosecution strategy was the UN's refusal to support its own prosecutors in one prominent indictment in 2003, along with the decision of the East Timorese leadership to distance itself from that indictment. The case was that of General Wiranto, the former minister of defence and commander of the Indonesian armed forces. When the indictment for General Wiranto and seven other men, including East Timor's former governor, Abilio Soares, was issued, East Timor's President Xanana Gusmao was quick to distance himself from it, expressing regret for not having been consulted on the matter and stating that it was not in East Timor's interest to hold such a trial, given the importance of good relations with Indonesia. While Gusmao tried to imply that the indictment had come from the United Nations, the United Nations countered by arguing that "while indictments are prepared by international staff, they are issued under the legal authority of the Timorese Prosecutor General. The United Nations does not have any legal authority to issue indictments."[116] This statement was insincere, because the SCU had been in charge of prosecutions even after East Timor gained its independence, whereas East Timorese prosecutors were predominantly involved with ordinary crimes.[117] It appears that this trial was politically unviable for both the United Nations and East Timor; the clear implication was that the impartial pursuit of justice does not apply to cases which have the potential to be politically destabilizing.

In addition to the lack of a fair and coherent prosecution strategy, the judicial process was marred by the lack of adequate defence counsel. While the United Nations set up a prosecution with experienced international lawyers and staff, and appointed international judges, the responsibility for public defence was placed entirely in the hands of inexperienced Timorese jurists: the United Nations established a small Public Defender's Office, manned it with local lawyers and mandated it with the responsibility for defending all types of cases, including those involving serious crimes.[118] While these lawyers had law degrees from Indonesian universities, none had any experience of litigation before being hired.[119] One observer argued that the appointment of public defenders came as an "afterthought" to the appointment of prosecutors and judges, and that such defenders were less able than their counterparts: "Simply put ... The public defenders were appointed out of what was left of candidates with law degrees."[120] And so initially fewer than 10 public defenders were hired for the whole territory.

The original expectation was that these lawyers would be able to work on the serious crimes cases. But eventually the gap in experience and skill between the Timorese defenders and the professional international prosecutors became impossible to ignore, and UNTAET offered to sponsor three international defence lawyers.[121] However, this and further offers by NGOs to sponsor international defenders were strongly resisted by the Timorese-administered Ministry of Justice.[122] This obstructionist behaviour was linked with the ministry's agenda to make Portuguese, as opposed to the predominant local dialect Tetun, or English, the official working language of the judicial system and the government sector.[123] As a result, experienced international defenders with NGO funding were directly blocked from joining the Public Defender's Office on the simple basis that they came from English-speaking countries.[124]

The International Foundation for Election Systems' offer to fund a second mentor in the Public Defender's Office also failed to lead to such an appointment before it expired in 2002, on similar grounds.[125] While eventually some international lawyers did manage to work in that office as either mentors or defenders, this did not happen without substantial resistance from the Ministry of Justice.[126] As will be demonstrated below, such obstructionism on the basis of language politics went beyond resistance to international defenders, and included resistance to the hiring of international judges and the acceptance of much-needed funding. Important to note is that language politics soured the relationship between the UN administration and the East Timorese relatively early on. There was a perception on the part of the Timorese that the United Nations wanted to impose the use of Bahasa Indonesia or English as a working language in East Timor, and in one instance Foreign Minister Ramos Horta threatened that he would prohibit the participation of any of his staff in a UN-organized training workshop if it was not conducted in Portuguese.[127] Given that only a small élite of approximately 5 per cent spoke Portuguese,[128] and that it was not spoken during most trials in the hybrid tribunals by either defendants, witnesses or defenders, the government's insistence on the use of Portuguese, and its resistance to vital international appointments on this basis, seems at best misplaced and at worst detrimental to the judicial system.[129]

While UNTAET had offered to sponsor three international defenders, the Justice Ministry's resistance to this offer meant that by 2003 only one of these positions had been filled. Even though the UNDP had managed to fund a further international defender temporarily, to assist with the mounting caseload,[130] and the NGO No Peace Without Justice had sponsored another international defender, these efforts were minimal in proportion to what was necessary so as to proceed with the trials at a reasonable pace and ensure that the quality of the defence was of a sufficiently high standard. As the *Los Palos* case demonstrates, there were serious shortcomings even though international defenders were hired: the very limited number of Timorese defenders meant that the three assigned to the case had to take on five clients between them, and the three international defence lawyers assigned to the case took on a further five clients.[131] The problem with this approach was that the representation of multiple clients by one lawyer had the potential to threaten the quality of the defence which each individual is guaranteed under international fair trial standards; this situation worsened further when two of the defenders left for Portugal, leaving the remaining lawyers to take over the defence of their clients.[132] Furthermore, while the issue was never raised in this case, there was nevertheless potential for a conflict of interest to arise for those defenders representing more than one person accused of the same crime.[133]

Moreover, the limited number of Timorese and international defenders, the high demand on their time and the limited resources available to them meant that they were not able to meet their clients with the desired frequency; this was true for ordinary and serious crimes cases.[134] For instance, in the *Los Palos* case one of the local defence lawyers sent a standardized letter to the investigators informing them that due to time constraints he would be unable to attend the questioning.[135] Eventually, defendants and witnesses in the case raised objections during the trial about their statements as they had been recorded or translated during questioning, and defence lawyers queried the use of statements taken under conditions where a lawyer was not present. The court nevertheless had to permit their use, arguing that in the act of testifying, after having been informed of his right to a defence lawyer, the defendant had waived his right to such counsel during questioning.[136] This incident was by no means the only one where a lawyer was unable to see a client at a key point, and serves to highlight the endemic lack of Timorese defence lawyers.

In addition to the fact that the low number and inexperience of the Timorese public defenders seriously undermined the quality of the defence, and eventually led to the creation of a backlog of cases, the quality of the international defence lawyers provided early on was also low:

none had experience of court work in crimes against humanity cases[137] and with international or even criminal law.[138] Furthermore, the two UNDP-funded mentors hired to assist and train the local defenders were not qualified for the position: the first mentor was a lecturer in commercial law, had never been a criminal defence lawyer and had no experience at litigation; and while the second had practised as a defence lawyer, he was unable to speak any of the four official languages used in court, which obviously rendered him virtually incapable of helping the Timorese defenders.[139]

The problem of insufficient numbers and lack of adequate experience plagued not only the Public Defender's Office but also extended to the local and international judges. Regulation 2000/15 required that "in the overall composition of the panels due account shall be taken of the experience of the judges in criminal law, international law, including humanitarian law and human rights law".[140] This was the first judicial appointment for the local judges, so *experience* as such, let alone with international law, was something they sorely lacked. But what made matters much worse was the fact that the international judges appointed to the special panels also lacked any prior experience in applying international law.[141] Thus the panels were made up entirely of judges who were inexperienced in matters of international law; and while groundbreaking cases were undertaken given that in practice the Rome Statute essentially applied, virtually none of the special panels' decisions contained references to international jurisprudence.[142]

The problem of having inexperienced international and local judges working on serious crimes cases was compounded by the fact that there were never enough judges for more than one panel to operate at any given time. Regulation 2000/15 envisioned the establishment of more than one special panel.[143] However, the scarcity of judges meant that only one panel was able to operate during all but one month of 2001, and subsequently five judges had to rotate between two panels.[144] This situation inevitably led to a large backlog of cases: once the *Los Palos* case got under way early in 2001, it effectively shut down the rest of the serious crimes cases,[145] and a backlog began which the United Nations was never able to remedy fully. Furthermore, the lack of judges meant that the Court of Appeal was unable to function for well over half a year between 2001 and 2002.[146] The problem was initially blamed in part on a lack of planning, a failure on the part of the United Nations and the Timorese to appreciate the importance of the right to an appeal and a misunderstanding between UNTAET and the Ministry of Justice over who was responsible for judicial appointments: while UNTAET held that the initiative for judicial recruitment lay with the Ministry of Justice, the ministry felt that it was UNTAET's responsibility.[147]

While the above is a valid assessment of some of the reasons why the Court of Appeal was unable to function, the Ministry of Justice was also at fault because it obstructed the appointments process. In addition to stalling some of the judicial appointments to the special panels,[148] the Ministry of Justice obstructed Court of Appeal appointments: when on 8 May 2002 the Transitional Judicial Service Commission recommended the appointment of one Irish and one Canadian judge to the Court of Appeal,[149] the Minister of Justice Anna Pessoa and the Department of Judicial Affairs resisted these appointments and the posts were not filled.[150] As one NGO observing all judicial proceedings, the Judicial System Monitoring Programme, put it: "There was a preference within the Ministry of Justice for Court of Appeal judges to come from Lusophone countries."[151] When Timor-Leste became independent, 39 cases were pending for appeal, eight of which were appeals from decisions made by the special panel.[152] Thus the Justice Ministry's obstinate behaviour towards judicial appointments had a negative impact on the right to appeal of those accused of both ordinary and serious crimes.

There were certainly many other factors which hindered the appeals process. Perhaps the most problematic of these was the absence of complete official written transcripts of court proceedings of any type made in the district courts, apart from some basic notes taken by judges in court.[153] The importance of a written record of trial proceedings for the launch of an appeals process is common knowledge to any lawyer:

> Having access to an accurate transcript of the proceedings is essential for the parties when preparing for any appeal, and for the judges during the appeal hearing. If the reasoning or outcome in the decision of the court at first instance is challenged, an accurate transcript is the primary basis upon which the appeal court is able to assess the challenge.[154]

This importance was acknowledged in two regulations – Regulations 2000/11[155] and 2000/30.[156] While video and audio recordings were made of the proceedings in front of the special panels, these records were not transcribed, and the common practice was for judges on the special panels to refer to their own notes taken during the proceedings and disregard these recordings.[157] Furthermore, the use of audio or video recordings of proceedings without a written transcript was highly problematic because it was very difficult for anyone to review specific sections of the record, since the recordings were only stored by date; and crucially, the recording of multiple interpretations from various languages on audio CDs or video is complex and problematic in itself.[158] The final decision in the *Joseph Leki* case clearly illustrates how the courts proceeded under the circumstances: "The rapporteur judge made a record after summarizing as accurately as possible on a portable computer the statements made by the parties and the questions, orders and decisions of judges during the hearing."[159]

This process led to a confused and unclear record of the trial proceedings. One case illustrates this particularly well, and also shows how important a clear, accurate and comprehensive written transcript of trial proceedings is for the appeals process. In the case of the first final appeal from a decision of the special panel, Judge Frederick Egonda-Ntende noted that the official record of the proceedings was inconsistent with the report contained in the special panel's judgment, arguing that "The imprecise language leaves the record somewhat confused"[160] and ultimately deciding that this lack of clarity and consistency between the panel's trial decision and the proceedings' record, which is vital for the appeals process, had led him to the conclusion, albeit the minority decision in this particular appeal case, that the panel's decision was not law-based and was thus a nullity.[161]

In addition to rendering trial decisions as potentially not based on law, the lack of comprehensive written trial records made it difficult to file an appeal, as can be illustrated in the *Los Palos* case. Following the judgment in the trial on 11 December 2001, the appeal notice filed states that the records of the proceedings will be used as evidence. By early February 2002 the special panel had to grant an extension for the appeal to be filed, given that no record of the proceedings was available, and also ordered that the court registrar make this transcript available. While the Court Registry made the video records available, it did not provide any transcript, as none existed.[162] The special panel ordered in late March 2002 once again that the records of the trial be made available to the appellants by mid-April, however, by the end of April 2002 no transcript had been provided, and thus the appeal proceedings were suspended.[163]

All in all, UNTAET allowed 13 trials to proceed to verdict without the provision of a written or recorded transcript.[164] A "very senior" official from the prosecutor's office is reported to have said that the special panels did not have to meet international standards because they were essentially domestic tribunals, and therefore "domestic" standards must apply.[165] However, given that it was the United Nations which established the justice system, a claim that domestic standards must apply is disingenuous, and attempts to hide the fact that the United Nations was unwilling to provide more expensive justice mechanisms, such as those offered at the ICTR and the ICTY.[166]

But even if written transcripts had been provided, this would not have surmounted the problem of the lack of adequate translation of court documents and adequate interpretation offered during the trials, a fact which would also have affected the quality and accuracy of such transcripts.

Regulation 2000/11 provides for the right to an interpreter in all cases,[167] and since the court was operating with four official languages,[168] the various combinations of Timorese and international judges, prosecutors, defenders, defendants and witnesses meant the demand for translation and interpretation was great, at times involving up to six languages in one trial if languages other than the four official ones had to be used.[169] However, during the entire mission no translation unit was established that could serve only the courts, which consequently had to use the seven interpreters working for the Justice Ministry. These *interpreters* had firstly no formal qualifications, secondly no legal training and thirdly no experience with court interpretation.[170] Yet as well as providing interpretation services in court and translating official court documents, these seven individuals had to offer their translation services to the National Parliament in addition to their regular work for the Justice Ministry; the most charitable way to describe the translation service is that it was "stretched to capacity".[171]

This overstretching of the translation and interpretation service, and its relatively low and dubious quality, were problematic in several key respects: firstly, it slowed down the proceedings of trials significantly; secondly, interpretation was provided only erratically during trials, thereby hindering a defendant's right to understand what was going on during the proceedings;[172] and thirdly, it led to a frequent problem of communication between the defence and a defendant. In the *Los Palos* case, for instance, two of the defenders spoke only English and were reliant on interpreters in order to communicate with the defendants; at times, if interpreters were not available, the defence had to ask members of the public for assistance.[173]

The quality of the translations also resulted in a lack of clarity. During a trial session, for instance, a defender spoke in English and enquired about "the hitting of Evaristo Lopez", but as he was unable to pronounce the English "h" at the beginning of a word, the question was translated into Bahasa Indonesia as the "eating ... of Evaristo Lopez".[174] A problem really arose when judges assigned considerable weight in their judgments on potentially faulty interpretation of quotes from the accused: in one case, the court impugned a defendant's credibility on the basis of inconsistencies in his testimony.[175] As the JSMP observed, "the possibility cannot be discounted that ... alleged inconsistencies [in a defendant's testimony] were simply the product of language difficulties between the participants in court".[176] And while faulty interpretation may have rendered some judgments of the special panels unfair, the limited capacity for translation also hindered the right to an appeal in several cases. For instance, an appeal filed in May 2001 was pending for over 18 months, primarily because a large number of documents needed to be translated from Indonesian to Portuguese so that the Portuguese-speaking judge would be able to review the appeal, but were not translated as a result of the lack of translators.[177]

Clearly, the lack of adequate resources, both human and non-human, was a major obstacle to the functioning of the judiciary. While the United Nations must bear part of the responsibility for this lack, some observers arguing that it was trying to get by "on the cheap"[178] on justice reforms, the Ministry of Justice itself was more than complicit. An offer from the US Agency for International Development (USAID) to write essentially a blank cheque to the judiciary was declined, shortly after which USAID donated US$8.2 million to various civil society organizations in the newly formed country.[179] The acceptance of an offer of such magnitude could have alleviated many problems: the mission's translation and interpretation capacity could have been increased, a stenographer could have been hired, the public defence capacity could have been increased, etc. The rejection of this offer, however, meant the continued provision of a judicial service which fell short of international standards in many respects.

Many of the above-mentioned problems led to lengthy pre-trial detention periods. The inability to have more than one special panel working at any given time, even when a second one became operational, along with some of the procedural delays led to a situation where in early 2001 some 700 cases in the category of serious crimes alone had still not been processed.[180] While some suspects were released without trial, many were kept for a year without a trial. Some defendants were also kept in pre-trial detention unlawfully, because the investigating judges issuing the warrants for their detention had no authority to detain these individuals; furthermore, some were also held unlawfully because their detention orders had expired and the judiciary was unable to hear applications for the extension of their detention orders.[181] But even in cases where detention was legal, the defendants were often unable to access legal representation for prolonged periods.[182] The long detention periods and the lack of access to defence lawyers were two of the key factors blamed when over half of the prison population of East Timor managed to escape in August 2002.[183] By August 2003 some of the detainees who had not escaped had been kept in pre-trial detention for three-and-a-half years without a trial date.[184]

Analysis and discussion

As in the Kosovo case study, the analysis here will consider the impact which the five elements[185] of the UN's approach had on the likelihood that the mission would succeed in its efforts to establish a sustainable legal system. Five sets of questions[186] are asked in assessing whether the approach enhanced or diminished the likelihood of establishing such a sustainable system, and thus in establishing whether the particular approach was suited to the task. The section is divided into five subsections, each of which aims to answer one set of key questions.

Adherence to Fuller's principles of legality

This subsection focuses on whether the UN's approach led to a violation of Fuller's principles,[187] and also on whether the adoption of the particular approach demonstrated the peacebuilders' aspiration to be in compliance with these principles. If a *total failure* of or *gross departure* from any of Fuller's principles occurred, or if it can be shown that even where no such failure occurred, the UN's efforts did not aim to be in line with these principles, the approach cannot be the appropriate method for building a sustainable legal system. The discussion begins with an exposition of the ways in which Fuller's principles were breached, and then links these breaches to the UN's approach.

As we have seen, one of Fuller's principles is the need for authorities to administer rules as they are announced and publicized. The discussion in the previous section demonstrated that there were many instances where UNTAET staff, the local authorities or the judicial appointees failed in this regard. One of the first and most detrimental failures of this principle relates to the appointment to the special panels of East Timorese and international judges who were not versed in international law. Section 23 of Regulation 2000/15 unequivocally required that in selecting the composition of the panels, the qualifications of the judges in criminal law and in international law must be taken into account. While the regulation as phrased[188] appears to leave some space for a judge less experienced in those areas to sit on a panel, it is clear the regulation requires that in the "overall" composition of the panels some of the judges have such qualifications. Yet, as we saw, East Timorese judges without any knowledge or experience of international law were permitted to sit on the panels together with international judges who also had no experience with international law; it is thus clear that this aspect of the law on the qualification of judges was administered differently from the way it was intended.

Furthermore, since the initial focus was on hiring exclusively East Timorese judges, no provision was made for the Transitional Judicial Service Commission (TJSC), which was responsible for the selection and recommendation of judges to the TA, to select and recommend international judges. However, as it became increasingly clear that relying only on local judges was not sustainable, especially because of the need for more experienced jurists for appellate proceedings and eventually also for the special panels, international judges were hired; some of the first judicial affairs officers who were working for UNTAET moved into judicial positions.[189] But since the United Nations initially wanted to appoint only local jurists, there was no provision in the law for the TJSC to review and recommend the applications of candidates of non-Timorese origin.[190]

While a change in that law would have been necessary for the TJSC to review and recommend persons of non-Timorese origin for judicial and prosecutorial posts, the appointment of international jurists to such offices continued through the regular recruitment procedures for UNTAET, and thus international jurists were appointed in a similar way as the first international judges who entered from UNTAET posts. One of the international Appeals Court judges, Frederick Egonda-Ntende, points out that this raised serious questions and doubts about the legitimacy of the appointment of international judges under UNTAET's own law.[191] Since UNTAET regulations amounted to laws, the appointment of international judges without an amendment to the relevant regulation did indeed amount to a failure of congruence between the rules as announced and as administered.

A further violation of this principle occurred as a result of the judges' frequent failure to apply international law, or to apply it properly. Regulation 2000/15 required the special panels to apply "where appropriate, applicable treaties and recognized principles and norms of international law, including the established principles of the international law of armed conflict".[192] However, judges' failure to apply international law or apply it correctly led to the handing down of very harsh sentences for relatively low-level perpetrators.[193] Furthermore, although the special panels could use as a source of guidance the jurisprudence of the ICTY and the ICTR, as well as the work of the International Law Commission and the Preparatory Commission for the International Criminal Courts, throughout 2001 none of the special panels' decisions contained references to any international jurisprudence.[194] The panels' lack of knowledge and experience with international law led to the failure to apply such law or apply it correctly, which clearly indicates that the special panels did not live up to the requirements concerning the law to be applied in serious crimes cases.

Moreover, in one case the presiding judge purposefully chose to disregard the law. The case was that of Victor Alves, a FALINTIL member regarded as a local hero.[195] Alves's defence had filed a petition for his release on the grounds that his detention was unlawful, and also that even if it had not been unlawful, the time limit of detention under Indonesia's Code of Criminal Procedure had expired. Fearing the destabilizing consequences of an early release of a local hero while pro-Indonesian militia leaders remained in detention, UNTAET quickly passed Regulation 2000/14, one day before Alves's court hearing. The regulation retroactively legalized all detentions which could have been deemed as potentially unlawful, and determined that in certain circumstances detainees could be held in pre-trial detention longer than the 110 days previously permitted prior to the commencement of the proceedings.[196]

Crucially, a further regulation also made it impossible for an individual judge to preside in cases that carry a sentence of over five years, which would have applied to Victor Alves. Understandably, the presiding judge felt that the regulation amounted to legislative interference designed to alter his potential decision.[197] Disregarding the law, the judge went on to rule that Alves's detention was unlawful. As the former prosecutor for the special panels, Suzannah Linton, put it:

> Rather than following the generally accepted practice of recording his concerns but nevertheless applying the law, the young East Timorese judge took a calculated decision not to apply a law he felt was unjust ... The first decision to emerge from the UNTAET administered District Court of Dili is therefore one where the judge refused to apply the law.[198]

After this decision, no appeal was possible because even though the Court of Appeal had been officially established, no judges had yet been appointed to it, for reasons discussed in the previous section. Thus Alves was released.

What this case highlights is that the law was not administered as announced, on three different counts. First was the issue of unlawful detention. Alves's case is by no means unique here, and had Regulation 2000/14 not retroactively validated all warrants for detention issued by an investigating judge or public prosecutor prior to 10 May 2000, then his detention would certainly have been unlawful. But the fact remains that for a brief period his detention, and that of many other suspects, was unlawful, not only because the time period allowed for pre-trial detentions had expired, but also because the investigating judge did not have the authority to issue such warrants: this was the case because Regulation 2000/11 establishing the courts was promulgated in March, by which time many warrants had been issued by judges appointed in January, and also because the position of *investigating judge* did not exist in the Indonesian criminal system.[199]

The second failure of congruence between the rules as announced and as administered is the judge's purposeful disregard of the law. He was right in his perception that Regulation 2000/14 was designed to ensure Alves's continued detention, and was meant to influence his decision.

However, the fact that he ruled in the way he did shows that the law was not upheld by those most expected to respect it. And the final failure of congruence between the rules as announced and as administered which the case demonstrates is the lack of an appeals procedure, despite the fact that the law establishing an appeals court had been promulgated through Regulation 2000/11. According to the law, it should have been possible for the prosecution to file an appeal not only on the grounds that the judge disregarded the law which would have validated the continued detention of the defendant, but also on the grounds that the judge was not competent to hold the hearing in this case as an individual judge, also as determined through Regulation 2000/14. However, the lack of judges to make up the Court of Appeals meant that the laws and procedures could not be administered in the way in which they were intended, and this violation occurred not just in this case but persisted for a large part of 2001, affecting many other cases.

A lack of congruence between the laws as determined by UNTAET and as administered by it also resulted from UNTAET's mandate to repatriate refugees. Militia leaders not only had a strong influence over these refugees, as discussed, but also held many of them captive in West Timor; the United Nations unsurprisingly saw cooperation with these leaders as vital for the return of the refugees. In his efforts to convince militia leaders to return, UNTAET's chief of staff made informal agreements with the general prosecutor regarding the prosecution of such leaders, who then received guarantees about their ability to return to East Timor frequently for negotiations.[200] As a result of these arrangements, some of the early warrants for arrest of some of these leaders were never executed.[201] The fact that these dealings became common knowledge across East Timor through community rumours[202] was damaging for the public's trust in the newly established judicial mechanisms. What these dealings demonstrate is that one key objective of the mission – the repatriation of refugees – trumped another key objective of the mission, namely the prosecution of those who had committed atrocities. They also demonstrate that prosecutors became involved in what was essentially a political process, that UN officials were evidently not administering the laws correctly and that they were thus violating a key legal principle.

There are a few more examples of the ways in which the justice administrators derogated from the law. It is understandable that the administration of justice was taking place in very difficult circumstances – essentially UNTAET had to oversee the creation of a new judiciary from the ground up; however, the failure to provide transcripts of the proceedings in court, and the persistent continuation of trials for a prolonged period of time in light of this inability to offer adequate means for an accurate transcript to be provided to either the defence counsel or the judges, were in violation of Regulations 2000/11 and 2000/30.[203] Since procedural law prescribed that such transcripts must be provided, but trials continued without them, it is clear that there was no congruence between the law's requirements and its administration. Although audio and video recordings of trials were eventually introduced, the UN's failure to ensure that written transcripts of the trials were provided on the basis of these recordings still meant that the law was not administered properly. While Regulation 2001/25 did eventually make it legal for recordings of trial proceedings to be offered instead of a written transcript, the fact remains that for over a year the law on criminal procedure was breached by the failure of the administration, local or international, to provide such a written transcript.

The final violation of Fuller's principle of the need for congruence between the rules as announced and as administered to be discussed here can be found in the promulgation of Regulation 2000/14 itself, which as mentioned saw the retroactive legitimization of detention orders[204] and the derogation from international standards, as enshrined in the ICCPR, regarding the deprivation of liberty of detainees.[205] Regulation 1999/1 made explicitly clear that all laws in the territory would need to be read subject to international human rights standards, and in particular subject to, among others, the ICCPR. While the ICCPR's Articles 9 and 14, which govern rights on the deprivation of liberty and a fair trial, are not among the covenant's non-derogable rights, the grounds upon which one may derogate from them are very narrow. The provision in the ICCPR states clearly that one may derogate from the articles only "In time of *public emergency* which threatens the life of the nation and the existence of which is officially proclaimed."[206] However, while the conditions on 10 May 2000, when Regulation 2000/14 was promulgated, were certainly difficult, it cannot be argued that they constituted circumstances which threatened the life of the nation; [207] moreover, neither the United Nations nor the East Timorese Transitional Administration had proclaimed a state of public emergency throughout the territory.

In light of the fact that Regulation 1999/1 required all laws in the territory to be in line with human rights standards, the promulgation of Regulation 2000/14 amounts to a violation of the rules as announced and administered on the grounds that a derogation from the right to liberty occurred in an unlawful fashion, as the prevailing circumstances in East Timor did not amount to a public emergency that threatened the territory's existence. The regulation was an effort on the part of the UN administration to address a difficult problem about which various organizations, including the United Nations itself, had expressed growing concerns – that of unlawful detentions; it was also designed to prevent a potential crisis that might have ensued with the release of Victor Alves. Regulation 2000/14 frequently refers to the prevailing circumstances in the territory as grounds for the extension of detention periods and the derogation from the right to liberty. However, if the United Nations had deemed the prevailing circumstances in East Timor to amount to a public emergency, it ought to have derogated from the relevant ICCPR articles already in Regulation 1999/1. That it did not attests to the fact it did not view the situation in East Timor as a public emergency warranting such derogation – not even at the very beginning of its mission – or at least that its desire to implement a full catalogue of human rights made it blind to the need for such derogation. Furthermore, so as not to promulgate a regulation that violated a key legal principle, UNTAET needed to announce a state of emergency in the territory. It did not, and so the passing of Regulation 2000/14 to suit its political needs and compensate for some of the errors already made essentially meant that UNTAET was not adhering to its own laws.

Aside from the above-mentioned failures with regard to the principle of congruence, there were also various violations of Fuller's principle that the law must be clear and understandable. This lack of clarity stemmed in part from UNTAET's failure to review the existing laws and strike those which were incompatible with human rights standards.[208] One particular incident between the UN Police (UNPOL) and a crowd of protesters is indicative of this lack of legal clarity:[209] protesters had gathered in a location, but UNPOL declared the gathering illegal; when challenged on the relevant law that made the protest illegal, UNPOL was unable to recall whether this judgement was based on a UNTAET regulation or an internal police directive. A further investigation into the matter revealed the judgement to have been based on an unofficial translation into English of an old Indonesian law which required demonstrators to have prior authorization from the Indonesian authorities before staging a protest. Evidently, the feasibility of this law had not been reviewed, and neither had its consistency with rights to freedom of expression.

Arguably, the confusion over this law stemmed from the fact that Regulation 1999/1 only requires the striking of laws deemed as incompatible with international human rights standards, and at first glance this law is not incompatible with such standards: it is common practice in democratic societies to apply for a permit to hold a protest, and as such this law does not appear to violate the right to freedom of speech. However, to Timorese protesters it would have been clear that during the Indonesian occupation this law was designed to curb freedom of expression, so they felt that with the Indonesian regime gone, they could exercise their right to demonstrate.

A similar incident occurred when a Japanese activist was arrested in August 2000 for criticizing Xanana Gusmao, Timor's former independence movement leader. After 18 days in detention he was released, and the TA issued an executive order declaring that defamation is not a criminal offence and repealing sections 310–321 of the Indonesian Criminal Code.[210] Thus some laws were evidently not in line with human rights standards and were clear neither to UNPOL nor to the East Timorese. These incidents were by no means unique, and UNTAET's failure to review the laws also resulted in a lack of clarity on the law among prosecutors and judges, and consequently to their failure to apply laws consistently and to the application of laws incompatible with human rights standards.[211]

As in Kosovo, the general problem of clarity of the legal regime stemmed from Regulation 1999/1's requirement that Indonesian laws be read in light of international human rights instruments. UNTAET's principal legal adviser admitted that "It is difficult for any lawyer ... to interpret the Indonesian Penal Code and Criminal Procedure Code through the lens of those international human rights instruments which are now part of East Timorese domestic law", let alone for Timorese lawyers who were not familiar with international law.[212] But even if these lawyers were familiar with such instruments, having to interpret domestic law through the lens of international law was bound to result in a situation where it was not always clear what the law was and what law must apply to a particular case. While the promulgation of the new Provisional Code of Criminal Procedure improved this situation slightly,[213] problems of clarity nevertheless remained throughout UNTAET's mandate.

Finally, problems of clarity were also the result of the UN's promulgation of regulations which were not clear. One example was the confusion surrounding the post of *investigating judge*: in January 2000 the United Nations appointed two investigating judges, even though no such post existed in the Indonesian criminal system, and initially failed to clarify the powers and duties of this office.[214] When the United Nations eventually passed Regulation 2000/11 establishing the court system in March 2000, it determined that "In criminal matters, there shall be at least one judge assigned as investigating judge at every District Court in East Timor" and that "The investigating judge shall have the powers defined in the Criminal Procedure Code and other relevant UNTAET regulations."[215]

However, as the applicable criminal procedure code was that of Indonesia, this section was nonsensical because, as already mentioned, there are no investigating judges in the Indonesian justice system, and there are also no UNTAET regulations which make any reference to the powers of an investigating judge.[216] So investigating judges were first introduced into the justice system before courts were established; and even though the confusions over their role were widely known by the time Regulation 2000/11 was promulgated,[217] the regulation still failed to specify what powers and duties these judges had. This led to a situation where the procedural rules were unclear, and thus to further confusion within the justice system.

The discussion of the legal and judicial reform developments in the previous section hinted at another key violation of Fuller's principles: the fact that the publication of the *Gazette*, which was to be the official way of publicizing UNTAET's laws, executive directives and other legislative acts, was initially irregular and then lapsed entirely in 2001[218] meant that Fuller's principle that the rules must be made known was violated. While perhaps an argument can be made that even if the *Gazette*'s publication was irregular, the laws were eventually publicized, the same cannot be claimed for the failure to publish the *Gazette* for over a year. Even if UNTAET regulations and other executive and legislative acts did become known in different ways, the public's expectation after the promulgation of Regulation 1999/4 establishing the *Gazette* was that it was going to be the main vehicle for the publication of new rules. And since Regulation 1999/4 was never amended, it cannot be assumed that the public's expectations changed and another mechanism for publicizing rules existed. Thus perhaps one of the most important principles of legality was clearly violated.

We have seen thus far that there were violations of Fuller's principle of congruence, his principle of clarity and his principle that the rules must be publicized. But can these violations be linked to the UN's approach to legal and judicial reform? The following few paragraphs will demonstrate that particularly when it comes to the violations of the first two of these principles, various elements of the UN's approach can indeed be linked to them. First, the problems with the lack of clarity in the law were the direct result of the UN's decision to apply from the beginning of the mission the Indonesian legal codes, and to make their applicability subject to international human rights standards, prior to reviewing the legislation – a decision which amounted to the intellectual equivalent of putting the metaphorical cart before the horse. While some of the obvious problem laws, such as the death penalty, were stricken in Regulation 1999/1, many provisions of the Indonesian legal code left questions open as to whether applying them would run counter to human rights standards. As the examples of the UNPOL-halted demonstration and the Japanese activist detained for defamation demonstrate, some of the provisions of that code did indeed run counter to international standards, but not in a sufficiently obvious manner as to alarm officials about their applicability.

Shortly after entering East Timor, INTERFET introduced an emergency legal regime based on Indonesian laws, and UNTAET had the option to continue the application of this legal regime until such time as it had the chance to review all the Indonesian laws for consistency with human rights standards, identify potential problem areas and devise guidelines on the applicability of the law and international standards as part of the legal regime. Doing so would also have given the United Nations more time to learn about the workings of Indonesia's judiciary; as we saw, though, the failure to learn enough about it led the United Nations mistakenly to assume that *investigating judges* existed within the judiciary. Even if the United Nations wished to introduce the position of an investigating judge, reviewing the Indonesian legal codes prior to making them applicable would have made it clear that the UN regulations needed to specify what powers and responsibilities such judges had. The resultant confusion about these posts was thus avoidable had sufficient time been allowed for a proper review of the Indonesian justice system and legal codes.

Furthermore, even if the review of the laws, which did not take place during the mission, had occurred in the first few months as was originally envisioned, the same problems of clarity would still have existed during that time period. The key point here is that deciding to establish a legal regime when it is evident from the outset that there will be points that need clarification certainly violates the spirit of Fuller's principle that the rules must be clear and understandable. As previously mentioned, the principle of clarity requires not only that the letter of the law be clear and understandable, but also that the rules be clear to the point where they can guide the behaviour of the law-enforcement authorities, the judiciary and the population at large. As demonstrated in this chapter, this was not the case with the legal regime in East Timor.

Moreover, the UN's decision to make a full catalogue of human rights applicable from the beginning of the mission led to many of the above-mentioned violations of the principle of congruence between the rules as announced and as administered. Clearly, the United Nations was in a difficult position in East Timor: while it had to build a new judiciary from the ground up with limited resources, it also had to process hundreds of detainees. In the first few months of UNTAET the situation on the ground was dire; INTERFET had managed to re-establish some security, but there were nevertheless still instances of reprisal violence.[219] Over 70 per cent of the infrastructure had been destroyed and there was a law-and-order vacuum; while INTERFET's legal regime and the Detainee Management Unit alleviated a part of that problem,[220] the situation was still an emergency to all intents and purposes, even if the existence of the nation was no longer at risk.

Given these circumstances, the UN's approach of applying a full human rights catalogue, including specific reference to the fact that all persons working in public office must adhere to, among others, the

ICCPR, proved to be detrimental. It was detrimental particularly from a legal perspective, because it led to many of the violations of the principle of congruence: the circumstances were such that longer permissible periods of pre-trial detention were needed than those allowed by the law and international standards, since the capability to process all the cases within the required time period simply did not exist. When the United Nations eventually passed Regulation 2000/14 and attempted to derogate from Articles 9 and 14 of the ICCPR, it was not only acting against its own initial decision to observe a full catalogue of human rights standards within the territory, but also derogated from the rights set out in those articles on grounds which were not permissible. Similarly, the UN's decision to apply the Indonesian legal code from the beginning of the mission meant that the 72-hour limit placed on the period after which suspects must be released if they have not seen a judge, and the 110-day limit on pre-trial detention before proceedings begin, also had to be observed.[221] The adoption of these laws meant once again that when the fledgling judiciary was unable to handle the cases in the specified times, the principle of congruence was violated.

As the following section will demonstrate, many of the violations of judicial norms were the result of the UN's decision to involve local actors in the judicial process from the beginning of the mission and to the fullest extent possible, which in the case of East Timor the United Nations deemed to be the complete handover of control of the judiciary to local officials. But before we discuss the violations of judicial norms, it is important to highlight that this approach also violated Fuller's principle of congruence. A prominent violation in this respect was highlighted in the discussion of the *Alves* case, and in particular the judge's decision purposefully to ignore the law. Linton concludes that the problem lay in the fact that "having appointed novices to such heavy responsibilities, UNTAET then failed to provide them with adequate training and mentoring".[222] But her conclusion tells only half the story, because even if adequate training and mentoring had been provided, the fact remains that such training and mentoring would have taken place while the respective judge was already in office, and not prior to it, thus still leaving the door open for inexperienced judges to apply the law wrongly or ignore the laws that did not suit them.

Thus it is not difficult to see how the UN's approach led first to the handover of judicial control to local authorities, and then to the early appointment of an inexperienced judge, who as a result of this lack of experience and training, and the position he nevertheless held, violated a key legal principle. Had judicial control not been handed over to the East Timorese so early on, the judge could have been reprimanded or removed and a mistrial could have been declared. However, as UNTAET had handed over the reins, it did not wish to interfere with this judicial decision and the work of the Ministry of Justice.

Finally, the UN's desire to address, or appear to address, the serious crimes committed during the conflict from the earliest stages of the mission led to a situation where this objective conflicted with another key objective, namely the repatriation of refugees. The result of this clash was that the prosecution of some individuals was put on hold, and warrants of arrest were not carried out as the law required. Essentially, the policy decision to pursue the perpetrators of atrocities early on did not leave sufficient time for the consideration of the policy's political repercussions and an evaluation of the UN's own political will for such an undertaking. This resulted in a failure to devise a clear and coherent prosecution strategy which would have reflected the political reality on the ground, the various objectives of UNTAET's mandate and the UN's political will. The outcome was an approach which led to relatively random prosecutions of small-time perpetrators, and the perception among the population that justice was not done, in terms of both the failure to prosecute the higher-ranked commanders in Indonesia and the unfairness of the random prosecution of some lower-ranked officials but not others. Importantly, the approach led to a situation where UNTAET's leadership felt the need to compromise its own laws in order to achieve its political goals, thereby violating the key legal principle that the laws must be upheld as promulgated.

Furthermore, the policy of pursuing prosecutions led to a situation where Timorese and international lawyers appointed to serve as judges on the special panels were allowed to participate in the proceedings even though they were not familiar with international law, as the relevant regulation indicated they needed to be. The United Nations was set in its approach, and this led to the decision to go ahead with the proceedings even if the judges' appointment to the panel meant that the legal requirement for the consideration of their qualification had to be ignored. Their appointment in turn led to the situation where they either failed to apply international law or failed to apply it correctly, even though Regulation 2000/15 had specifically set out that international law must apply in serious crimes cases. And finally, the desire to prosecute the perpetrators of atrocities led the United Nations to continue with the trials even after it realized that various rules of procedure were being broken, such as the requirement for the provision of written transcripts of the proceedings. Once again, we see that this aspect of the UN's approach to legal and judicial reform led it to several important violations of a key Fullerian principle.

Compliance with basic judicial norms

This subsection focuses on the question of whether any violation of the judicial norms[223] resulted from any of the five elements of the UN's approach. It will first outline how some of the 10 judicial norms were violated, and then demonstrate how it was in particular the UN's approach of involving local actors early in the judicial process to the fullest extent possible, as well as its insistence on pursuing serious crimes trials, which led to most of the violations.

While there were virtually no problems with the lack of independence of judges and also no problems of impartiality in East Timor, as there were in Kosovo, the discussion of the various developments has highlighted several key violations of judicial norms. The first of these, which can be linked directly to the approach of involving local actors early in the judicial process, was the lack of provision of adequate defence. Firstly, the UN's desire to involve local actors in the judicial process early on led the Office of the Principal Legal Adviser to take this to the extreme and recommend the complete handover of the task of public defence into local hands.[224] The hired public defenders were selected from a group of local jurists whose only legal experience was to have attended law school, and who were the least capable from that group.[225]

Apart from lacking experience, the small number of available defenders meant they were unable to meet their clients frequently and had to defend more than one client in the same case, opening up the potential for a conflict of interest; moreover, the caseload these defenders had to contend with meant less preparation time for each case.[226] In comparison to the UN prosecutors, these defence counsellors were novices, and consequently the quality of the defence provided in the early cases violated the defendants' right to effective counsel.[227] As one observer put it: "What justification can there be that a tribunal to which the United Nations lends its name provides outstanding international defence counsel to Rwandan or Serb defendants and novice law school graduates with no trial experience to Timorese accused of similar crimes?"[228]

Furthermore, the premature decision to hand over full ownership of the judicial process into local hands resulted in a situation where inexperienced local actors were incapable of managing this task without allowing politics to affect their decisions: as we saw, after the United Nations and various NGOs recognized that there was a lack of adequate defence, the Ministry of Justice turned down or stalled many of the offers of funding for international defenders or mentors for the existing defenders; similarly, the Justice Ministry's obdurate refusal to approve judicial appointments of non-Portuguese-speaking jurists for the appellate level, along with the difficulty of finding enough and sufficiently qualified local jurists to staff the appeals panel, led to a situation where the appeals court was not functioning for over one year, and thus clearly to a violation of the right to an appeal. Essentially, the ministry allowed language politics to get in the way of the provision of the best possible judicial service.

Even though a few international defenders and mentors were eventually hired, some of them were not suited for their posts, and the international defenders were not of the same standard as the international defence provided in other UN *ad hoc* tribunals. This in turn meant that another judicial norm was violated, namely that of delivering justice across different judicial bodies in a consistent manner. While this norm usually should only apply within a national judicial system, given that the special panels were a hybrid between national and UN *ad hoc* courts, the norm must also apply, and thus the manner in which the United Nations delivers justice through its courts in East Timor should be similar to the manner in which it delivered justice in, for instance, the ICTR and the ICTY. The special panels were part of a community of internationalized courts and tribunals that attempted to enforce international criminal law, and as such justice ought to be delivered equally in all such judicial bodies.[229] While it is not difficult to see how the UN's approach directly contributed to violations of judicial norms, particularly as a result of the decision to hand over judicial powers to the local authorities too soon and the appointment of inexperienced lawyers to act as defence counsel, the perception that one must involve local actors early in the judicial process, and that handing over ownership of this process sooner rather than later is beneficial from the perspective of creating a sustainable legal system, contributed to many more judicial violations, especially in combination with the UN's perception that it should prosecute serious crimes early on in the mission.

Many of the problems of the judicial system, such as the failure to provide written transcripts, the frequent lack of adequate translation and interpretation during judicial proceedings and the slow progress of the trials leading to prolonged pre-trial detention periods, resulted from a lack of funding and adequate resources. However, while this link is more immediately apparent, few links have been established between these problems, the UN's approach to legal and judicial reform, UNTAET's obdurate unwillingness to alter its approach even in the face of overwhelming evidence that the judicial process did not live up to international standards and the resultant failures of judicial norms.

It is indeed true that the lack of funding and resources was the cause, for instance, of the failure to provide adequate transcripts during proceedings: better funding could have seen the appointment of professional stenographers, who in turn could have produced the written transcripts needed for appeals from the trials to be filed; it could have paid clerks to transcribe the recordings of the proceedings; and could also have seen the hiring of more professional interpreters and translators, very much needed so that the proceedings and judgments could be fair. However, as we saw, the Ministry of Justice turned down substantial offers of external funding from NGOs and governmental aid agencies, once again because of domestic political considerations. Evidently, the UN's desire to involve local actors in the judicial process early on backfired, in that those who were handed ownership over the judicial process refused to accept the funds so sorely needed to make the judicial system function according to international standards, and thus this aspect of the UN's approach had a direct impact on the violations of key judicial norms.

However, it was the UN's desire at least to appear to prosecute the perpetrators of serious atrocities from the early stages of the mission which contributed more to the violations of judicial norms than even the premature handing over of the reins of the justice system. The initial reasons for failing to provide written transcripts, hindering the appeals process; failing to provide adequate translation during trials, making the judgments based on these translations potentially unfair; having a back-log of cases, leading to a failure to hear cases within a reasonable amount of time, etc., may have indeed been related to problems of resources and funding. But the UN's obdurate continuation with the trials under these circumstances, despite warnings and its own recognition that the trials were failing to live up to international standards, led to a situation where violations of judicial norms continued to be perpetrated. If UNTAET was unable to guarantee fair trials which did not violate very basic judicial norms, the right course of action would have been to discontinue them and search for other solutions.

By 2003, three years after the serious crimes prosecutions began, the political climate in East Timor was beginning to shift in favour of amnesties as a result of the inadequacies of the judicial process.[230] But many unfair trials had already taken place by then, and a consideration of, for instance, amnesties was needed much sooner and at the initiative of UNTAET. However, as discussed in Chapter 1, from 1997 onwards the United Nations wanted to move away from amnesties and impunity for serious atrocities; thus it is not difficult to see how the UN's obdurate continuation with its approach of pursuing prosecutions contributed to the violations of the above-mentioned judicial norms. It allowed many such violations to take place which, after the UN's realization that there were indeed serious flaws with the judicial system, can no longer be simply blamed on resource and funding problems.

The incorporation of human rights principles as part of the legal framework

As was the case in Kosovo, none of the five elements of the UN's approach led to a failure to incorporate the 10 basic human rights principles.[231] UNTAET succeeded in incorporating these principles as part of the legal framework by stating that the applicable laws would have to be interpreted through the lens of various human rights instruments.

However, the incorporation of a full catalogue of human rights within the legal framework early on did, as we saw, lead to a host of violations of legal principles and judicial norms.

The legal and judicial framework and its acceptability within the community

As discussed, a legal system cannot be regarded as acceptable within a society if there is either major public opposition or major opposition from within the legal community to that system, if such opposition leads to substantial changes to the legal framework or judicial structure or if there is a major competing parallel legal or judicial framework in operation.[232] This subsection focuses on answering the question of whether any of the five elements of the UN's approach led to any of these factors which indicate that the legal system was not acceptable.

As we saw, while UNTAET's approach of applying the Indonesian legal codes from the beginning of the mission was not rejected in the same way as the application of Serbian law was rejected in Kosovo, the application of Indonesian law was not only unpopular, but eventually also led to the major judicial rift between the special panels and Dili District Court on the one hand and the Court of Appeal on the other, as well as to a significant political crisis. As discussed, if major competing parallel legal frameworks or judicial mechanisms operate in a territory during or shortly after a UN mission, then the legal system as established cannot be deemed to be acceptable. This was the case when the Court of Appeal decided that Portuguese law was applicable, and began applying it to cases at the same time as the hybrid tribunals and the Dili District Court were applying Indonesian law.

The failure in this regard is arguably the result of the UN's belief that the initial legal framework must be based upon prior legal codes from the beginning of the mission. It should be stressed here that the application of Indonesian laws *per se* was not the problem: INTERFET had already drafted an emergency legal framework on the basis of laws emanating from Indonesia's criminal code, a decision it based on the fact that in requiring the continued application of prior legal codes, Geneva

Convention IV intended to avoid retrospectivity and ensure that the laws were familiar to the population.[233] Thus, even though Portuguese law applied in East Timor *de jure*, the fact that Indonesian laws were applied for nearly 25 years *de facto* made the selection of an *emergency* legal regime on the basis of Indonesian laws the sensible choice.

However, in applying Indonesian laws from the beginning of its mission, UNTAET failed to appreciate the difference between the emergency legal framework which INTERFET had established for a limited period of a few months, so as to restore law and order, and the transitional legal framework which would be in place at least for the duration of its mission, and possibly beyond that time frame. Believing that applying Indonesian laws would be appropriate was not a wrong assumption; the wrong assumption was that the transitional legal framework could be selected from the beginning of the mission, before UNTAET had had the chance to consult local actors as to whether the Indonesian legal code would be acceptable, and before allowing a public debate on the matter of whether Indonesian, Portuguese or other laws should be used.

Such a debate would have been highly beneficial, because while pragmatism is likely to have won the day, as most lawyers found in East Timor were trained in Indonesian law, it would have given the public and the legal community the sense that the decision over the law was theirs, thereby providing them with a sense of ownership over the judicial process and a feeling that the decision was not externally imposed. Furthermore, once a decision on the applicable law was taken publicly, the likelihood of rogue jurists going against it would have decreased. And finally, such a debate is likely to have revealed any potential problem candidates for judicial posts, and would have given UNTAET the opportunity to consider more carefully the appointment of certain individuals.

It should be noted, however, that even though there was some initial opposition to the application of Indonesian laws and some jurists were angered by the promulgation of certain regulations, such as Regulation 2000/15, these incidents by themselves do not amount to *major opposition*, neither from the public nor from the legal community, to the legal framework or institutional structure as set up. While the application of Indonesian laws was unpopular, it was accepted for pragmatic reasons; as such, these incidents cannot be considered to have substantially detracted from the goal of establishing a sustainable legal system. However, the actions of the rogue judges from the Court of Appeal did, in that they led to a situation where a parallel legal framework applied for some time.

The fact that in 2006 the legal system initially based on Indonesian laws, and eventually altered through the introduction of other transitional codes, was replaced by civil and penal codes based on Portuguese law[234] does serve as an indication that the UN-introduced system did not take root in the society. While this change occurred four years after UNTAET's mission ended, it came only one year after the special panels ceased to operate in Timor-Leste, and it was a fairly substantial change to the legal framework that was in operation until then. UNTAET's failure to put in place a long-lasting legal framework cannot be blamed directly on any elements of the UN's approach, since any sovereign state has the right to alter its legal codes as it sees fit; but perhaps an earlier recognition that the nation favoured Portuguese legal codes would have led the United Nations to encourage their introduction instead of any other transitional legal codes, thereby contributing sooner and more directly to the establishment of a sustainable legal system.

Legal and judicial reform and its security-related implications

The final question to be asked in relation to the UN's legal and judicial reform efforts is whether any of the five key elements of its approach can be linked to any violence in the territory once the mission began, whether it aggravated any prior tensions which had led to violence in the past and whether it created new conditions which could have potentially led to a resurgence of violence in the territory. While there is clear evidence of reprisal violence in East Timor after the conflict ended,[235] this was relatively short-lived and on a small scale. Unlike in Kosovo, there is no evidence to suggest that any of this violence was the direct result of the UN's reform efforts. However, the UN's approach did lead to a situation which slightly increased the potential for a resurgence of violence in East Timor: the reference here is to the prison break in August 2002, when half of East Timor's prison population escaped. Academics blamed the prison break on the long detention periods and the lack of access to defence lawyers,[236] and as argued, these two failures can be linked to the UN's approach. The premature return of a large number of detainees into the community had the potential to increase criminality and also to lead to reprisal violence against former enemies, witnesses who had given evidence against these detainees and the individuals responsible for their detention.

Conclusion

As this chapter has demonstrated, the UN's approach to legal and judicial reform detracted from its aim of establishing a sustainable legal system in East Timor in several important respects: in essence, it led to a number of violations of Fuller's principles of legality and of key judicial norms, to the temporary split of the judiciary into two opposing camps and to a situation which had the potential to lead to increased levels of violence.

Perhaps most detrimental to the UN's goal was its desire to involve local actors in the judicial process from the beginning of the mission. As we saw, the principal legal adviser's decision to hand over the responsibility for judicial administration to locals, along with the UN's decision to include local actors in the judicial process as jurists, had many negative consequences. Firstly, appointed officials were insufficiently qualified for their posts, particularly not for the special panels where knowledge of international law was essential, leading them to apply the law incorrectly. Secondly, public defenders' lack of experience and heavy caseload meant they were unable to provide effective defence.[237] Thirdly, the lack of qualified individuals meant that many key posts could not be filled quickly enough, leading to significant delays to trials, a large backlog of cases and a failure to uphold the right to an appeal.

The initial focus on appointing only local jurists failed to account for the possibility that international jurists might need to be hired eventually; when international judges and defence counsellors were drafted in, the UN's failure to amend the relevant legislation led to the unlawful employment of such individuals. Finally, the premature handing over of ownership of the judicial process to the Timorese Justice Ministry placed local justice officials in a position to block crucial appointments and funds, which they did; such funds and appointments, however, would have alleviated many of the problems of the legal system. Thus while some of the judiciary's resource and financial problems can be blamed on the UN's failure to provide them, many can be blamed on the UN's decision to hand over ownership of the judiciary to local actors from the beginning of the mission.

Also detrimental to the establishment of a sustainable legal system was the UN's perception that impunity must necessarily end, and that amnesties or other policy options were no longer desirable. This perception led to an approach which failed to achieve the desired *justice* for past atrocities which Timorese victims' groups demanded. In the first instance, justice was not blind in the case of the special tribunals: prosecutors and other UN officials looked the other way when it came to pursuing pro-independence militia leaders who were seen as politically indispensable for refugee returns. Furthermore, neither UN nor Timorese leaders were prepared to rock the Indonesian political boat. From the UN's perspective, stability in the region depended on Indonesia's political stability, and so it was unprepared to back even its own prosecutors when it came to charging high-level Indonesian military officials implicated in bearing ultimate responsibility for the atrocities. Even though it was evident that the Jakarta show trials were not undertaking the desired prosecutions,[238] the United

Nations was content with the continuation of a random prosecution process which saw the charging of certain low-level perpetrators but not others. The fact that such a system was regarded as unfair by those who had been prosecuted for crimes and those who demanded justice for the atrocities is unsurprising.

This pursuit of what appeared to be a cover for an end to impunity, rather than real justice, in spite of the evident shortcomings of the system, such as the lack of an adequate translation and interpretation service, the lack of written transcripts, the lack of judges and adequate defence counsel, the lack of an adequate appeals procedure and the backlog of cases as a result of the slow proceedings, led to various violations of legal principles and judicial norms. While resource and funding problems were indeed at fault for many of these shortcomings, the continuation of the trials, rather than a consideration of a change to the approach, directly contributed to the failures to provide written transcripts, the right to an appeal, the right to adequate defence, the right to interpretation and the right to a trial within a reasonable amount of time. Finally, the decision to pursue prosecutions without having an adequate judicial system also meant that many detainees were kept in pre-trial detention for periods which are unacceptable under international standards.

The UN's approach of applying previously applicable legal codes from the beginning of the mission led it to choose the Indonesian legal codes as the applicable law. But its failure to consult local actors and organize public debates on the choice of law eventually led to a split in the judiciary and the application of parallel legal frameworks. This split had the potential to undermine or cancel out over three years' worth of judicial reform efforts, simply because the choice of law issue had not been addressed properly at the beginning of the mission. Furthermore, the decision to implement Indonesian legal codes prior to reviewing their content for consistency with human rights standards led to a situation where the law-enforcement authorities and local jurists were unclear as to the applicability of certain laws; thus, as with Kosovo, the UN's decision to implement the previously applicable laws early on led to the creation of a confusing legal regime.

The decision to apply a full human rights catalogue early on was also legally detrimental. International human rights standards required that pre-trial detention periods be shorter than those the fledgling judicial system was able to offer; applying such standards too soon not only led the United Nations to violate them, but also to the UN's legally dubious decision to derogate from them under circumstances which did not allow for such derogation. Furthermore, this derogation was aimed at preventing the release of a serious crimes suspect and amounted to executive interference with the judiciary, which sets a bad example for good governance.

Unsurprisingly, the judge unlawfully ignored the relevant regulation, arguing that the continued detention of the individual in question violated the suspect's human rights. As in Kosovo, the initial implementation of a more limited human rights catalogue, and the specific derogation from articles which set guidelines on the period of pre-trial detention, would have prevented this violation of the principle of congruence between the rules as announced and as administered.

Finally, while the approach of establishing a regular court structure from the beginning of the mission led to the least number of judicial problems, it nevertheless contributed to the creation of the large backlog of cases and the consequent problem of prolonged pre-trial detention periods: UNTAET's focus on the establishment of a full court system led its officials to ignore the need for a more immediate and temporary judicial arrangement and to a situation where for two months – between 7 January, when the United Nations appointed the first jurists,[239] and 6 March, when the courts were established – the INTERFET detainees who had been handed over to UNTAET were not brought to trial. While this did not violate any laws regarding the time period during which detainees may be held in pre-trial detention, because at that point no limits had been broken, it did clearly contribute to the eventual backlog of cases, as a result of which detainees eventually suffered prolonged and illegal pre-trial detention periods. Thus a more temporary judicial arrangement might have offered a practical solution to the immediate detainee problem.

While the lack of resources and funding, and managerial problems, as reported in various international organization and NGO reports, partly explain the multitude of difficulties which the fledgling legal system experienced, these factors fail to account for the more fundamental root of the problems: as in Kosovo, the answer as to why the UN's approach to legal and judicial reform led to the above-mentioned violations of legal and judicial principles and norms, and to the establishment of a legal system that was marred by so many problems, lies in the fact that the approach either aggravated or failed to strike the right balance between the key tensions at the heart of the UN's governance operation. The first tension related to UNTAET's need to balance demands for order and security on the one hand and justice on the other; and the second tension required UNTAET to balance its mandate to govern the territory to a high standard with its need to empower the local community through local participation in or ownership of institutional processes, thereby helping to establish locally sustainable institutions.

Peacebuilders concluded regarding the UN's approach to justice sector reforms in Kosovo and East Timor that various tasks would have to be carried out from the beginning of the mission and to the fullest extent possible. This meant that human rights standards would not only have to be observed, but that all laws would have to be interpreted through the prism of a full catalogue of human rights; that local individuals would not only become involved in the judicial process, but that they would control the justice ministry, would be solely in charge of public defence and would work as judges, despite their lack of experience. Furthermore, it meant that previously applicable legal codes would not only guide legal reforms, but would become the applicable law. And finally, it meant holding to account those responsible for perpetrating gross atrocities through hybrid courts within the national judicial system, since an international tribunal, which would have guaranteed the highest standards of justice, was regarded as financially and politically unfeasible.

As it did in Kosovo, this approach confused the ends with the means, and failed to ease the above-mentioned tensions. Firstly, UNTAET's decision to hand ownership over the judicial process to local jurists and to staff judicial posts with inexperienced local lawyers from the beginning of the mission entirely failed to address the tension between the need for governance, a task the United Nations was mandated with, and the need for local empowerment; instead of aiming to strike a careful balance between these opposing tasks, this approach not only ignored the tension but actually aggravated it. Even though the United Nations initially empowered local actors to take charge of judicial affairs, it nevertheless proceeded to pass a regulation which was designed to influence the judicial process, and which was interventionist. Demonstrating to local actors that the executive can interfere with the judiciary to influence the outcomes of the judicial process does not set the type of example needed when aiming to establish a sustainable legal system.

Similarly, empowering locals with the running of judicial affairs but then failing to consult them on key alterations to the judicial structure and legal framework, as was the case when the United Nations wished to promulgate Regulation 2000/15, establishing the special panel for serious crimes, and Regulation 2000/30, establishing the transitional rules for criminal procedure, inevitably led to hostile reactions from local jurists. High-level judicial officials were upset at not having been consulted prior to the promulgation of Regulation 2000/15 despite the fact that the law required that they be consulted.[240] And when the United Nations showed local jurists a draft of the transitional code of criminal procedure a few days before it was meant to be made law, these jurists, who had not even been consulted at the drafting stage, decided to reject it and requested major alterations – not because there were substantial flaws in it, but because they felt angry about having been disempowered by the process by which this regulation was created.[241] The resultant difficult relations between the United Nations and local authorities, who became suspicious of the United Nations, were to be expected.

The premature empowering of local actors, in terms of both owner-ship of the judicial process and employment within the judiciary, meant the United Nations was unable to achieve the high standards of justice which the mission required, in part because these local actors proceeded to block various international initiatives aimed at rectifying the problems. Thus instead of easing the tensions between these two divergent objec-tives, the UN's approach only aggravated them. As with Kosovo, the early introduction of international judges and prosecutors, with a gradual in-crease in the number of local jurists operating within the judicial system, would have had the potential to prevent many of the violations that did occur: it would have provided sufficient time to train and mentor some of the local jurists, and introduce them to the human rights laws which they had to apply, and would ultimately have prepared them better for ownership of the process, thereby creating a more solid foundation for a sustainable legal system.

The UN's approach of using previously applicable laws as the initial legal framework also failed to strike the right balance between interna-tional governance and local empowerment. While UNTAET was pre-pared to hand over ownership of the judicial process early on, it seemed oblivious to the fact that the involvement of local actors in the selection of the law was important. By failing to strike the right balance at the right time between international leadership on this matter and local in-volvement in the process, the United Nations created the unsatisfactory situation where a matter that needed to be publicly debated early on was not debated, and this led to a political and judicial crisis. The United Nations had the simple option of continuing to apply the emergency legal code implemented by INTERFET until the matter of the applicable law had been publicly discussed and decided; its failure to do so had evident negative repercussions.

A further tension in UN governance operations, as mentioned above, is between the need to establish order and security and the need to do so within a framework of internationally recognized human rights standards, while also aiming to educate the local population about human rights and seek justice for past atrocities. A mission aiming for success would try to ease or resolve this tension, so as to succeed at both its security-related responsibilities and its justice- and rights-related tasks. But the UN's approach of incorporating a full catalogue of human rights from the beginning of the mission failed to strike the right balance between the two goals. In particular the failure to derogate in Regulation 1999/1 from the provisions regarding the right to liberty as enshrined in Articles 9 and 14 of the ICCPR led to many of the problems.

The failure to recognize officially that the circumstances in East Timor warranted such derogation meant that the United Nations set unreasonably high expectations about what was achievable in terms of standards in the judiciary. Instituting such rights early on meant that for a while the United Nations itself was in breach of them, as it was unable to process cases rapidly enough. However, the United Nations was unwilling to free many of the detainees, and particularly not high-profile individuals whose release might have caused tensions to flare up or resentment leading to calls for the release of other detainees from opposing groups. When the United Nations eventually saw it as necessary to derogate from the right to liberty, allow for longer pre-trial detention periods and retroactively legitimate detentions which were illegal, it was in breach of rights and the law, since the circumstances at that stage no longer mandated such derogation, as per the ICCPR, which the United Nations had to uphold. The initial derogation from certain human rights provisions, the introduction of a more limited human rights catalogue and the gradual reintroduction of rights as the overall security situation improved and judicial capacity grew would have struck a better balance between the need for order, and the consequent need for prosecution of criminals, and the need for rights.

The problem with the lengthy pre-trial detention period highlights a tension which is particular to justice sector reform, namely the need for accountability on the one hand and the need to deliver justice in accordance with human rights on the other. The United Nations found itself in a situation where the victims of violence, as well as other members of the community, demanded accountability for past atrocities; it had itself decided upon an approach that would seek to end impunity. However, its dilemma was that while there was a demand for accountability, the United Nations also had to deliver justice in accordance with fair trial standards, which was not an easy undertaking given that it was establishing a new judiciary from the ground up. The method it chose – trials in hybrid courts – did very little to balance the tension between these two demands, and in fact achieved neither of the goals: the trials did little to satisfy local demands for justice, as most of those tried were relatively low-level perpetrators, and the standard at which these trials were held fell short of international fair trial standards.

Arguably, the UN's approach was indeed intended to balance the need for order and the demand for justice: by not pursuing the perpetrators who had fled to Indonesia or trying high-level Indonesian military officials, the United Nations wished to maintain regional stability and refrain from upsetting the fragile relations between Indonesia and its new neighbour; and by trying some of the perpetrators caught in East Timor, the United Nations tried to show that it wanted to put an end to impunity, and perhaps even to set some sort of example that amnesties would no longer be tolerated. However, while order and security were maintained, justice was evidently not done. Once again, the UN's approach failed to strike the right balance between the competing demands, leading to the pursuit of what amounted to unfair trials. A different approach, focused on an alternative justice mechanism, as will be discussed in the next chapter, would have helped to balance this tension better, and could have prevented many of the problems.

Notes

1. For more on the colonial history of East Timor see *Encyclopaedia Britannica Online*, available at www.britannica.com/nations/East-Timor; for a good overview of East Timor's conflict with Indonesia see Martin (2001); Greenless (2002).
2. Martin (ibid.: 15).
3. Ibid., p. 16.
4. Ibid.
5. Ibid.
6. Ibid.
7. See, for instance, UN Security Council (1975, 1976).
8. Kondoch (2001: 247).
9. Katzenstein (2003: 248); the statistic of 200,000 includes thousands who died in forced resettlement camps as a result of lack of food and medicine.
10. Kondoch (2001: 247).
11. Katzenstein (2003: 248).
12. Matheson (2001: 81).
13. Martin and Mayer-Rieckh (2005: 105).
14. Ibid., p. 107.
15. Katzenstein (2003: 249).
16. Linton (2002: 104).
17. See UN Security Council (1999c); on this see also Katzenstein (2003: 249).
18. Katzenstein (ibid.).
19. For a good overview of the UN's administration of East Timor see Ruffert (2001); Stahn (2001). For some lessons learned from UNTAET see Vieira de Mello (2000). For critiques of the mission see Chopra (2000); Beauvais (2001); Wilde (2004).
20. See UN Security Council (1999e).
21. Ibid., Article 6.
22. Ibid., Article 1.
23. Pritchard (2001: 185); on this see also UN Security Council (2000a: paras 40–62).
24. UN Security Council (1999e: para. 39).
25. UNTAET (1999b). Caplan (2005: 94–95) writes that "The NCC comprised seven representatives of the National Council of the Timorese Resistance (CNRT); one from the Catholic Church; three from pro-autonomy groups: the Forces of the East Timorese People (BRTT), the Timorese Nationalist Party (PNT), and the Forum for Unity, Democracy and Justice (FPDK); and four UNTAET representatives."
26. Similar councils were also established at the municipal and district levels in East Timor, however, they ceased to function when East Timor gained its independence in 2002; see Caplan (ibid.: 94).
27. UNTAET (2000e).

28. Caplan (2005: 100).
29. Ibid.
30. It should be noted, however, that the members of the council were appointed by the TA.
31. For more on the relative merits of the co-administration model in East Timor see Caplan (2005: 99–108); Vieira de Mello (2000, 2001).
32. See UN Security Council (2002).
33. See UNTAET (1999a), section 3.1; Strohmeyer (2000: 267) makes this point.
34. Australia was one of the major exceptions in the international community: it had recognized East Timor as an integral part of Indonesia in 1989.
35. Strohmeyer (2000: 267); Chesterman (2004: 170 n. 56) also highlights this point.
36. *Mutatis mutandis* is a Latin phrase meaning "that having been changed which had to be changed", or more commonly "with the necessary changes".
37. The relevant wording of section 3.1 on the "Applicable Law in East Timor" of UNTAET (1999a) reads: "the laws applied in East Timor prior to 25 October 1999 shall apply in East Timor insofar as they do not conflict with [international human rights] standard[s] ... the fulfilment of the mandate given to UNTAET under United Nations Security Council Resolution 1272 (1999), or the present or any other regulation and directive issued by the Transitional Administrator."
38. Chesterman (2004: 170).
39. The wording of section 2 on "Observance of Internationally Recognized Standards" of UNTAET (1999a) is slightly more detailed than that of section 2 of UNMIK (1999c) in that it refers particularly to the international instruments to be taken into consideration when observing the international standards on human rights. The regulation states that: "In exercising their functions, all persons undertaking public duties or holding public office in East Timor shall observe internationally recognized human rights standards, as reflected in particular in: The Universal Declaration on Human Rights of 10 December 1948; The International Covenant on Civil and Political Rights of 16 December 1966 and its Protocols; The International Covenant on Economic, Social, and Cultural Rights of 16 December 1966; The Convention on the Elimination of All Forms of Racial Discrimination of 21 December 1965; The Convention on the Elimination of All Forms of Discrimination Against Women of 17 December 1979; The Convention Against Torture and other Cruel, Inhumane or Degrading Treatment or Punishment of 17 December 1984; The International Convention on the Rights of the Child of 20 November 1989. They shall not discriminate against any person on any ground such as sex, race, colour, language, religion, political or other opinion, national, ethnic, or social origin, association with a national community, property, birth or all other status."
40. Linton (2001a: 137).
41. See UNTAET (1999a), section 2.
42. Ibid., section 3.
43. Ibid., section 3.3.
44. Ibid., section 3.2: The Law on Anti-Subversion; Law on Social Organizations; Law on National Security; Law on National Protection and Defense; Law on Mobilization and Demobilization; and the Law on Defense and Security.
45. District courts were established for the following locations in East Timor: Dili, Baucau, Los Palos, Viqueque, Same, Maliana, Ermera and Oecussi.
46. See UNTAET (2000a), section 7.
47. See UN General Assembly (1999: para. 42).
48. See UN General Assembly and Security Council (2000a).

49. Ibid., para. 152.
50. Cohen (2002: 2).
51. Kofi Annan is cited here in Cohen (ibid.: 3; quotation taken from *India Times*, 15 February 2000).
52. Conflict Security and Development Group (2003b: para. 258).
53. Ibid., para. 259.
54. Ibid.
55. See UNTAET (2000a), section 10.1; note that the court would have exclusive jurisdiction over the latter three "only insofar as the offence was committed in the period between 1 January 1999 and 25 October 1999", as stipulated in section 10.2.
56. See UNTAET (2000c), sections 1.1 and 1.2; for a good introduction to the workings of these panels see Linton (2001b).
57. Katzenstein (2003: 245 n. 2); had the Kosovo War and Ethnic Crimes Court been established, it would have been granted such exclusive jurisdiction.
58. See UNTAET (2000c), sections 22.1 and 22.2.
59. Conflict Security and Development Group (2003b: para. 268).
60. UNTAET (2000d).
61. Ibid., section 6.1.
62. Linton (2001b: 418).
63. Strohmeyer (2001b: 50); see also Strohmeyer (2000, 2001a).
64. See UN Security Council (1999c: para. 33).
65. Strohmeyer (2001b: 50).
66. See UN Security Council (1999c: para. 51).
67. Strohmeyer (2001c: 175); on this problem see also Beauvais (2001: 1153–1154); Chesterman (2004: 170).
68. Chesterman (ibid.: 170–171).
69. Strohmeyer (2001b: 54).
70. Ibid.; on this see also Chesterman (2004: 171).
71. Strohmeyer (ibid.: 54–55).
72. Chesterman (2004: 171).
73. Strohmeyer (2001c: 175).
74. Ibid.
75. Chesterman (2004: 171).
76. Strohmeyer (2001b: 51, 2001c: 175).
77. See UNTAET (1999c).
78. Strohmeyer (2001c: 176).
79. Chesterman (2004: 171).
80. Katzenstein (2003: 254); it should be noted, however, that the Serious Crimes Unit and special panels did remain primarily UN entities (see ibid., n. 48).
81. Beauvais (2001: 1149).
82. Chesterman (2004: 170).
83. Linton (2001a: 137).
84. Strohmeyer (2001c: 174).
85. Linton (2001a: 137).
86. Beauvais (2001: 1151).
87. Court of Appeal, Democratic Republic of Timor-Leste (2003a).
88. De Bertodano (2004: 90); see also Special Panel for Serious Crimes, Democratic Republic of Timor-Leste (2002).
89. On this see Judicial System Monitoring Programme (2003).
90. Court of Appeal, Democratic Republic of Timor-Leste (2003a: 5).

146 UNITED NATIONS JUSTICE

91. Court of Appeal, Democratic Republic of Timor-Leste (2003b: 1).
92. See Special Panel for Serious Crimes, Democratic Republic of Timor-Leste (2003), section B; see also No Peace Without Justice (2003).
93. Judicial System Monitoring Programme (2003: 4).
94. De Bertodano (2004: 91).
95. National Parliament, Democratic Republic of Timor-Leste (2003).
96. East Timor and Indonesia Action Network (2003).
97. See Judicial System Monitoring Programme (2006), section 2.2; see also the CIA's country profile for Timor-Leste, available in the World Factbook at www.cia.gov.
98. Strohmeyer (2000: 267).
99. Linton (2001a: 148).
100. Ibid., pp. 148–149.
101. Ibid., p. 140.
102. UNTAET (1999d).
103. Conflict Security and Development Group (2003b: para. 228).
104. See UNTAET (2000b), section 2, which states that "Until such time as additional District Courts are established in East Timor, District Courts shall be established in the following locations: (a) Baucau (b) Suai (c) Oecussi and (d) Dili"; on this see also Beauvais (2001: 1154 n. 221).
105. Linton (2001a: 134).
106. On this point see Katzenstein (2003: 256).
107. Suzannah Linton (2001a: 134) also makes this point; as discussed in the Kosovo case study, Article 9 of the ICCPR requires that a person may not be the subject of an arbitrary arrest or detention, and that if such a detention takes place it can only be made in accordance with the grounds and procedures established in the legal code. No criminal procedure code would allow for such detentions, and the Indonesian one itself certainly does not.
108. UNTAET (2000b), section 12a.10; see also Linton (2001a: 134). For a more detailed discussion of the particular detentions and their illegal nature see Judicial System Monitoring Programme (2002a).
109. There were circa 200,000 such refugees who had fled East Timor in the wake of the ballot results of 4 September 1999.
110. De Bertodano (2004: 81–82).
111. Tanaja (2001), quoted in De Bertodano (ibid.: 82).
112. De Bertodano (ibid.).
113. UN Security Council (1999e: para 16); for a discussion of the lack of a coherent prosecution strategy see De Bertodano (ibid.: 83–84).
114. De Bertodano (ibid.: 83).
115. Ibid., pp. 83–84; De Bertodano, one of the public defenders in East Timor, argues that the SCU should have had one of two prosecution strategies: "it should either have concentrated exclusively on the high command, prepared its cases, issued indictments and arrest warrants, and then reported back to the Security Council that it was unable to fulfil its mandate because Indonesia's failure to cooperate meant that it was unable to carry out arrests. Alternatively, it could have acted like an ordinary domestic justice system, and investigated and prosecuted anyone within its jurisdiction against whom there was evidence, regardless of their role in the overall command structure."
116. See UNMISET (2003), cited in De Bertodano (ibid.: 85); for a more detailed discussion on the failure of the United Nations to support its own prosecutors in this case see De Bertodano (ibid.: 84–86).
117. Ibid., p. 85.

118. Conflict Security and Development Group (2003b: para. 270).
119. Katzenstein (2003: 263).
120. Malunga and Alagendra (2002: 30), cited in Katzenstein (ibid.); Shyamala Alagendra worked as one of the prosecutors and Siphosami Malunga as one of the public defenders in East Timor.
121. Katzenstein (ibid.).
122. Cohen (2002: 6).
123. Ibid.
124. Ibid.; some of the applicants were British and Australian.
125. Katzenstein (2003: 269).
126. Ibid.
127. Dodd (2001); see also Katzenstein (ibid.).
128. See UNDP (2002: 36); on the language problem see Chesterman (2001a: 13).
129. On this, David Cohen (2002: 8 n. xii) makes a valid point: "This kind of neo-colonialism does not bode well in a country where the new Portuguese-speaking governing elite has made Portuguese one of the two official languages but more than 95% of the population do not speak or understand it."
130. Katzenstein (2003: 263).
131. Judicial System Monitoring Programme (2002a: 16–17).
132. Ibid.
133. Ibid.
134. Katzenstein (2003: 263).
135. Judicial System Monitoring Programme (2002a: 17).
136. Ibid.
137. Human Rights Watch (2002b), section III, A.5.
138. De Bertodano (2004: 89).
139. Katzenstein (2003: 267).
140. UNTAET (2000c), section 23.2.
141. Judicial System Monitoring Programme (2001: 10).
142. Ibid.
143. Sections 10.3 and 15.5 of UNTAET (2000a) and section 1 of UNTAET (2000c) specifically refer to the establishment of *panels* in the plural, within both Dili District Court and the Court of Appeal, to hear appeals arising from the special crimes cases.
144. Katzenstein (2003: 271).
145. Judicial System Monitoring Programme (2001: 14).
146. Judicial System Monitoring Programme (2002b: 9).
147. Ibid.; on this see also Katzenstein (2003: 271).
148. Katzenstein (ibid.: 268).
149. Judicial System Monitoring Programme (2002b: 11); see also Katzenstein (ibid.: 271).
150. Katzenstein (ibid.).
151. Judicial System Monitoring Programme (2002b: 11).
152. Ibid., p. 12.
153. Ibid., p. 18.
154. Judicial System Monitoring Programme (2002a: 28).
155. UNTAET (2000a), section 26.1, explicitly states that "the court shall ensure that, in each hearing by a judge or panel of judges, written or recorded notes of the proceedings are taken".
156. UNTAET (2000f), section 31, states that in criminal cases the record of the proceedings must be used to produce transcripts, and that the official record must contain "a shorthand, stenographic or audio recording of the proceedings ... [and that] Recorded media shall be used as necessary during further proceedings to produce transcripts and

otherwise facilitate the functions of reviewing authorities." See also Judicial System Monitoring Programme (2002b: 18).

157. Judicial System Monitoring Programme (ibid.).
158. This point has been made in several JSMP reports: see, for instance, Judicial System Monitoring Programme (2001: 23, 2002a: 28, 2002b: 18).
159. See Special Panel for Serious Crimes, East Timor (2001); the judgment is also cited in Judicial System Monitoring Programme (2001: 23).
160. See Court of Appeal, East Timorese Transitional Authority (2001), cited here in Judicial System Monitoring Programme (ibid.); for a discussion of this decision see Linton (2001b: 318–323).
161. See Judicial System Monitoring Programme (ibid.).
162. Arguably, the failure of the court registrar to make available a full written transcript of the record of the proceedings was the result of the promulgation of UNTAET (2001): when comparing section 26 of UNTAET (2000a), which requires that "the court shall ensure that ... a transcript of the proceedings [is] taken and that the transcript is made available ... to all parties to the proceedings", to section 26.1 of UNTAET (2001), which states that "the court shall ensure that ... written *or recorded* [emphasis added] notes of the proceedings are taken and made available ... to all parties", it becomes clear that over a year after the courts were established, UNTAET must have realized the courts would be unable to make available transcripts of proceedings, and thus the regulation had to be altered to reflect the reality of what was feasible given the difficult circumstances. On this point see Judicial System Monitoring Programme (2001: 22 n. 64).
163. Judicial System Monitoring Programme (2002b: 18).
164. Cohen (2002: 6).
165. Ibid.
166. Ibid.
167. See UNTAET (2000a), section 23.
168. English, Tetun, Bahasa Indonesia and Portuguese.
169. Conflict Security and Development Group (2003b: para. 269); at times, other local dialects or languages were used.
170. Ibid.
171. Judicial System Monitoring Programme (2002b: 19).
172. Katzenstein (2003: 261) observed the following during a detention review hearing in Dili on 23 July 2002: "The judge, prosecutor, and defender spoke in English. An interpreter would translate what they said into Indonesian, and a second would translate the Indonesian into Tetun. Even for this minor straightforward review hearing, the translation significantly slowed the proceedings. For certain periods of the proceedings, it simply did not occur. Only when the counsel or judge reminded the first interpreter were statements translated. The defendant, it seemed, missed most of what was said in the proceeding."
173. Judicial System Monitoring Programme (2002a: 28); for more on the effect which the dubious interpretation service had on trial proceedings see Judicial System Monitoring Programme (2001: 26–28, 2002a: 27, 2002b: 19).
174. Judicial System Monitoring Programme (2002a: 27).
175. See the factual findings in Special Panel for Serious Crimes, East Timor (2001: 4–7); reference is made to this in Judicial System Monitoring Programme (2001: 27).
176. Judicial System Monitoring Programme (ibid.).
177. Judicial System Monitoring Programme (2002b: 19); see also Katzenstein (2003: 261 n. 91).
178. See Cohen (2002: 1).

179. Katzenstein (2003: 268).
180. Beauvais (2001: 1155).
181. Judicial System Monitoring Programme (2001: 12); on this problem see generally Linton (2001c).
182. Conflict Security and Development Group (2003b: para. 250).
183. Chesterman (2002a: 8).
184. De Bertodano (2004: 87).
185. See Chapter 2, p. 33.
186. See Chapter 2, p. 45.
187. See Chapter 2, pp. 35–37.
188. Section 23.3 of UNTAET (2000c) states in part that "In the overall composition of the panels due account shall be taken of the experience of the judge in criminal law, international law, including international humanitarian law and human rights law."
189. Conflict Security and Development Group (2003b: para. 231).
190. Article 8.1 on "Review of Applications" of UNTAET (1999c), which established the TJSC, clearly states that the commission "shall receive and review individual applications of legal professionals of *East Timorese origin* for provisional service in judicial or prosecutorial office", emphasis added.
191. See Egonda-Ntende (2001).
192. See UNTAET (2000c), section 3.1(b).
193. Katzenstein (2003: 253).
194. Judicial System Monitoring Programme (2001: 10); this was so also in the case of the *Public Prosecutor v Joseph Leki*, where both the defence and the prosecution made clear references to the decisions of the ICTY and the ICTR in their submissions to the court, both written and oral. See Special Panel for Serious Crimes, East Timor (2001).
195. For a full discussion of the case see Linton (2001a: 140–144).
196. See UNTAET (2000b), section 12a.
197. Linton (2001a: 142).
198. Ibid.
199. Linton (ibid.: 139); for a discussion of the UN's early concerns about the possibility that detentions were unlawful see Conflict Security and Development Group (2003b: para. 145); UN Security Council (2000d); Amnesty International (2000b); Devereux (2000).
200. Conflict Security and Development Group (ibid.: para. 280).
201. Ibid.
202. Ibid.
203. Katzenstein (2003: 260); both regulations set out the requirement that an official transcript has to be provided.
204. UNTAET (2000b), section 12a.10.
205. Ibid., section 12a.
206. See Article 4(1) of the ICCPR; emphasis added.
207. Suzannah Linton (2001a: 145) makes the same point regarding the relative conditions in East Timor in 2000.
208. On the lack of clarity see Conflict Security and Development Group (2003b: paras 239–240).
209. This incident is described in detail in Conflict Security and Development Group (ibid.: para. 239 n. 243).
210. Linton (2001a: 137).
211. Conflict Security and Development Group (2003b: paras 239–240).
212. Strohmeyer (2000), cited here in Beauvais (2001: 1152).
213. See UNTAET (2000f).

214. Linton (2001a: 139).
215. See sections 12.1 and 12.2 of UNTAET (2000a).
216. On this see Linton (2001a: 139); Linton (ibid.: n. 67) offers a potential explanation for this confusion and misunderstanding: "Under the *Indonesian Code of Criminal Procedure*, there is a clear distinction between the roles of interrogator, investigator, prosecutor and judge. There are provisions for a judge to review detention after the first 110 days; that judge is not an 'investigator' and may in fact try the case. UNTAET appears to have considered at the time that this official equated with the European model of the investigating judge (for example an *Untersuchungsrichter* in the German legal system)." Given that UNTAET's principal legal adviser, Strohmeyer, was a German judge, it is conceivable that he may have made this erroneous interpretation of the Indonesian Code of Criminal Procedure.
217. Ibid.
218. Conflict Security and Development Group (2003b: para. 228).
219. For a good overview of the issue of reprisal violence in East Timor see Boyle (2005).
220. For an introduction to the Detainee Management Unit's activities see Oswald (2000); Kelly (2000).
221. These were the procedural regulations according to the Indonesian legal code.
222. Linton (2001a: 142).
223. See Chapter 2, pp. 37–39.
224. Katzenstein (2003: 254).
225. Ibid., p. 263.
226. Cohen (2002: 5).
227. On this point see Cohen (ibid.); Katzenstein (2003); Linton (2001c); Judicial System Monitoring Programme (2002a).
228. See Cohen (ibid.: 7).
229. For a discussion on the notion of a community of courts see Burke-White (2002); for a discussion on the role of internationalized courts in the enforcement of international criminal law see Cassese (2004); for a broad discussion on second-generation UN-based tribunals see Shraga (2004).
230. De Bertodano (2004: 86).
231. See Chapter 2, pp. 39–41.
232. See Chapter 2, pp. 41–42.
233. Kelly (2000: 4).
234. See Judicial System Monitoring Programme (2006), section 2.2; see also the CIA's country profile for Timor-Leste in the World Factbook, available at www.cia.gov.
235. For more on this topic see Boyle (2005).
236. Chesterman (2002a: 8).
237. This changed later on in the mission, when international lawyers took over virtually all defence responsibilities for serious crimes trials.
238. See Human Rights Watch (2002b); Amnesty International (2002b).
239. UN Security Council (2000a: para. 44).
240. Linton (2001a: 150) points to section 10.3 of UNTAET (2000a), which states: "The Transitional Administrator, *after consultation of the Court Presidency*, may decide to establish panels with the expertise to exercise exclusive jurisdiction vested in the court by Section 10.1 of the present regulation", emphasis added.
241. Linton (ibid.: 174).

5

Legal and judicial reform reconsidered

The preceding case-study chapters demonstrate that the UN's approach to legal and judicial reform detracted from the goal of establishing a sustainable legal system; part of the reason for this detraction was the failure of the approach to address adequately the key tensions of a governance operation and justice sector reform. This chapter will highlight and sum up the issues raised by the UN's experience, particularly as they relate to the five elements of the UN's approach, and consider how these issues have been presented in the literature on justice sector reform and transitional administration more broadly. In discussing these issues, the chapter will contend with some of the assumptions underlying the UN's approach; in locating them within the literature, the chapter will seek to find answers that academics or practitioners who have written on the subject may offer as to ways in which a different approach to legal and judicial reform might better address the tensions discussed.

Filling the legal vacuum

Issues raised

We saw in the Kosovo case study that Albanian jurists rejected the UN's initial decision to apply the laws of Serbia, and the United Nations had to reverse its decision on the applicable law six months into its mission. In East Timor the UN's initial decision to apply the Indonesian legal code

United Nations justice: Legal and judicial reform in governance operations
Trenkov-Wermuth, United Nations University Press, 2010, ISBN 978-92-808-1173-5

eventually led to a legal and political crisis in the territory. In both cases the problems were rooted in the UN's failure to consult with local actors on the choice of applicable law and allow sufficient time for discussions on the matter to take place locally. Furthermore, we also saw that the decision to implement in Kosovo the legal codes of 1989, and the resultant need to fill legal gaps with laws from Serbia and the Federal Republic of Yugoslavia, led to the creation of a confusing legal regime.

Similarly, the UN's failure to review the Indonesian legal code for consistency with human rights standards and principles before it was implemented in East Timor led to a lack of clarity and confusions with the law. And thus it became clear that the UN's initial decision to implement a previously applicable legal code from the very beginning of its missions directly led to the establishment of a confusing legal regime, and therefore to the violation of Fuller's principle that the rules must be understandable, and also to further legal and political problems in both territories. Based on this experience, it is clear that sufficient time must be allowed for debates on the choice of applicable law to take place and consultations on the matter to be held with local actors, and that consequently the introduction of a comprehensive transitional legal framework based on previously applicable laws from the very beginning of a mission is not a productive undertaking when filling the initial legal vacuum.

Responses from academics and practitioners, analysis and discussion

The question of how to fill a legal vacuum effectively is addressed early on in the literature on the subject, and the initial responses were formulated in relation to the UN's failures to address this problem effectively in Cambodia.[1] Recognizing the problems with the UN's hasty efforts to devise legal codes for Cambodia, and the eventual shortcomings of these UN codes, the then foreign minister of Australia, Gareth Evans, argued in 1993 in favour of UN pre-prepared *justice packages*,[2] based on universal legal principles and made up of criminal laws and criminal procedure codes.[3] In 1998 Mark Plunkett, who had served as the UN's special prosecutor for Cambodia, also proposed the use of justice packages which contain "the generic nuts and bolts of law and order restoration, as well as local social and cultural dynamics for its acceptance by the population".[4] The basis for his argument was that:

> Usually there will not be any law in the host country because the state and the rule of law will have collapsed ... To use the laws of one group over the other will imperil the neutrality of the peace operation. Furthermore, a peace opera-

tion can use existing local laws and local courts to enforce the law only when those laws and courts reasonably meet international standards. Usually there will be no domestic substantive or procedural law that is competent, credible and independently administered.[5]

As we saw, however, the United Nations did not heed calls for the creation of such justice packages containing interim legal codes, opting instead for the direct application of previously applicable laws in Kosovo and East Timor. The UN panel which reviewed peace operations in 2000 recognized that there were problems with the UN's method for filling the legal vacuum in the two territories. As mentioned in the Kosovo chapter, the panel observed that "in both places, the law and legal systems prevailing prior to the conflict were questioned or rejected by key groups considered to be the victims of the conflicts",[6] and also argued that UNMIK's and UNTAET's "tasks would have been made much easier if a common United Nations justice package had allowed them to apply an interim legal code in which mission personnel could have been pre-trained while the final answer to the 'applicable law' question was being worked out".[7] It would also circumvent the problem of international lawyers having to take at least six months to learn local laws which they would only then be able to apply, a time during which criminals and other powerful local actors might exploit the legal vacuum or fill it with their own parallel administrations.[8] Consequently, the panel's report recommended that the Secretary-General should convene a panel of experts to assess the feasibility and utility of an interim criminal code.[9] The panel of experts, however, quickly dismissed the practicality and desirability of such an interim legal code, doubting that it would be feasible on the grounds of "the diversity of countries' specific legal traditions".[10]

Despite this dismissal, and recognizing the errors of the UN's approach to legal reform, and perhaps also his own responsibility for these errors, UNTAET's principal legal adviser, Hansjoerg Strohmeyer, argued in 2001 for the "Creation of an immediately applicable legal framework", the availability of which he viewed as a "prerequisite for the building of judicial institutions".[11] He believed that this body of "law-enforcement-related legislation should be developed as part of a 'quick-start package' for UN administered territories", and also that "Readily applicable criminal procedure and criminal codes, as well as a code regulating the activities of the police, are essential to the unimpeded functioning of the UN civil police component of peace-building missions."[12] Similar arguments followed in 2001: Joel Beauvais, for instance, stated that "UNTAET's experience demonstrates the potential usefulness of an interim, off-the-shelf U.N. criminal law, particularly given the two-month delay between INTERFET's arrival and UNTAET's definition of applicable law."[13] And in 2003 Megan Fairlie continued along these lines, claiming that a "generic legal framework" is a "necessary prerequisite for effective and immediate international assistance ... [and] a means for assuring that the arrests and prosecutions, initiated under the auspices of the U.N., are aligned with the U.N.'s own standards".[14]

And while there were some variations and differences on this theme of *interim legal codes*, or *transitional* or *model codes*, particularly regarding their scope,[15] any and all of these propositions could not be further from the UN's stance against the "ill-advised" notion of "pre-packaged" solutions, and its recommendation to "Avoid the imposition of externally imposed models."[16] As these quotations from the Secretary-General's report of 2004 on "The Rule of Law and Transitional Justice in Post-Conflict Societies" indicate, little changed in four years from the expert panel's initial stance on the practicality and desirability of an interim code.

But despite the expert panel's initial position, the US Institute of Peace and the Irish Centre for Human Rights,[17] in cooperation with the UN Office of the High Commissioner for Human Rights (OHCHR), drew inspiration from the Brahimi Report and decided to develop transitional model legal codes.[18] In mid-2002 a specialist panel was convened, and over the course of the next year it developed a Transitional Criminal Code, a Transitional Code of Criminal Procedure, a Transitional Detention Act and a Transitional Law Enforcement Powers Act.[19] They were created by blending codes from a variety of legal systems – civil, common and Islamic – rather than using just one. The codes were presented at a review conference in June 2003, and over the course of the following year there were a set of consultations with experts in an attempt to improve the transitional codes.[20] By the time they were complete they had grown into something not originally envisaged in the Brahimi Report, which only sought to investigate the potential for codes that would deal with crimes such as murder, rape and arson.[21] At the review conference, the transitional codes received much criticism: Afghanistan had signalled the beginning of the *light-footprint* approach, and with the UN's eschewing of further executive missions, there would be no way to promulgate such codes; legitimacy problems, as well as the difficulty in applying them in different regions of the world, were also cited as challenges to these transitional codes.[22]

This climate of criticism led to a change in the focus and terminology of the project. The codes were no longer referred to as *transitional* codes, but as *model* codes, and their use would no longer be envisaged as codes that could be applied in a post-conflict society, but as a reform tool that could help national and international personnel charged with providing technical assistance for legal reforms.[23] Whether or not the model codes will ever be used in any of the ways which the creators envisioned remains to be seen,[24] but it is clear that the UN's stance is essentially that while they can be useful tools in helping local actors design their own justice system, they should not be imposed in a post-conflict context, as evidenced by the Secretary-General's August 2004 report on the rule of law and transitional justice.

The report casts a positive light on the notion of transitional codes in several instances: for example, it regards transitional criminal codes as "policy tools",[25] and elsewhere refers to the development of transitional codes as "progress"[26] in the aim "to address ... lacunae"[27] in the approach to date. However, more frequently the report argues against foreign-imposed models: at the beginning, the summary states that we "must learn ... to eschew one-size-fits-all formulas and the importation of foreign models, and instead, base our support on national assessments, national participation and national needs and aspirations".[28] Furthermore, the report argues that "too often, the emphasis has been on ... foreign models and foreign-conceived solutions to the detriment of durable improvements and sustainable capacity".[29] This point is repeated frequently: "Pre-packaged solutions are ill-advised ... Instead, experiences from other places should simply be used as a starting point for local debates and decisions."[30]

Ultimately, the report argues that "no rule of law reform, justice reconstruction, or transitional justice initiative imposed from the outside can hope to be successful or sustainable", and that "countless pre-designed packages or imported projects, however meticulously well-reasoned and elegantly packaged, have failed the test of justice sector reform".[31] While this basic point is repeated several times, the concluding section makes no direct mention of the need to implement transitional codes. However, there is a recommendation that Security Council mandates should "Avoid the imposition of externally imposed models."[32]

In the same report, the Secretary-General writes that the "role of the United Nations and the international community should be *solidarity, not substitution*", and that "peace operations must better assist national stakeholders to develop their own reform vision, their own agenda, their own approaches to transitional justice and their own national plans and projects".[33] Furthermore, the report argues that the "most important role we can play is to facilitate the processes through which various stakeholders debate and outline the elements of their country's plan to address the injustices of the past and to secure sustainable justice for the future", reminding us that this must be done "in accordance with *international standards*, domestic legal traditions, and national aspirations".[34]

While the United Nations clearly wishes to give local actors the upper hand in shaping their justice systems, the statement above clearly demonstrates some of the inherent contradictions and flaws in the UN's position: the suggestion that legal reform must occur in accordance with international standards is already a foreign-conceived notion and an external imposition of sorts in itself. Furthermore, the Secretary-General proposes that the United Nations must show solidarity with local actors, but this presumes that there are actors who can be shown such solidarity and helped with their own vision. While this is feasible in the long run, it does not address the immediate problems when there is a legal vacuum and there are virtually no jurists left in a territory whose reform visions the United Nations can support. The UN's argument that its role should be "solidarity, not substitution" is more of a programmatic statement which reflects its wishes to refrain from taking on further responsibilities for governance and administration than a feasible assessment of what can be done to help reform a legal system in a post-conflict environment where such a system needs to be rebuilt from the ground up, without the local capacity for doing so.

The Secretary-General's report on the rule of law and transitional justice in post-conflict societies accurately identified foreign-imposed transitional legal codes as problematic. Furthermore, the UN's stance is that foreign-conceived transitional codes should only be used to guide local actors in reforming their legal framework. However, this broad position clearly fails to provide any practical guidance as to how the organization should deal with a legal vacuum in a post-conflict territory. The UN's stance starts from the assumption that the organization will no longer undertake governance-type operations, and that any future role it will have in post-conflict territories will only be in an advisory and assistance capacity to local or other international authorities. Judging by the UN's recent missions, where it has adopted a *light-footprint* approach, such as in Afghanistan, this is indeed likely.[35] However, the possibility that it will at some stage need to undertake governance functions cannot be disregarded, and thus it is important to have a clear understanding of the options the United Nations has if it is in a situation again where it faces a lack of local capacity for governance and a legal vacuum at the same time. And thus the crucial question is how a legal vacuum can be filled quickly, until such time as local actors have had the opportunity to debate and decide upon a transitional legal framework.

There is one option proposed in the literature which has the potential to be perceived as less intrusive than foreign-conceived generic legal codes; it partly stems from a territory's own legal codes and customs, and may therefore be potentially more acceptable to UN peacebuilders. The approach is Simon Chesterman's suggestion that:

> In an immediate post-conflict environment lacking a functioning law enforcement and judicial system ... the law imposed ... should be simple and consistent. If it is not feasible to enforce the law of the land, martial law should be

declared as a *temporary* measure, with military lawyers (especially if they come from different national contingents) agreeing upon a basic legal framework.[36]

Thus the initial and temporary imposition of martial law, with military agreement upon a basic legal framework, is one option that has been devised so far. The root of this proposal arguably lies in the method and the basic legal framework which INTERFET applied to deal with the initial legal vacuum upon its arrival in East Timor in September 1999. In order to understand the essence and practicability of Chesterman's proposal, it makes sense to take a closer look at INTERFET's approach.

INTERFET established "basic, short-term legal and practical provisions for preventive detention, in consultation with UNAMET and the International Committee of the Red Cross (ICRC)".[37] These provisions essentially amounted to the ability for INTERFET troops to detain individuals temporarily where there was sufficient reason to suspect that a person either had committed, was in the process of committing or was going to commit a serious offence.[38] However, it soon became clear that in the absence of a functioning judicial system, INTERFET would have to balance the demand for order and security with the demand for justice and due process. It quickly decided to do this by providing detainees with legal representation and regular detention reviews conducted by an independent reviewing body,[39] so the commander of INTERFET passed the Detainee Ordinance on 21 October 1999.

This ordinance, along with the Force Detention Centre Orders, was for the most part based on the provisions of Geneva Convention IV,[40] and in particular those which address the issues of the maintenance of security and of a military force's handling of detainees.[41] Essentially, the ordinance established the Detainee Management Unit (DMU), an emergency military regime designed to help INTERFET re-establish law and order in the territory. The DMU consisted of an authority which could review cases, a prosecutor, a defending officer, a police expert and two visiting officers, and this emergency and "quasi-judicial regime" was designed to provide a temporary review process for individuals held in INTERFET's detention centre.[42]

INTERFET chose as applicable law the prevailing *de facto* legal regime, namely Indonesian law. The reason why Indonesian law was chosen rather than the *de jure* legal regime – i.e. the legal codes of Portugal – is because of the intention of GC IV to avoid retroactivity and ensure that the laws are familiar to those to whom they will apply: while the Portuguese legal code applied *de jure* during the time of Indonesia's occupation, the fact that Indonesia had not applied Portuguese laws for 25 years, applying Indonesian laws instead, meant that the law was *de facto* that of Indonesia, so INTERFET considered it *efficacious* to rely on Indonesian laws.[43] Importantly, however, Indonesian laws applied only to the extent that they were meant to guide behaviour, and did not extend to various procedural laws. The procedural framework within which Indonesian criminal laws would apply was different to Indonesia's code of criminal procedure, in that it was based on international humanitarian law principles, and in particular on GC IV.[44]

The ordinance initially placed several key limitations upon the DMU's operation. Firstly, only those who committed crimes which would be punishable with more than five years under Indonesia's penal code (i.e. *serious offences*) were to be held in continued detention, and all other detainees were to be released; this limitation was designed on the basis of the realization that serious crimes would need to be prioritized, and also to ensure that individuals having committed minor offences were not incarcerated for prolonged periods as a result of the inability of the system to process their cases quickly.[45] And secondly, the DMU would only hold in continued detention those individuals who were suspected of having committed serious offences *after* INTERFET's deployment on 20 September 1999. The rationale for this was firstly that Article 70 of GC IV forbids the occupying power to prosecute and punish any crimes, other than war crimes, committed prior to a territory's occupation; and secondly that under the 5 May Agreement the Indonesian government had the responsibility for law and order until INTERFET's arrival, and therefore such crimes would be a matter for it to address.[46]

However, it became clear fairly soon that allowing individuals suspected of committing crimes prior to 20 September to remain free in East Timor would potentially encourage the local population to address matters themselves, which would of course undermine INTERFET's goal of re-establishing peace and security throughout the territory.[47] Thus INTERFET's commander decided to allow such individuals to be held as *security detainees*, and to hold them until a civilian judiciary could address their cases. Along with security detainees, the three other classes of detainees were voluntary detainees,[48] individuals held on suspicion of committing a serious criminal offence and individuals committed for trial as a result of a suspected commission of a serious offence.[49] Slightly different procedures[50] were adopted for dealing with the different types of detainees, but importantly, INTERFET's DMU was able to strike the right balance between the need for order and the need for justice. By the time the UNTAET civilian judiciary was established in early January 2000 and INTERFET handed over 25 detainees to the UNTAET civilian police,[51] the DMU had reviewed the cases of over 60 individuals.[52]

Chesterman's proposal for the imposition of martial law and the implementation of a basic legal framework, which is essentially what INTERFET did in East Timor, is one option proposed in the literature as to how a legal vacuum can be filled quickly in a post-conflict society. Such a proposal hints at the need for an emergency legal framework to apply temporarily, and makes the distinction between a short-term and a long-term solution. While most prior proposals for generic and pre-prepared interim legal codes envisioned such codes applying for a prolonged period of time, the initial application of martial law by a security assistance force along with a basic legal framework would apply only temporarily, as Chesterman states, and until such time as a transitional legal framework has been discussed and selected.

When UNTAET came into existence it shied away from continuing to apply the INTERFET-created emergency framework. However, continuing to apply such a framework, or implementing a similar framework until the discussion and consultations on a transitional legal framework had taken place and a transitional framework had been chosen, would have spared it many of the problems it eventually created.

Chesterman's proposed approach would much better balance two of the key tensions of governance operations. Firstly, the approach would not only make it possible for an acceptable transitional legal framework to be chosen, thereby preventing any frequent changes in the law and potential legal and political crises, but would also be likely to strike a better balance between the need for international governance on the one hand and local empowerment on the other: the ultimate decision over the transitional legal framework would still lie with the transitional administrator, but it would provide an opportunity for local actors to feel involved in the legal process to an extent that they should indeed be involved, namely the selection of the law.

The approach would also give sufficient opportunity for any transitional legal codes to be, in the first instance, identified, collected and organized. As Scott Carlson highlights in the *Primer for Justice Components in Multidimensional Peace Operations* he authored for the UN Department of Peacekeeping Operations, gathering and organizing the applicable laws is essential after the arrival of a mission, but given that these can be difficult to locate, and that linguistic challenges make matters even more complicated, this can be a time-consuming task. Furthermore, the approach would also create an opportunity for the laws to be reviewed for compatibility with human rights standards, and for jurists to be familiarized with such standards and with the legal codes themselves before they have to begin applying them. Finally, it would also strike the right balance between the need for order and security and the need for justice based on international human rights standards: while detainees would receive adequate due process and a hearing with a reviewing authority, as they did with the DMU, the system would allow for security detentions, including for individuals suspected of having committed atrocities prior to the UN's arrival, and for prolonged pre-trial detention periods.

Human rights in a post-conflict legal context

Issues raised

The notion that a full catalogue of human rights must necessarily apply as part of a legal framework in situations where a UN civilian administration mission takes charge of a post-conflict territory dominated the thinking of both UNMIK and UNTAET; consequently the two administrations implemented such a complete catalogue from the beginning of the respective missions. The analysis presented in the case-study chapters, however, demonstrates that while basic human rights should indeed apply broadly, the notion that a full catalogue of such rights can apply in the immediate aftermath of violence is misguided: such an approach led to the violation of key legal principles, most importantly the need for congruence between the rules as announced and as administered, and also the need for clarity; furthermore, it led to the violation of various judicial norms, and in particular key due process rights related to the length of pre-trial detention periods.

Responses from academics and practitioners, analysis and discussion

As we saw, various human rights NGOs and some international institutions were unsurprisingly critical of the UN's failures to uphold human rights standards in its missions. The criticisms were made in particular in relation to the violation of detainees' rights to liberty and to a fair trial: in Kosovo, this was largely the result of the executive detentions, as highlighted by the OSCE,[53] the Ombudsperson Institution,[54] Amnesty International[55] and Human Rights Watch,[56] for instance;[57] and in East Timor it was as a result of the violation of various due process and other fair trial standards, as highlighted by the Judicial System Monitoring Programme[58] and various academics.[59] But while many of the reports and papers which discuss the subject of human rights in a post-conflict legal context are very quick to condemn the international community's failures and call for an end to problematic practices, such as executive detentions, virtually none offers any suggestions as to how a UN mission can adequately balance its obligations on the one hand to re-establish law and order on the ground in what is frequently a very challenging security situation, and on the other hand to observe and protect human rights to the fullest extent possible.

At the end of one of the most violent centuries in human history, and at a time when human rights are still broadly violated in most societies, the protection of human rights has rightfully become the focus for many organizations, and has also begun to have a very slight influence on some states' relations with each other. However, the fact that the protection of human rights has become the be all and end all of some practitioners' and institutions' existence, and that many academics subscribe to the unswerving protection of such rights with an almost dogmatic fervour, has evidently prevented lateral thinking on the matter, particularly when it comes to addressing human rights problems in the context of post-conflict reconstruction. Furthermore, the problems of extraordinary rendition, particularly as practised by the United States, of extra-judicial security detentions in locations such as Guantanamo Bay and of human rights abuses during the military occupation of Iraq have been at the forefront of intellectual discussions and debates on the matter of how adequately to balance a state's need for order and security versus human rights and justice, arguably to the detriment of any discussions on the matter in the context of post-conflict reconstruction, particularly if carried out by a non-state entity.

The United Nations is open to suggestions on the matter: in the Secretary-General's report on rule-of-law reform in conflict and post-conflict societies, he recognizes that:

> lawlessness can seriously undermine the efforts of an entire peace operation ... we must, together with Member States, *rethink* our current strategies for addressing the rule of law vacuum into which we are deployed, including the role, capacities and obligations of military and civilian police components.[60]

This statement does imply a recognition on the part of the United Nations that its reform strategies have not worked, and the fact that the organization is willing to *rethink* these reform strategies indicates that it is broadly open to suggestions on the matter.

While some academics and practitioners have heeded this call and have provided suggestions on some issues, as we saw in the previous section, the discussion about how the United Nations can effectively administer human rights in a post-conflict context has largely focused on discovering how to ensure that international human rights standards are not violated through the UN's legal and judicial reform process.[61] The literature on this topic implies that better funding and resourcing could help to avoid a number of problems, which is indeed true, but it fails to address the problems which are inherent in the task of building a new legal system from the ground up, namely that the reform efforts take place in an environment where order and security have not been re-established, and they require time. Unless these factors are taken into account, it is unlikely that the United Nations will come up with a successful approach.

It is interesting to note that while international legal instruments, and more specifically the law on belligerent occupation, guided the UN's legal and judicial reform efforts, particularly regarding the initial choice of law and institutional framework, neither the United Nations nor any academics have looked towards such legal instruments for an answer to the human rights dilemma and how to deal with it in times of public emergencies, which is essentially what a post-conflict environment amounts to. However, perhaps with the exception of the Universal Declaration of Human Rights[62] and the African Charter of Human and Peoples' Rights,[63] most human rights instruments do provide some answers about how to deal with this problem, and those answers lie in the division of human rights between non-derogable and derogable rights.[64] For instance, Article 4.1 of Part II of the ICCPR states that:

> In time of public emergency which threatens the life of the nation and the existence of which is officially proclaimed, the States Parties to the present Covenant may take measures derogating from their obligations under the present Covenant to the extent strictly required by the exigencies of the situation, provided that such measures are not inconsistent with their other obligations under international law and do not involve discrimination solely on the ground of race, colour, sex, language, religion or social origin.[65]

The European Convention on Human Rights and the American Convention on Human Rights have similar provisions for derogations from certain rights.[66] Furthermore, international humanitarian law makes provision for such derogation in Geneva Convention IV, as set out in Articles 41–43, 68 and 78 of the convention.[67] Certain rights remain non-derogable under these conventions, such as the right to life, freedom from torture, protection against slavery and protection against retrospective criminal penalties, but in essence these articles provide the ability for either national governments or an occupying power to derogate from some rights in times of a public emergency so as to be able to re-establish law and order effectively. Among the derogable rights are articles which pertain to arrests and detention, such as Articles 9 and 14 of the ICCPR.

Perhaps it was the UN's past efforts to encourage states to uphold the highest human rights standards which prevented it from invoking emergency powers when it was in a governing position itself. However, as the case studies demonstrated, no matter what good intentions the United Nations may have had in avoiding the issue of derogation, the decision not to derogate led it to violate its own laws and to be rightfully accused of failing to live up to the very standards it had implemented. Derogation from key rights did occur under the INTERFET regime in East Timor, and if they had publicly acknowledged the need for derogation from certain rights, only then derogating from such rights, both UNMIK and UNTAET would have prevented the violation of their own laws and key legal principles.

There is nothing new about the notion that a society where the regular law-and-order mechanisms have broken down is in need of emergency legal measures to try to restore security. Traditionally, states have dealt with such situations through constitutional provisions permitting the implementation of martial law. All in all, derogating from certain human rights has the potential to balance better the need for order and security on the one hand and justice within a framework of human rights on the other hand. In the approach taken in Kosovo and East Timor, the balance was too much in favour of human rights. But derogation in particular from rights pertaining to arrests and detentions in both UNMIK and UNTAET would have left these missions in a better position to ensure the security and stability of the territory without having to be in breach of the law. In essence, such derogation would simply have legalized *preventive* and *security* detentions, which did take place in Kosovo in the form of the SRSG's executive detentions, thereby helping to keep legally behind bars individuals who were already detained and who posed a threat to security and stability if released, and by holding other detainees, such as suspected perpetrators of gross atrocities or other suspected criminals, for longer periods pending trial. Derogation would also have ensured accountability for past and more recent crimes without having to keep individuals illegally detained, and without feeling forced to begin trial proceedings at a time when such proceedings cannot be held in conditions that fulfil internationally expected standards.

While it is perhaps understandable that the United Nations has not wanted to invoke emergency rights in its governance operations, even though the situation on the ground would certainly have constituted the equivalent of a national emergency and such derogation could have been justified on these grounds, it is noteworthy that the issue of derogation has been left out from the literature on transitional administration broadly and on justice sector reform more specifically, and this presents a significant gap in the literature.

Establishing an institutional structure

Issues raised

The decision to establish a comprehensive and regular court structure from the beginning of the mission was the aspect of the UN's approach to legal and judicial reform which caused the least number of problems and violations. However, as we saw in the East Timor case study, the focus on establishing a comprehensive regular court structure early on turned UNTAET's attention away from the more pressing need to implement some temporary institutional measures so that the newly appointed judges could function within some sort of judicial framework, rather than extra-judicially as they did. UNMIK's establishment of mobile courts was a step in the right direction in this respect; however, the similarity of these mobile courts to regular courts implies that the United Nations was not willing to contemplate establishing anything but such regular courts. Furthermore, in East Timor the approach also led to the implementation of a structure which was larger than was feasible, and consequently the need for UNTAET to downsize the number of district courts it had initially envisioned from eight to four.

In essence, this approach does not account for the fact that a post-conflict society has judicial needs which have to be addressed instantly, and that what may be desirable may not be feasible, and may initially and unnecessarily raise local expectations about the ability of the legal system to deliver justice quickly; thus the approach does not leave sufficient time for the consideration and design of an appropriate institutional structure. Moreover, the approach does not allow sufficient time for considering whether and how any customary justice and/or dispute resolution mechanisms and practices may be integrated into or work together with or within that institutional structure.[68]

Certainly, whether or not customary justice mechanisms and practices should be integrated into a statutory judicial system is debatable. The approach taken may be advantageous, in that it may help to root out some extreme customary practices which are not deemed to be in line with international human rights standards. Such practices may include, for instance, ones which are similar to the Punjab Tribal Council's ordering of the gang rape of Mukhtaran Bibi in 2002, in retribution for her very young brother's alleged affair with an older woman.[69] On the other hand, the approach may be disadvantageous in that it may potentially ignore useful customary justice mechanisms and practices: in many societies there are, for instance, village- or tribal-level justice mechanisms which in minor disputes between parties may ease the pressure on the statutory justice system, particularly if the courts are distant and the claims are small. As we saw in East Timor, the United Nations ignored the cultural importance of *forgiveness* in its approach to justice, which may have been detrimental to its decisions on whether or not to prosecute the lower-ranked individuals who had committed atrocities during the conflict. Finally, an approach that ignores local customs may in fact contribute to the creation of two parallel legal systems – one based on customs and one which is statutory, rendering the statutory system potentially ineffective if such customs are strongly embedded in the local culture.[70] Either way, the early establishment of a regular institutional structure pre-empts any discussions on the potential integration of customary justice practices and mechanisms into the statutory judicial system.

Responses from academics and practitioners, analysis and discussion

Among the academics and practitioners writing on transitional justice and rule-of-law reform, there is virtually no discussion or debate on the establishment of a judicial institutional structure in a post-conflict society. The lack of scholarly treatment of this issue would appear to suggest that the current approach is regarded as largely unproblematic and not worthy of further investigation. While this book confirms that the institutional structure was the least contentious area of reform, and that the establishment of a regular court structure was the least problematic of all the elements of the UN's approach, the above discussion of the issues raised does indicate that the approach is not without flaws.

What is interesting to note in this context is that there is some scholarly treatment of the issue of how the security forces dealt with the absence of a court structure in East Timor: Bruce Oswald and Michael Kelly have both addressed the establishment of the Detainee Management Unit.[71] INTERFET's approach to the problem of establishing an institutional and procedural framework in order to maintain law and order clearly holds many valuable lessons for the United Nations, since INTERFET's task of dealing with detainees in a chaotic post-conflict environment, in the absence of any functioning structures, is not very different to the tasks the United Nations has to carry out in administering justice. Importantly, INTERFET did not follow the GC IV regulation that the regular courts have to continue to function as before in a territory under military occupation. INTERFET's leadership recognized that even though INTERFET was essentially an Australian-led security force, the fact that its mission had been sanctioned by the Indonesian government and was welcomed by the Timorese factions meant that its presence in East Timor did not amount to military occupation, and it was therefore free to design the law-and-order functions of its operation as it saw fit. In the absence of any local legal and judicial capacity, it established a mechanism through which its own personnel could deal with law and order, and through which detainees could be guaranteed some due process rights.

But while there was still no functioning judiciary in East Timor, and the local legal and judicial capacity was still absent when the United Nations took over responsibility for the DMU detainees in early January 2000, the United Nations chose a different route to dealing with these and other detainees. As we saw, the United Nations employed some local jurists, and did not recognize the inherent problem in permitting such individuals to issue detention orders etc. in the absence of any judicial structures. Moreover, it let the new and the DMU detainees stay in pre-trial detention for a prolonged period of time without any real mechanism through which their detention could be challenged. The important lesson for the United Nations here is that there must be a recognition that the establishment of a mechanism to deal with detainees cannot be delayed simply because the UN's policy preference is to establish a regular court system before dealing with such detainees. In this respect, Scott Carlson's suggestion that Emergency Mobile Courts "may be needed in the emergency phase to deal with the most acute needs" is very helpful, as is his conclusion that such mobile courts "can also provide a long term solution to some endemic access to justice challenges".[72]

INTERFET's establishment of the DMU helped the security forces to balance better the tensions between the need for order and security on the one hand and justice within a framework of international human rights standards on the other: while detentions, including security and preventive detentions, were carried out, they were carried out legally. Importantly, such security detentions occurred within a framework which gave detainees the right to a prompt hearing regarding their detention, as well as the right to challenge that detention. Detainees were released either conditionally if they were not deemed to be a security threat or a flight risk, or unconditionally if there was insufficient evidence against them. Such releases also helped to prevent prolonged and unnecessary pre-trial detention periods. Certainly, the United Nations has much to learn from INTERFET's approach, and the way in which it helped to balance the key tensions of its operation, and it would also be wise to heed the advice of Scott Carlson on the potential use of emergency mobile courts.

Addressing past atrocities and serious crimes

Issues raised

The evidence presented in this work has shown that burdening a newly established judiciary with cases that concern war, inter-ethnic or other serious crimes committed during a conflict is highly problematic, in that it draws away much-needed resources from the judicial system, contributes to a burgeoning backlog of cases and expects local jurists to work on cases that demand the expertise of much more experienced and better-qualified individuals. Furthermore, particularly the UN's experience in East Timor highlighted that if it is agreed that some sort of trials for past atrocities are held, it is important for the entire judicial process that a clear prosecution strategy is agreed upon prior to the commencement of any trials.[73] The problems in both Kosovo and East Timor highlighted that the United Nations cannot afford to proceed *on the cheap* so that it can avoid the greater expenditures of *ad hoc* tribunals such as the ICTR

and ICTY:[74] in trying to avoid large expenses, it has not only been unfair towards the persons who have been convicted in trials which cannot
be deemed to be fair, but it has actually undermined several key objectives of the UN's rule-of-law reform efforts, such as the advancement of
high standards of justice through the tribunals and the establishment of
a sustainable legal system. Where up-to-standard prosecutions cannot be
undertaken, other policy options need to be considered, and thus the
stance taken here is that something is not better than nothing when it
comes to justice, and standards of justice cannot be compromised for the
sake of *appearing* to prosecute.[75]

Responses from academics and practitioners, analysis and discussion

The broad question of how to address past atrocities in the aftermath of
a conflict, or after the fall of a dictatorial regime, has been the subject of
countless studies. The answer to this question has completed a full cy-
cle: starting with the Nuremberg and Tokyo trials after the Second World
War, which saw the prosecution of war criminals, there was a prolonged
period during the Cold War when impunity ruled the day. During the
1980s and early 1990s the commonly accepted approach was the granting
of amnesties, frequently coupled with a truth and reconciliation process.
In the mid-1990s the establishment of the ICTY and ICTR saw the first
major attempts since the end of the Second World War to prosecute the
perpetrators of genocide, war crimes and crimes against humanity. The
notion that there can be no peace without justice took a firm hold among
peace researchers, and there have been few challenges to the argument
that a sustainable peace requires justice.[76] The push for prosecutions
for past atrocities led to the establishment of hybrid internationalized
national panels in Kosovo, East Timor and Bosnia; of the International
Criminal Court; and of internationalized criminal courts for Cambodia,
Sierra Leone and Lebanon.

However, the view that there can be no peace without justice, and that
challenging impunity is always in the best interest of a war-torn society,
was not embraced by all, and found some of its most ardent critics in
communities which have suffered some of the worst atrocities. For instance, Peter Onega, the chairman of the Ugandan Amnesty Commission and a leading figure of Uganda's Acholi community, one of the worst
affected by the Lord's Resistance Army (LRA), went to the Hague to
complain about the ICC's decision to issue warrants for various LRA
members. Fearing that the LRA leaders could react to such warrants as
"desperately as a wounded buffalo" and that this could in turn lead to
more atrocities, he argued that "The priority should be peace first and

justice later."[77] Similarly, in a report of October 2004, the Sierra Leone Truth and Reconciliation Commission argued that "disallowing amnesty in all cases would be to deny the reality of violent conflict and the urgent need to bring such strife and suffering to an end", and further that "those who argue that peace cannot be bartered in exchange for justice, under any circumstances, must be prepared to justify the likely prolongation of an armed conflict".[78] Furthermore, East Timor's President Xanana Gusmao stated that it is "not necessarily" true that the "absence of justice ... is a fundamental obstacle in the process of building a democratic society".[79]

But despite such objections, it is unlikely that the trend to prosecute will change in the near future. It may be true that criminal prosecutions are not always regarded as a "categorical good": Chesterman highlights, for example, that "there seems to be a general acceptance of South Africa's decision to grant amnesties rather than prosecute".[80] Nevertheless, the establishment of the *ad hoc* tribunals for Yugoslavia and Rwanda, and of the various internationalized criminal courts, chambers and tribunals suggests that the notion that the perpetrators of atrocities must be held accountable for their crimes rather than granted amnesties seems to have taken root in the international community.[81]

While the trend is unlikely to change soon, academics and practitioners have recognized a number of the problems which prosecuting past atrocities created in Kosovo and East Timor. In the first instance, the approach the United Nations took was overly concerned with prosecutions for the sake of prosecutions, or for the sake of appearing to prosecute: in regard to East Timor in particular, the co-founder of one of the NGOs which monitored the judicial reform efforts, the Judicial System Monitoring Programme, observed that appearing to do something about prosecuting atrocities was more important than actually prosecuting atrocities, and that prosecutions were more about making gestures and seeming to do the right thing than actually pursuing justice; according to him, the hybrid tribunal that was set up was like a "trophy to be put on UN bookshelves", presumably meaning nice to show off, irrespective of the substance of the achievement.[82] Trials in both territories were undertaken without regard for the fairness and standards of the proceedings, and in the case of East Timor without regard for the fairness of trying low-level perpetrators while giving concessions to some of their higher-ranked colleagues in exchange for the return of refugees, and of not prosecuting Indonesian military commanders.

As Suzannah Linton, who worked within the East Timorese system, argued, the hybrid model might encourage the international community wrongly to equate prosecutions with actual justice, lead them to "a false sense of accomplishment" and complacency, and inadvertently to undermine "the very standards of justice and the rule of law" that it was intended to promote.[83] Linton's overall assessment was that:

> The Serious Crimes project best illustrates the need for UNTAET to take a more realistic and practical approach that considers the actual conditions in East Timor. It is highly commendable to have a "state of the art" legal regime for prosecuting international crimes in domestic courts but, before embarking on the exercise, it is fundamental to consider whether the existing (or incoming) system can support such a venture ... In a still fragile and volatile society, dangerously high expectations have been created. Failure of the enterprise may have serious consequences for the future peace and stability of East Timor.[84]

Such assessments have led some observers, such as Suzanne Katzenstein, to argue that since opting for a compromised justice mechanism in the short term may actually undermine future efforts to establish justice, choosing no justice at all may in fact be preferable to a justice mechanism that is compromised.[85] While this assessment has some merits, the UN's desire to put an end to impunity and shift away from amnesties means that it is unlikely to opt for a course of *no justice* and is likely to continue to follow a policy of pursuing prosecutions, irrespective of whether it is involved in governance operations again or whether it does so in the context of peace assistance missions.

Given that the pursuit of prosecutions is likely to be the preferred UN choice in addressing past atrocities, and that academics and practitioners have recognized some of the problems that occurred in Kosovo and East Timor, the literature on the subject holds surprisingly few answers as to the ways in which some of the problems can be surmounted. As indicated above, Suzannah Linton does suggest that a clear prosecution strategy has to be agreed upon prior to the commencement of any trials; and David Cohen indicates that the United Nations cannot pursue justice "on the cheap"[86] in an effort to avoid the expensive mechanisms of the ICTY and the ICTR.[87] But apart from these few suggestions and the occasional critique of the hybrid court model, such as that of James Cockayne, the literature largely fails to discuss what alternatives there may be to that model.

This may be the case partly because some academics and practitioners are at a loss as to what other methods there may be,[88] and partly because, despite the problems, a number of academics feel that internationalized or hybrid national criminal courts are "globally to be praised".[89] For instance, Antonio Cassesse strongly believes that "in the long term, resorting to mixed or internationalized criminal courts and tribunals may prove to be one of the most effective societal and institutional devices of the many which are at present available to international law-makers".[90] Luigi

Condorelli and Theo Boutruche also write favourably of the *nationally based* hybrid court model, because they feel that "it is necessary that the international judge not be distant, but close to the country, and that he is perceived as such" and that the perception must be advanced that "international justice is not the monopoly of a unique court but also belongs to some tribunals composed of national judges".[91]

However, one academic in particular – Alain Pellet – is not only critical of the problems with internationalized criminal courts, but also offers an alternative proposal as to how past atrocities can be addressed in the aftermath of a conflict. He does recognize that one of the hybrid court model's "main advantages over truly international bodies is their 'proximity' – proximity to the place where the crime has been committed, proximity to the evidence, proximity to the population more directly concerned".[92] However, he believes there is a danger that proximity may result in partiality, and argues that "trials rendered 'on the spot' in a post-trauma context are more open to criticism and to the dangers of revenge than expatriated trials in more remote countries where the heat can be more easily taken out of the situation".[93] Furthermore, Pellet makes the case that "when ... serious crimes are at stake they are 'of concern to the international community as a whole', as stated in the Preamble to the Rome Statute of the ICC, and it is therefore important that they not be confiscated by any particular state, including the one in which the crime has been committed or of which the victims or the authors are nationals".[94] Also, he feels that essentially "internationalized criminal courts cloud the issues"[95] because:

> They are an expression of the international community's concerns but, at the same time, they are part of the reconstruction enterprise of a new judicial system in countries where the entire administration had been destroyed by civil wars (Kosovo, East Timor) or they facilitate acceptance of accountability to justice of former national rulers (Cambodia and, in some respects, Sierra Leone) in view of a purely national process of reconciliation. They bear witness to the will of the international community to have its own peremptory norms respected and to fight impunity but, at the same time, they will generally answer a national need and, at least to some extent, fulfil national purposes.[96]

He is willing to concede that mixed criminal tribunals "are a lesser evil than purely national justice in the absence of a truly international competent tribunal", but is nevertheless highly critical of the fact that the "tribunals are created much more with a view to strengthening the local judiciary than to rendering *international* justice and punishing the perpetrators of *international* crimes as such".[97]

As the case studies have demonstrated, the internationalized criminal courts in Kosovo and East Timor have anything but strengthened the local judiciary, and have not rendered the type of *justice* with which the international community would wish to associate. Pellet's criticisms of internationalized criminal courts lead him to ask the question whether instead of *internationalizing* national courts, a case can be made for *nationalizing* international tribunals, a result which he argues would not be that far off what was achieved with the Special Court of Sierra Leone, which "comes close to a truly international criminal tribunal but with an important nuance: it is statutorily, and then symbolically, a national court".[98] In making this proposal for the nationalization of international tribunals, he also points to Antonio Cassesse's proposal for dealing with the drug-trafficking problem in Colombia, namely that it would be appropriate to create an international tribunal which can have the competence to address drug trafficking and related crimes which would not normally fall within the realm of a crime against humanity or a war crime.[99]

While Pellet only speculates about the particulars of establishing a nationalized international tribunal, such as its composition and location, issues of safety and security, the manner by which it would be created and the type of cases it would take on, he is adamant that "such a new judicial body would be a permanent structure, not an ad hoc creation such as ICTY or ICTR or the existing mixed tribunals".[100] The key element of such an international body would be the inclusion of national judges, which could help to reassure countries, such as the United States, that have major objections to the current ICC arrangement. The major difference between an internationalized national tribunal and an international tribunal with national judges is that in the first case "the international component is, so to speak, secondary, incidental; those tribunals (including their mixed nature) answer primarily national concerns".[101] In the second scenario, on the other hand, "the concerns of the international community as a whole become predominant while at the same time, the special interests of one or some given States would be taken into consideration".[102]

This proposal is interesting, and has certain similarities with the proposed Kosovo War and Ethnic Crimes Court (KWECC).[103] But while the proposal has merit, Pellet's apparent aversion to internationalized processes which deal with anything but international crimes ignores the need for certain crimes and criminals to be tried by foreign jurists and panels. In a society which has recently experienced or is experiencing high levels of violence, local judges may not be in a position or may not wish to be in a position to try certain individuals or certain crimes: this may be the case either out of fear for their own safety or because of pressures from their local communities or ethnic or religious groups. For instance, in cases where local war heroes are put on trial, there would be enormous pressure on a local judge to release that individual, as was frequently the case in Kosovo. Even if such an individual is not charged with a crime against humanity or a war crime, but is linked to the illegal arms trade, prostitution rings, drugs, murders, human trafficking or petty crimes, the individual may be immune to prosecution because of his or her status in the community.

Thus a nationalized international tribunal which can hear cases relating to non-international crimes would in fact be much more useful in a post-conflict context than simply a panel that can hear international crimes cases. The KWECC structure was a step in the right direction, but interestingly, even Pellet does not discuss the potential benefits which that court would have brought to Kosovo. His proposal, coupled with the need for certain non-international crimes cases to be heard by international judges, points towards the potential benefits which marrying the KWECC structure with that of the Regulation 64 panels, as Kosovo's mixed courts came to be known, would have had in Kosovo. If national and international judges sitting on nationalized international panels had been able to hear not only high-profile cases where a crime under international law had been committed, but importantly also high-profile cases of crimes which would not normally be classed as an international crime, such as drug trafficking, extortion, money laundering, kidnapping etc., as was the case with the Regulation 64 panels, this would have alleviated the substantial backlog created by such complex cases within the regular courts, freed up much-needed resources and thus benefited the entire judicial reform effort in Kosovo.

The idea of a *nationalized* international tribunal has clear merits, since it would help to remove war and at least some of the serious crimes trials from the domestic courts – trials which we saw placed an unacceptable burden on a newly formed judiciary. The involvement of national judges in such international tribunals has the potential not only to help to reassure countries that have objections to an internationalized process, but also to give such countries a degree of ownership over the justice process, and in this respect also over justice, which they might otherwise not have. However, the view that such a nationalized international tribunal should have a permanent structure may be overly ambitious: given the recent establishment of the ICC, there may be less incentive in the international community for the establishment of a further permanent structure. Thus the establishment of nationalized international panels locally and *ad hoc* may find more favour.

A case for the establishment of such an *ad hoc* tribunal can be made on the grounds of the argument mentioned above that proximity to the population which was affected, to the evidence and to the location where the crime was committed has certain benefits. While trials held in a post-conflict environment do carry the risk that they may be polarizing and can result in increased tensions, they also have the benefit of rendering justice where it is needed most. Some academics have argued that locating *ad hoc* tribunals far away from the place where the crimes were committed has not helped the country in question to re-establish its judicial system and rebuild the rule of law.[104] In delivering justice locally, internationalized national panels which have heard serious crimes cases were perhaps considered to be a step in the right direction; however, as this book has shown, such panels have themselves frequently undermined the very goal of the establishment of a sustainable legal system. In this respect, the nationalization of international panels, which can be located in the territory where the crimes took place, can be a move in the right direction when it comes to remedying the problems which the current approach creates.

It could also be argued that a case for such a panel can be made on the grounds that the legal regime established under the Rome Statute for the ICC is not all-encompassing, and it is possible to imagine situations where international crimes are committed neither in a state party to the statute nor by a national of a state party to the statute.[105] In such circumstances, and when a state has not given consent for the ICC's jurisdiction,[106] the proposed court would have jurisdiction over such cases and try them within the territory where the crimes were committed. Addressing the atrocities of Saddam Hussein's regime in Iraq through such a process would have given the trials more international legitimacy, and shielded them from the criticisms that victors' justice was rendered in the trials of Saddam and his former high-level officials.

What remains unclear about the proposed nationalized international tribunal is the nature of its relationship with the ICC, and particularly the question as to whether it would have concurrent jurisdiction with the ICC or would simply be designed to complement the work of the ICC. Mariacarmen Colitti's proposal for symbiosis between the ICC and internationalized national panels, where the panels focus on low-rank suspects of international crimes and the ICC targets the high-profile individuals, could potentially offer an answer to this unaddressed question.[107] Colitti's suggestion as applied to the proposed tribunal would see the nationalized international tribunals defer to the competence of the ICC in high-profile cases, and in this way the burden of trials could be shared between the ICC and Pellet's proposed court.

A further issue that remains unclear in relation to the establishment of such a court is that of funding. As we saw in Chapter 3, the problem of funding was arguably the biggest obstacle to the creation of KWECC. There is no question that the type of court proposed by Pellet can be a big expense for a mission with a limited budget, and funding would be problematic.[108] However, given the level of involvement of international judges and prosecutors in Kosovo and East Timor, it is unclear what the budgetary difference would be in allocating some internationals to a separate court and providing them with an international staff. It would certainly be a great expense, but such financial questions are often a matter of political will, and should political will exist, along with the realization that addressing certain serious crimes in internationalized national panels is detrimental to the establishment of a sustainable justice system, it is conceivable that enough assets will be freed up for the creation of such a court.

Overall, there needs to be a change in attitude within the international community as far as legal and judicial capabilities for governance or even peacebuilding missions are concerned. The Brahimi Report pointed out in 2000 that "the United Nations has faced situations in the past decade where the Security Council has authorized the deployment of several thousand police in a peacekeeping operation but has resisted the notion of providing the same operations with even 20 or 30 criminal justice experts".[109] While a nationalized international court may be expensive, the investment in other rule-of-law reform efforts may be a waste if a sustainable legal system is not created. There may indeed not be enough political will in the international community to create such nationalized international tribunals. Certain states may not wish to set a precedent that may at some stage become a problem for them, and this hurdle might be more difficult to overcome than any budgetary problems. However, unless such budgetary and political hurdles are overcome, the United Nations may find itself repeating its peacebuilding efforts in regions which deteriorate into violence after the withdrawal of the international community, and where the organization has failed to advance high standards of justice and effectively create sustainable mechanisms of justice.

A nationalized international panel would not only ensure that complex cases do not drain the resources of the fledgling judiciary, but also that the high standards of international justice required for the trial of the most serious atrocities and high-level officials would be observed. This could be ensured by exclusively recruiting the most talented international lawyers to work within such a court. Furthermore, ensuring that such a court operates outside the regular justice system would force UN administrators to consider options other than prosecution, such as amnesties, if there is not sufficient will locally and internationally to provide the court with adequate funding and resources. Finally, the establishment of such a court would better balance the tension that exists between the need for accountability for past atrocities and the need to deliver justice in accordance with international standards. Importantly, it is imperative that the establishment of such nationalized international courts, or of any mechanisms designed to deal with past atrocities for that matter, should follow and not precede any decisions on a prosecution strategy for past atrocities. While in some cases this would include only a select few high-level officials responsible for the past violence, as was the case in Sierra

Leone,[110] other arrangements may adopt a broader prosecution strategy and also hold lower-ranked officials to account.

Local actors in the legal and judicial reform process

Issues raised

The Kosovo and East Timor case studies have clearly demonstrated that local empowerment early on in a mission can be detrimental to the goal of establishing a sustainable legal system. In Kosovo the UN's decision to allow local jurists to take on all types of cases from the outset created many problems with judicial impartiality and independence; and the decision to hand over outright ownership of the judicial process virtually from the beginning of the mission in East Timor had negative consequences for overall judicial reconstruction and the integrity of the judicial process. What the East Timor case study in particular has demonstrated is that while local ownership over the judicial process must indeed be the end goal of a mission, it cannot be the means to the end of establishing a sustainable legal system. And what both case studies have shown is that allowing poorly trained local actors to work as jurists can lead to frequent legal complications resulting from the jurists' lack of qualifications and the potential for ethno-religious or political bias.

Responses from academics and practitioners, analysis and discussion

The broad problem with the international community's desire to hand over ownership too quickly in governance operations has been recognized in the literature: in his book *You, the People*, Simon Chesterman addresses the problem and correctly asserts that "Local control of political power is appropriately seen as the end of a transitional administration, but if an international actor has assumed some or all governmental power then local ownership is surely not the means."[111] He goes on to explain that:

> It is both inaccurate and counter-productive to assert that transitional administration depends upon the consent or "ownership" of local populations. It is inaccurate because if genuine local control were possible then a transitional administration would not be necessary. It is counter-productive because insincere claims of local ownership lead to frustration and suspicion on the part of local actors.[112]

What is broadly true for the international governance of territory is also particularly true for legal and judicial reform. Chesterman recognizes the particular problem with the granting of too much power too quickly in relation to judicial reform: he argues that while "any foreign involvement" in justice sector reform must "be sensitive to the particularities of that population ... this is not to say that ... locals must drive this process in all circumstances".[113] His assertion that "international engagement will sometimes abrogate the most basic right to self-governance on a temporary basis"[114] is something that future peacebuilders will be wise to take into consideration when planning for justice sector reform. The case studies have clearly highlighted what the consequences are if ownership is handed over too soon: we saw in the East Timor chapter, for instance, that there is a clear danger that handing over such ownership early on can make judicial reform the hostage of local politics, with all the negative repercussions which that entails. As one observer put it, "The experience of East Timor reveals all too well the risks of allowing the Tribunal or the defence function to become the hostage of local politics to the detriment of the right of each defendant to a fair trial and an adequate defence under international standards."[115] As a consequence of these and similar negative repercussions on the overall reform efforts, judicial administration needs to be one of the last areas of governance over which the international community should relinquish its ownership.

But even if ownership over the judicial administration process remains in the hands of international actors working in a particular territory, what answers does the literature hold for the problem of employing local actors with very basic legal qualifications, little legal experience and a potential for ethno-religious or political bias to work within a fledgling judiciary? Academics and practitioners alike have recognized the problems with the prior approach, and in essence their response lies in the suggestion for a more rapid and immediate introduction of international jurists into the judicial system. Carlson highlights that staffing numbers for international judicial positions have been abysmal in comparison to those allocated for police reform, civil affairs, and human rights units, and argues that the provision of "a sufficient number of international staff in mission budgets" must be "commensurate with the mission mandate and needs on the ground". He also recognizes that "Delays in staffing rule of law components undermine credibility and harm mission start-up" thus arguing for a more rapid deployment of international jurists.[116] In this respect, Chesterman proposes that "Measures to create a standby network of international jurists who could be deployed at short notice to post-conflict areas would facilitate the establishment of a judicial system."[117] While Chesterman envisages that such jurists would operate primarily as trainers and mentors, Strohmeyer's similar proposal envisions that they would also work as international judges and prosecutors within the system. Strohmeyer writes that:

> It is ... imperative for the United Nations to develop a standby network (as opposed to a standing capacity) of experienced and qualified international jurists that can be activated at any given time. In view of the significant practical differences between the common-law and civil-law systems, experts in both systems should be recruited in sufficient numbers to ensure that they can adequately respond to the specific needs of the territory to be administered. Since quick deployment is crucial to the effectiveness and credibility of an operation in its early stages, the United Nations should create a network based on standby agreements with member states, agencies, and academic institutions to facilitate mobilization of these jurists on short notice, within a few days, if required. If provided with ongoing training in international legal and human rights standards, and updated information on international instruments and judicial developments, the members of this network would eventually constitute a sufficient number of qualified international lawyers, who could work as trainers, mentors, judges and prosecutors.[118]

The proposal for an early introduction of international jurists into the local judicial system appears to be very sound given the evidence presented in the case-study chapters. Such a move would not only fill recruitment gaps and increase the capacity of the judiciary to hear cases early on, thereby preventing once again the build-up of a backlog of cases, but would also ensure that international jurists could act as mentors and/or advisers to local jurists. Certainly, however, the implementation of this proposal would have its own complications: firstly, states are jealous of their competent legal experts, and may not be prepared to spare them for UN missions;[119] and secondly, Chesterman himself doubts whether such a network of jurists would "be able to deploy in sufficient time and numbers to establish even an ad hoc system on their own".[120]

However, if these political and operational obstacles can be surmounted, introducing international jurists from the very beginning of a governance operation where a judiciary has to be established anew, while broadly retaining ownership over the judicial process, holds the potential to strike a better balance between the need for international governance to a high standard and local empowerment for the purposes of establishing a sustainable judicial system. The UN's initial approach in Kosovo and East Timor shifted this balance too much in favour of local empowerment, to the detriment of the overall legal and judicial reform in both territories. But retaining ownership over the judicial process and the introduction of international jurists from the beginning would address this tension in a way which would not undermine the UN's efforts: it would prevent many of the violations of legal principles and judicial norms and standards which did occur, and would focus the UN's approach on local ownership as the end goal of its efforts and not the means to the establishment of a sustainable legal system.

Notes

1. See Chapter 1.
2. Evans (1993: 56).
3. Ibid.
4. Plunkett (1998: 68).
5. Plunkett (2003: 215).
6. UN General Assembly and Security Council (2000b: para. 79) (Brahimi Report).
7. Ibid., para. 81.
8. Ibid., para. 80.
9. Ibid., para. 83. This particular recommendation was based on the advice of Christopher Lord. See Annex II of the Brahimi Report; on this see also Oswald (2004).
10. UN General Assembly and Security Council (2000c: para. 31); see also Chapter 1.
11. Strohmeyer (2001b: 62).
12. Ibid.
13. Beauvais (2001: 1156–1157).
14. Fairlie (2003: 1059).
15. While some propose the implementation of comprehensive model codes (Fairlie, ibid.), others argue that a model code should not provide any comprehensive and universal definitions of criminal laws and/or procedures, but "should be limited to serious crimes and the set of procedural issues surrounding searches, seizures, and pre-trial detention" (Beauvais, 2001: 1157, paraphrasing an interview with Hansjoerg Strohmeyer).
16. UN Security Council (2004: paras 16 and 64(h)).
17. Colette Rausch at the US Institute of Peace and Vivienne O'Connor at the Irish Centre for Human Rights, based at the National University of Ireland at Galway, led this project.
18. The fact that the project was organized in cooperation with the UN's Office of the High Commissioner for Human Rights (OHCHR) was not initially clear to the OHCHR itself, a point clarified in an interview. This indicates the UN's initial level of involvement and interest in such an endeavour.
19. Interview with academic present at the review conference, June 2005.
20. Ibid.
21. See UN General Assembly and Security Council (2000b: para. 82) (Brahimi Report).
22. Interview with academic present at the review conference, June 2005.
23. This matter is discussed at length by Vivienne O'Connor (2005); O'Connor and Rausch (2005).
24. Five potential uses were particularly identified by the codes' creators: see O'Connor and Rausch (2007).
25. UN Security Council (2004: para. 57).
26. Ibid, para. 30.
27. Ibid.
28. Ibid., p. 1.
29. Ibid, para. 15.
30. Ibid., para. 16.
31. Ibid., para. 17.

32. Ibid. para. 64(h).
33. Ibid., para. 17, emphasis added.
34. Ibid., emphasis added.
35. For a good discussion of the UN's approach in Afghanistan see Chesterman (2002b).
36. Chesterman (2004: 181–182), emphasis added.
37. UN Security Council (1999c: para. 13); cited here in Kelly (2000: 4).
38. Kelly (ibid.); as Kelly (ibid., n. 11) explains, a "serious offence included murder, manslaughter, grievous bodily harm, rape, possession of a weapon with intent to injure, carrying a weapon with criminal intent, causing an explosion likely to endanger life or property, kidnapping, and looting".
39. Conflict Security and Development Group (2003b: para. 218).
40. "Convention Relative to the Protection of Civilian Persons in Time of War" – see Treaties list.
41. Kelly (2000: 4).
42. Conflict Security and Development Group (2003b: para. 218); see also Kelly (ibid.).
43. Kelly (ibid.).
44. Michael Kelly (ibid.) explains that "while GC IV did not apply *de jure* in this situation because the Indonesian Government had consented to INTERFET's deployment, the Convention did provide a helpful framework for the regulation of the relationship between INTERFET and the civilian population in East Timor".
45. Ibid., p. 5.
46. Ibid. See "Agreement between the Republic of Indonesia and the Portuguese Republic on the Question of East Timor" – see Treaties list.
47. Kelly (ibid.).
48. Article 42(2) of Geneva Convention IV allows for voluntary detentions: "If any person, acting through the representatives of the Protecting Power, voluntarily demands internment, and if his situation renders this step necessary, he shall be interned by the Power in whose hands he may be." On this see also Kelly (ibid.: 5).
49. Kelly (ibid.: 6).
50. Ibid.; essentially, non-voluntary detainees would be held for up to 96 hours at the discretion of the force commander, after which the reviewing authority would need to make a decision within 24 hours on the continued detention of an individual, a decision which could have one of three outcomes: firstly, release with or without condition; secondly, detention pending trial by a competent court or other tribunal; and thirdly, detention of an individual pending trial by a competent court or tribunal or for a fixed period of time, whichever would come first.
51. UN Security Council (2000a: para. 45).
52. Kelly (2000: 3).
53. OSCE Mission in Kosovo (2002), section 4.
54. Ombudsperson Institution in Kosovo (2001a).
55. Amnesty International (2001a).
56. Human Rights Watch (2002a: 386).
57. See also Caplan (2005: 65); Chesterman (2004: 168).
58. Judicial System Monitoring Programme (2001).
59. See, for instance, Friman (2004: 336).
60. UN Security Council (2004: para. 28), emphasis added.
61. See, for instance, Judicial System Monitoring Programme (2001, 2002b); Cohen (2002).
62. See "Universal Declaration of Human Rights" – see Treaties list.
63. See "African Charter on Human Rights and Peoples' Rights" – see Treaties list.
64. For a good overview on the topic of states of emergency and derogations from human rights see Livingstone (2002).

65. See Article 4(1), ICCPR.
66. See Article 15 of the ECHR and Article 27 of the ACHR.
67. Article 42 of Geneva Convention IV, for instance sets out that "The internment or placing in assigned residence of protected persons may be ordered only if the security of the Detaining Power makes it absolutely necessary." Article 78 reiterates that "If the occupying power considers it necessary, for imperative reasons of security, to take safety measures concerning protected persons, it may, at the most, subject them to assigned residence or internment." Certainly, such procedures are subject to the right to an appropriate appeal system, as required by further provisions in Article 78.
68. For an overview of the challenges of reconciling customary justice mechanisms with the statutory judiciary in East Timor see Hohe and Nixon (2003); Mearns (2002); Judicial System Monitoring Programme (2002c).
69. See International Commission of Jurists (2002).
70. Such a parallel customary-statutory legal system has been in existence in Afghanistan for many decades, and the statutory system has been ignored; on this see Lau (2002); Thier (2004).
71. See Oswald (2000); Kelly (2000).
72. UN Department of Peacekeeping Operations (2006), p. 27. Scott Carlson authored this document.
73. On the importance of a coherent prosecution strategy see De Bertodano (2004: 83–84).
74. Cohen (2002: 7) also makes the point that the "United Nations should not commit itself so deeply to achieving a tribunal that it is willing to compromise the integrity of an institution to which it attaches its name".
75. On the negative impact which *appearing* to prosecute has on justice sector reform see Linton (2001a); Katzenstein (2003) also makes the point that no justice may be preferable to a flawed justice.
76. On the issue of whether there can be no peace without justice see Chesterman (2001b).
77. Mr Onega is cited here in OCHA (2006: 10).
78. Ibid., p. 11.
79. Ibid., p. 13.
80. Chesterman (2004: 164).
81. Please note in this regard Colette Rausch's (2006) excellent discussion of various specialized mechanisms to prosecute and adjudicate past atrocities, but also to combat serious crimes in a post-conflict context. As for the notion that prosecutions for past atrocities must be pursued, note that it led the Inter-American Court of Human Rights to require the government of Peru to repeal two controversial amnesty laws.
82. Katzenstein (2003: 272), citing an interview with Christian Ranheim of the JSMP.
83. Suzannah Linton (2001a: 177), cited in Katzenstein (ibid.: 278).
84. Linton (ibid.: 178).
85. Katzenstein (2003: 277–278).
86. Cohen (2002).
87. The UN's willingness to pay a substantial portion of the expenses of the Extraodinary Chambers for Cambodia is an indication that it may have learned this lesson: the United Nations agreed to pay US$43 million of the US$56.3 million budget for the trials and the Cambodian government agreed to provide the remaining $13.3 million; see UN News Service (2007).
88. This was my impression in a number of the interviews I conducted on the matter.
89. Pellet (2004: 437). Pellet is critical of the internationalization of national criminal courts, and states that he is not persuaded by the suggestion that such hybrid courts are to be praised.
90. Cassese (2004: 13). Antonio Cassese is currently the president of the Special Tribunal for Lebanon and is a former president of the ICTY.

91. Condorelli and Boutruche (2004: 435).
92. Pellet (2004: 438); Alain Pellet is a professor at University of Paris X – Nanterre, and a member and former chairman of the International Law Commission.
93. Ibid.
94. Ibid.
95. Ibid.
96. Ibid.
97. Ibid., p. 440.
98. Ibid., p. 441–442; by *nationalizing* Pellet implies here that certain elements which would normally be associated with domestic courts, such as judges from a particular national jurisdiction, statutes, etc., could be introduced into international tribunals.
99. Ibid., p. 442; see Cassese (2004: 10).
100. Pellet (ibid.).
101. Ibid., p. 443.
102. Ibid.
103. As we saw in Chapter 3, KWECC was in essence envisioned as an international tribunal with national representatives sitting as judges on mixed panels; it was to hear cases that the ICTY did not have the capacity to take on, and was to have concurrent jurisdiction with both the ICTY and the domestic courts.
104. See, for instance, Colitti (2004: 425).
105. Colitti (ibid.: 419–420) explains that "Article 12 of the Statute provides that the Court may exercise jurisdiction when either the state of the territory where the crime is committed (ie the *territorial state*), or the state of nationality of the accused (ie the *national state*), is party to the Statute."
106. Colitti (ibid.: 420) further explains that paragraph 3 of Article 12 of the Statute "also allows states which are not party to the Rome Statute to give their consent to the Court's jurisdiction by way of an ad hoc declaration filed with the Registrar". For a good introduction to the Rome Statute of the International Criminal Court see Politi and Nesi (2001).
107. See Colitti (ibid.: 426); she explains in footnote 48 that this is "exactly what ICTY and the Office of the High Representative in Bosnia Herzegovina ... planned to do to help ICTY complete its mission". For a further discussion of the co-existence of the ICC and other internationalized criminal bodies see Benzing and Bergsmo (2004).
108. For more on the financing of internationalized criminal courts and tribunals see Inga-dottir (2004).
109. UN General Assembly and Security Council (2000b: para. 40).
110. For a good introduction to the Special Court for Sierra Leone see Linton (2001c); Cerone (2002); Schabas (2003).
111. Chesterman (2004: 5).
112. Ibid., p. 239.
113. Ibid., p. 182.
114. Ibid.
115. Cohen (2002: 7).
116. Carlson (2006: 10).
117. Chesterman (2004: 181).
118. Strohmeyer (2001b: 61–62).
119. Interview with former judge working as an international official in Kosovo, August 2003.
120. Chesterman (2004: 182).

Conclusion

This book set out to demonstrate that in its governance operations, the UN's approach to legal and judicial reform was not well suited to the organization's goal of establishing sustainable legal systems in the territories it administered, most notably in Kosovo and East Timor. When the UN took on the Security Council's mandates for the governance of these two territories in 1999, precedents as to how the organization could undertake rule-of-law reform responsibilities in such missions were few, and understandably it leaned to a certain extent on models derived from military occupation. However, the portrayal of the UN's approach as comprising a number of *ad hoc* decisions taken on the basis of the particular exigencies and circumstances of the situation which UN administrators found in the territories under consideration is not valid. In fact, the key decisions clearly fit within a broader pattern of assumptions and ideas which guided the approach to reform, though their practical application was hampered by lack of funding and adequate resources.

These assumptions were that impunity had to be ended, the transitional legal framework had to be based on previously applicable legal codes, the court structure had to reflect and be similar to the structure that had existed previously in the territory, internationally recognized human rights standards had to be incorporated into the locally applicable legal framework and there had to be local participation in the judicial process. And thus peacebuilders chose to implement legal frameworks based on previously applicable legal codes in the respective territories from the

United Nations justice: Legal and judicial reform in governance operations
Trenkov-Wermuth, United Nations University Press, 2010, ISBN 978-92-808-1173-5

beginning of the missions, and to resurrect the basic institutional structures as they had previously existed; they decided to push for an end to impunity through the early commencement of the prosecution process for those accused of perpetrating atrocities during the respective conflicts; they made the applicable law subject to a full catalogue of human rights; and finally, they gave ownership over the judicial process to local actors, or involved such actors in this process as judges, prosecutors and defence counsellors.

However, instead of bringing the United Nations closer to its goal, this approach did not make the establishment of a sustainable legal system more likely, but detracted from that goal. In this study, Lon Fuller's *eight principles of legality*, crucial to the notion of a legal system, were used to assess the UN's efforts at establishing and administering a legal regime in Kosovo and East Timor, and this assessment showed in the case-study chapters that the UN's approach did lead to the violation of a number of these principles. Furthermore, 10 judicial norms derived from various international legal instruments were employed to evaluate the UN's judicial reform efforts, an evaluation which demonstrated that key aspects of the UN's approach also led directly to the violation of these norms. And it was shown that the approach led to major local opposition to various UN decisions on justice sector reform in both Kosovo and East Timor, and in some instances to increased levels of violence and legal and political destabilization.

Among the reasons why the main elements of the UN's approach were not suited to establishing a sustainable legal system in these territories is the fact that they fail to balance adequately some of the key tensions at the heart of governance operations. These tensions stem from the antinomies of the missions' need to balance the demands for order and security on the one hand and justice and rights on the other; the need to govern to a high standard while empowering the community through local ownership of institutional processes; and the need to hold the perpetrators of crimes accountable while delivering justice within a framework of human rights. Experience suggests that failure to balance these tensions risks popular rejection, increases the risks of political instability and violence in a territory and holds the potential for key legal and judicial principles to be violated.

The book also expounded several issues raised by the UN's experience of legal and judicial reform in Kosovo and East Timor, and explored some of the responses from academics and practitioners on the various challenges which a mission faces in regard to such reforms, trying to link these issues to ideas which have emerged in the literature on methods that would be more suited to the re-establishment of a legal system in a post-conflict environment. The case studies show that implementing a comprehensive transitional legal framework based on prior legal codes from the beginning of a mission ignores the need for local actors to debate the choice of law and be involved in the selection of the applicable law, so that the legal framework can be locally acceptable and thus sustainable. In this respect, the book hints at the need for an emergency framework which can quickly fill a legal vacuum. Simon Chesterman's proposal for the initial imposition of martial law and the implementation of a basic legal framework as a potential solution to the problem is thus sensible; INTERFET essentially adopted such an approach in East Timor, and its Detainee Ordinance could serve as a model for future emergency legal frameworks.

Furthermore, the application of a full catalogue of human rights from the beginning of a mission not only ignores its security needs during the emergency phase, but also forces a mission to violate the standards and principles that it has itself implemented. While the literature does not offer any suggestions as to how a UN mission can adequately balance its obligations on the one hand to re-establish law and order on the ground in what is frequently a very challenging security situation, and on the other hand to observe and protect human rights to the fullest extent possible, an answer to this dilemma can be found in international legal instruments which allow for the derogation of certain rights in times of public emergency. The issue of derogation not only needs to be explored further in the literature, but importantly it has to be taken seriously if problems like those encountered in Kosovo and East Timor are to be avoided in the future.

The case studies showed that local ownership of the judicial process from the beginning of a UN governance operation cannot be the means to the end of achieving a sustainable legal system, and that the involvement of poorly trained local actors in the judicial process as judges and prosecutors leads to various legal and judicial problems. Thus this work argues that judicial administration must be one of the last areas of governance over which the United Nations should relinquish its ownership; however, the question of which areas of governance must remain under international control the longest in administration missions is still insufficiently explored in the literature, and further research on this topic is warranted.

Moreover, on the issue of the extent to which local actors can be involved in the judicial process early on in a mission, the book has shown that where there is no meaningful local capacity, the early involvement of international jurists in the judicial process is imperative. Hansjoerg Strohmeyer's and Simon Chesterman's suggestions that there is a need for a standby network of international jurists who could be deployed quickly and at short notice to post-conflict areas which lack local judicial capacity, to work either as mentors and trainers or as actual judges and prosecutors, have merit. But even in the absence of such a standby network of jurists, which may be difficult to create, the book highlights that unless international jurists are involved early on in the reform process, various legal principles and judicial norms are likely to be violated, which will in turn undermine the overall justice sector reform initiatives.

The study argued further that the upholding of international standards of justice is more important than the pursuit of prosecutions. While Suzannah Linton presents a similar argument in her work, she does not offer any suggestions about what approach international administrators can adopt to ensure that such standards are respected but also address past atrocities. In this respect, since it became clear that burdening a newly established judicial system with trials of war or other serious crimes cases can be counterproductive, Alain Pellet's proposal for the nationalization of international tribunals may offer an interesting alternative to the current hybrid court model, which has addressed serious crimes within national courts. However, his aversion to internationalized processes which deal with anything but international crimes ignores the urgent need for certain non-international crimes and criminals to be tried by international jurists and panels. Thus an international tribunal which also employs national judges, and which can deal with both international and national crimes, may be an improvement upon the current model.

The need for national crimes to be tried by international tribunals has been recognized by the international community, as the Special Tribunal for Lebanon (STL), launched on 1 March 2009, demonstrates. It was established with the primary and narrow purpose of trying, under Lebanese criminal law, those suspected of involvement in the assassination of the former Lebanese Prime Minister Rafiq Hariri on 14 February 2005. It has a majority of international judges and an international prosecutor, but also includes national judges, as was the case with the Special Court for Sierra Leone. As such, the STL is a step in the direction of Pellet's idea of having national judges brought into international tribunals, and also in the direction of trying non-international crimes through international panels. However, the STL has only a very limited mandate, and as such international criminal and humanitarian law does not apply. The final result is that this tribunal is quite close to the Lockerbie trial, which also had a rather limited mandate, was sanctioned by the Security Council and took place (under Scottish law) in the Netherlands, also the location of the STL.[1] Especially the fact that the STL can only try cases under Lebanese law shows that a key hurdle still needs to be overcome in the attempt to create a nationalized international tribunal which can try cases under national and international law, and which employs both national and international judges and prosecutors.

If trials are chosen over amnesties or any other methods for addressing past atrocities, the book argues that a clear prosecution strategy is crucial. While Suzannah Linton and Sylvia De Bertodano also argue for the need of a clear prosecution strategy, their work and the literature on the subject more broadly do not substantively cover the relative merits of different prosecution strategies, and this is an area that is certainly open to further investigation.

Finally, the study showed that while implementing a regular court structure early on in a mission is not very problematic, it does not leave the time needed for the design of an institutional structure which will be appropriate for the particular circumstances and which can incorporate traditional justice mechanisms; importantly, however, establishing a mechanism that can deal with detainees has to be prioritized over the UN's desire to establish a regular court structure. In this respect, Scott Carlson's recommendation for the use of emergency mobile courts in the short or long term should be given serious consideration; and INTERFET's approach with the establishment of the Detainee Management Unit in East Timor may present an interesting model for future UN or other governance operations mandated with the responsibility for law and order.

In addition to the above-mentioned areas that warrant further investigation, there are a few more topics which were outside of the scope of this work, as indicated in the Introduction, which remain unexplored in the literature and require further study. One of these areas relates to the question of the integration of customary law and traditional justice mechanisms into a Western statutory legal system based on civil or common law. The lack of serious scholarly treatment of this subject presents a gap in the literature which must be urgently filled, because the successful integration of such customary laws and practices within a modern legal system can arguably determine the outcome of any legal and judicial reform initiatives in a war-torn territory. The protracted violent conflicts in Afghanistan and Somalia demonstrate clearly that when a statutory justice system collapses because of war, traditional justice mechanisms and laws will resurface: in the case of Afghanistan authority reverted back to traditional chiefs, who went on to apply various tribal and Islamic legal customs in the territories under their control, and in Somalia warlords applied a host of different customary laws and practices.[2] While the rule-of-law reform failures in Afghanistan can in part be blamed on the security challenges and the lack of central government control over the territory, they are arguably also in no small part the result of the failures to consider seriously and explore ways in which traditional justice mechanisms can be integrated into the modern and statutory legal system which the international community wished to help establish in the country. Thus ignoring such customary laws and practices in a territory which has been ruled by them for several decades has been detrimental to the rule-of-law reform efforts in Afghanistan, and may have a similar effect in other war-torn societies.

A closely related subject for further study is the method by which peacebuilders can contend with legal pluralism in a post-conflict context. In the aftermath of decolonization, many newly independent governments decided to undertake various legal reforms aimed at integrating customary and modern laws.[3] Arguably, scholars can learn much about the challenges of integrating customary and modern legal practices from the post-colonial African experience of legal reform, for instance, where a range of different approaches were tried. But while it is clear that this post-colonial experience has the potential to hold many valuable lessons for peacebuilders on the integration of customary and modern laws, and also on how to contend with legal pluralism, no extensive study which aims to explore ways in which these problems can be surmounted in a peacebuilding context has been published to date.[4]

Boutros Boutros-Ghali's administration wrote in 1995 that "The United Nations is, for good reasons, reluctant to assume responsibility for maintaining law and order, nor can it impose a new political structure or new state institutions."[5] This reluctance is understandable: the United Nations was inexperienced in the maintenance of law and order, and felt that its place was not to impose structures and institutions on states. However, the Security Council mandated the organization with the task of governing several territories, and thereby also with the responsibility for the very tasks it was reluctant to carry out. The operational challenges of administering territories left the organization with little desire for further ventures of a similar nature, and in Afghanistan it essentially backed away from taking on a substantial role again, preferring a *light-footprint* approach instead – rather than governing per se it essentially assists a transitional administration. Similarly, the United Nations wishes to back away from any substantial responsibilities in the realm of legal and judicial reform, as the Secretary-General's 2004 report on rule of law and transitional justice in post-conflict territories also clearly shows,[6] perhaps because of its past failures and mistakes.

However, irrespective of whether or not the United Nations goes down the path of governance in the future again, or if it acts predominantly in a supporting role to a state in transition, it is important for the organization as well as other entities involved in peacebuilding work to understand and learn from the mistakes of the UN's past approach to one of the most challenging yet crucial areas of peacebuilding, namely legal and judicial reform. Such lessons will not only affect how justice sector reform efforts are undertaken by future UN missions, but also how other organizations or governments address these matters. As an example, the

UN's formulation of the applicable law in Kosovo and East Timor served to inspire the US choice of law for its occupation of Iraq: the Coalition Provisional Authority's Regulation No. 1 stated that the "laws in force in Iraq as of April 16, 2003, shall continue to apply in Iraq, insofar as the laws do not prevent the CPA from exercising its rights and fulfilling its obligations, or conflict with the present or any other Regulation or Order issued by the CPA".[7] This formulation went well beyond what is envisaged by Geneva Convention IV for the law that should apply in an occupied territory;[8] and when juxtaposed to either UNMIK's or UNTAET's formulation of the applicable law in Kosovo or East Timor, respectively, it becomes evident that the Coalition Provisional Authority's choice of law essentially grafted the UN's approach on to the CPA's administration of Iraq.[9]

In the twenty-first century various national, international, supranational or non-governmental entities will continue to be involved in legal and judicial reforms in war-torn territories. In Kosovo, the European Union (EU) officially took over the rule-of-law reform efforts from UNMIK in December 2008 through its EU Rule of Law Mission in Kosovo (EULEX). What happened during the initial stages of the UN's reform efforts in terms of choice of law, incorporation of human rights into the legal framework, creation of court structures, addressing past atrocities, involvement of local actors in the reform process, etc., will continue to inform the EU's current legal and judicial reform strategy and efforts. The international community will also continue to seek ways to deliver justice for past atrocities. The establishment of the International Criminal Court, the Extraordinary Chambers in Cambodia, the War Crimes Chamber in Bosnia and Herzegovina, the Special Court for Sierra Leone and the Special Tribunal for Lebanon, and most recently the ICC's indictment of President Omar al-Bashir of Sudan for war crimes and crimes against humanity, attest to this. The role the United Nations will play in future justice sector reforms and transitional justice is yet to be determined, but what is clear is that its approach thus far will have a lasting impact on the efforts of other entities involved in legal and judicial reform in war-torn societies.

Notes

1. International Center for Transitional Justice (2008: 38).
2. Mani (2002: 81).
3. Ibid., pp. 82–83.
4. It should be noted, though, that the US Institute of Peace is currently undertaking a project on "The Role of Non-State Justice Systems in Fostering the Rule of Law in Post-Conflict Societies" which may produce interesting results. Some institutions have begun

to work on questions of customary justice systems and legal pluralism, and have done recent noteworthy work in this area: DFID, IDEA, Max Planck, NRC, PRI, UNDP, USAID, USIP and the World Bank.

5. UN General Assembly and Security Council (1995: para. 14).
6. See UN Security Council (2004).
7. See section 2 of Coalition Provisional Authority (2003).
8. Article 64 of the convention stipulates that the occupying power may deviate from the domestic law, which must continue to apply, only if this law constitutes a threat to the security of the occupier or prevents the application of the convention.
9. As indicated in Chapter 3, the wording of Section 3 on the "Applicable Law in Kosovo" of UNMIK (1999c) reads: "The laws applicable in the territory of Kosovo prior to 24 March 1999 shall continue to apply in Kosovo insofar as they do not conflict with [international human rights] standards ... the fulfilment of the mandate given to UNMIK under the United Nations Security Council Resolution 1244 (1999), or the present or any other regulation issued by UNMIK." On this point see Stahn (2008: 672).

References

ABA/CEELI (2002) *Judicial Reform Index for Kosovo*, April, Washington, DC: American Bar Association.

AFSOUTH NATO Regional Headquarters Allied Forces Southern Europe (2003) "Operation Joint Guardian", 14 July, available at www.afsouth.nato.int/operations/kfor.

Amnesty International (1998) "Fair Trials Manual", AI Index POL 30/02/98, December, available at www.amnesty.org/ailib/intcam/fairtrial/fairtria.htm.

——— (2000a) "Federal Republic of Yugoslavia (Kosovo): Amnesty International's Recommendations to UNMIK on the Judicial System", AI Index EUR 70/006/2000, 4 February, available at http://web.amnesty.org/library/Index/engEUR700062000.

——— (2000b) "Building a New Country Based on Human Rights", AI Index ASA 57/05/00, 29 August, available at http://web.amnesty.org/library/Index/ENGASA570052000?open&of=ENG-TMP.

——— (2001a) "East Timor: Justice Past, Present and Future", AI Index ASA 57/001/2001, 27 July, available at http://web.amnesty.org/library/index/engASA570012001?OpenDocument.

——— (2001b) "FRY/Kosovo: Amnesty International Protests the Unlawful Detention of Afrim Zeqiri", news item, available at www.amnesty.org.uk/news_details.asp?NewsID=13229.

——— (2002a) "Kingdom of Cambodia: Urgent Need for Judicial Reform", AI Index ASA 23/004/2002, 23 April, available at http://web.amnesty.org/library/Index/ENGASA230042002?open&of=ENG-313.

——— (2002b) "Public Statement – Indonesia: East Timor Trials Deliver neither Truth nor Justice", AI Index ASA/21/121/2002 (Public), 15 August, available at http://web.amnesty.org/library/index/engASA211212002!Open.

——— (2002c) "Federal Republic of Yugoslavia (Kosovo): International Officials Flout International Law", AI Index EUR 70/008/2002, 1 September, available at http://web.amnesty.org/library/index/engeur700082002.

——— (2004) "Serbia and Montenegro (Kosovo): The Legacy of Past Human Rights Abuses", AI Index EUR 70/009/2004, 1 April, available at www.forumnvo. org.yu.docs/Amnesty%20International-Serbia&20and%20Montenegro_ Kosovo_The%20legacy520og%20past%20human%20rights%20abuses.pdf.

Baskin, Mark (2002) *Lessons Learned on UNMIK Judiciary*, Pearson Papers 8, Clementsport, Nova Scotia: Canadian Peacekeeping Press.

Bass, Garry John (2000) *Stay the Hand of Vengeance: The Politics of War Crimes Tribunals*, Princeton, NJ: Princeton University Press.

Bassiouni, M. Cherif (1996) "Searching for Peace and Achieving Justice: The Need for Accountability", *Law and Contemporary Problems* 59(4), pp. 9–28.

Beauvais, Joel (2001) "Benevolent Despotism: A Critique of U.N. State-Building in East Timor", *NYU Journal of International Law & Politics* 33(4), pp. 1101–1178.

Benzing, Markus and Morten Bergsmo (2004) "Some Tentative Remarks on the Relationship between Internationalized Criminal Jurisdictions and the International Criminal Court", in Romano Cesare, André Nollkamper and Jann K. Kleffner, eds, *Internationalized Criminal Courts: Sierra Leone, East Timor, Kosovo and Cambodia*, Oxford: Oxford University Press, pp. 407–416.

Berdal, Mats and Michael Leifer (1996) "Cambodia", in James Mayall, ed., *The New Interventionism 1991–1994: United Nations Experience in Cambodia, Former Yugoslavia and Somalia*, Cambridge: Cambridge University Press, pp. 25–58.

Betts, Wendy S., Scott N. Carlson and Gregory Gisvold (2001) "The Post-Conflict Transitional Administration of Kosovo and the Lessons Learned in Efforts to Establish a Judiciary and the Rule of Law", *Michigan Journal of International Law* 22(3), pp. 371–390.

Boothby, Derek (2004) "The Political Challenges of Administering Eastern Slavonia", *Global Governance* 10(1), pp. 37–51.

Boyle, Michael (2005) "The Prevention and Management of Reprisal Violence in Post-Conflict States", PhD dissertation, University of Cambridge.

Brownlie, Ian (1992) *Basic Documents on Human Rights*, 3rd edn, Oxford: Oxford University Press.

Bull, Carolyn (2008) *No Entry Without Strategy: Building the Rule of Law under UN Transitional Administration*, Tokyo: United Nations University Press.

Burke-White, William (2002) "A Community of Courts: Toward a System of International Criminal Law Enforcement", *Michigan Journal of International Law* 24(1), pp. 1–101.

Cady, Jean-Christian and Nicholas Booth (2004) "Internationalized Courts in Kosovo: An UNMIK Perspective", in Romano Cesare, André Nollkamper and Jann K. Kleffner, eds, *Internationalized Criminal Courts: Sierra Leone, East Timor, Kosovo and Cambodia*, Oxford: Oxford University Press, pp. 59–78.

Caplan, Richard (2002) *A New Trusteeship? The International Administration of War-Torn Territories*, Adelphi Paper No. 341, Oxford: Oxford University Press/ International Institute for Strategic Studies.

—— (2004a) "Partner or Patron? International Civil Administration and Local Capacity Building", *International Peacekeeping* 11(2), pp. 229–247.

—— (2004b) "International Authority and State-building: The Case of Bosnia and Herzegovina", *Global Governance* 10, pp. 53–65.

—— (2005) *International Governance of War-Torn Territories: Rule and Reconstruction*, Oxford: Oxford University Press.

Carlson, Scott N. (2006) "Legal and Judicial Rule of Law Work in Multidimensional Peacekeeping Operations: Lessons-Learned Study", UN Department of Peacekeeping Operations Lessons-Learned Series, New York: United Nations.

Cassese, Antonio (2004) "The Role of Internationalized Courts and Tribunals in the Fight against International Criminality", in Romano Cesare, André Nollkamper and Jann K. Kleffner, eds, *Internationalized Criminal Courts: Sierra Leone, East Timor, Kosovo and Cambodia*, Oxford: Oxford University Press, pp. 3–14.

Cerone, John (2002) "The Special Court for Sierra Leone: Establishing a New Approach to International Criminal Justice", *ILSA Journal of International & Comparative Law* 8(2), p. 379.

Cerone, John and Clive Baldwin (2004) "Explaining and Evaluating the UNMIK Court System", in Cesare Romano, André Nollkamper and Jann K. Kleffner, eds, *Internationalized Criminal Courts: Sierra Leone, East Timor, Kosovo and Cambodia*, Oxford: Oxford University Press, pp. 41–58.

Chesterman, Simon (2001a) "East Timor in Transition: From Conflict Prevention to State-Building", International Peace Academy Project on Transitional Administrations, May, available at www.jsmp.minihub.org/Resources/2001/IPA%20-%20East%20Timor%20in%20Transition.pdf.

—— (2001b) "No Justice Without Peace? International Criminal Law and the Decision to Prosecute", in Simon Chesterman, ed., *Civilians in War*, Boulder, CO: Lynne Rienner, pp. 145–164.

—— (2002a) "Justice Under International Administration: Kosovo, East Timor and Afghanistan", International Peace Academy Project on Transitional Administrations, September, available at www.ipacademy.org/PDF_Reports/JUSTICE_UNDER_INTL.pdf.

—— (2002b) "Walking Softly in Afghanistan: The Future of UN Statebuilding", *Survival* 44(3), pp. 37–46.

—— (2003) "You, the People: The United Nations, Transitional Administration, and State Building", International Peace Academy Project on Transitional Administrations, November, available at www.ipacademy.org/PDF_Reports/.

—— (2004) *You, the People: The United Nations, Transitional Administration, and State-Building*, Oxford: Oxford University Press.

Chopra, Jarat, ed. (1998) *The Politics of Peace-Maintenance*, Boulder, CO: Lynne Rienner.

—— (2000) "The UN's Kingdom of East Timor", *Survival* 42(3), pp. 27–39.

Coalition Provisional Authority (2003) "Coalition Provisional Authority Regulation No. 1", CPA/REG/16 May 2003/01, 16 May, available at www.sigir.mil/hardlessons/pdfs/4-CoalitionProvisionalAuthorityRegulation1.pdf.

Cockayne, James (2005a), "The Fraying Shoestring: Rethinking Hybrid War Crimes Tribunals", *Fordham International Law Journal* 28(3), pp. 616–680.

Cockayne, James (2005b), "Hybrids or Mongrels? Internationalized War Crimes Tribunals as Unsuccessful Degradation Ceremonies", *Journal of Human Rights* 4, pp. 1–19.

Cohen, David (2002) "Seeking Justice on the Cheap: Is the East Timor Tribunal Really a Model for the Future?", *AsiaPacific Issues* 61, pp. 1–8.

Colitti, Mariacarmen (2004) "Geographical and Jurisdictional Reach of the ICC: Gaps in the International Criminal Justice System and a Role for Internationalized Bodies", in Romano Cesare, André Nollkamper and Jann K. Kleffner, eds, *Internationalized Criminal Courts: Sierra Leone, East Timor, Kosovo and Cambodia*, Oxford: Oxford University Press, pp. 417–426.

Common Security Forum (1997) "Seminar Report: Promoting the Rule of Law in Post-Conflict Societies", 26 September, Cambridge, MA: Harvard University.

Condorelli, Luigi and Théo Boutruche (2004) "Intenationalized Criminal Courts and Tribunals: Are They Necessary?", in Romano Cesare, André Nollkamper and Jann K. Kleffner, eds, *Internationalized Criminal Courts: Sierra Leone, East Timor, Kosovo and Cambodia*, Oxford: Oxford University Press, pp. 427–436.

Conflict Security and Development Group (2003a) *A Review of Peace Operations: A Case for Change – Kosovo*, 10 March, London: King's College.

—— (2003b) *A Review of Peace Operations: A Case for Change – East Timor*, 10 March, London: King's College.

Court of Appeal, Democratic Republic of Timor-Leste (2003a) "Decision", *Armando Dos Santos v Prosecutor General*, 15 July, available at www.unmiset.org/legal/court-decisions/court-decisions.htm.

—— (2003b) "Judgment (Dissenting Opinion Concerning the Law as Applied in This Case: Jacinta C. Da Costa)", *Augustinho da Costa v Prosecutor General*, 18 July.

Court of Appeal, East Timorese Transitional Authority (2001) "Separate Opinion of Judge Egonda Ntende", *Joao Fernandes v Prosecutor General*, Criminal Appeal 2/2001, 29 June, available at www.unmiset.org/legal/court-decisions/court-decisions.htm.

Cousens, Elizabeth M. and Chetan Kumar, eds (2001) *Peacebuilding as Politics: Cultivating Peace in Fragile Societies*, Boulder, CO: Lynne Rienner.

De Bertodano, Sylvia (2004) "East Timor: Trials and Tribulations", in Romano Cesare, André Nollkamper and Jann K. Kleffner, eds, *Internationalized Criminal Courts: Sierra Leone, East Timor, Kosovo and Cambodia*, Oxford: Oxford University Press, pp. 79–98.

De Soto, Alvaro and Graciana Del Castillo (1994) "Obstacles to Peacebuilding", *Foreign Policy* 94 (Spring), pp. 69–83.

Devereux, Annemarie (2000) "Strengthening the Judicial Process in East Timor", issues paper prepared for Jesuit Refugee Service, 30 June.

Dickinson, Laura (2003a) "The Promise of Hybrid Courts", *American Journal of International Law* 97(2), pp. 295–310.

—— (2003b) "The Relationship between Hybrid Courts and International Courts: The Case of Kosovo", *New England Law Review* 37(4), pp. 1059–1072.

Dobbins, James, Seth G. Jones, Keith Crane, Andrew Rathmell, Brett Steele, Richard Teltschik and Anga Timilsina (2005) *The UN's Role in Nation-Building: From the Congo to Iraq*, Santa Monica, CA: Rand.

Dodd, Mark (2001) "Ramos Horta Lashes UN in Language Row", *Sydney Morning Herald*, 25 August, p. 17.

Domingo, Pilar and Rachel Sieder, eds (2001) *Rule of Law in Latin America: The International Promotion of Judicial Reform*, London: University of London, Institute of Latin American Studies.

Doyle, Michael (1995) *UN Peacekeeping in Cambodia: UNTAC's Civil Mandate*, Boulder, CO: Lynne Rienner.

―――― (1997) "Authority and Elections in Cambodia", in Michael Doyle, Ian Johnstone and Robert Orr, eds, *Keeping the Peace: Multidimensional UN Operations in Cambodia and El Salvador*, Cambridge: Cambridge University Press, pp. 134–164.

Doyle, Michael and Nicholas Sambanis (2000) "International Peacebuilding: A Theoretical and Quantitative Analysis", *American Political Science Review* 94(4), pp. 779–801.

Doyle, Michael, Ian Johnstone and Robert C. Orr, eds (1997) *Keeping the Peace: Multidimensional UN Operations in Cambodia and El Salvador*, Cambridge: Cambridge University Press.

East Timor and Indonesia Action Network (2003) "Parliament Passed Law on Applicable Law", news item, available at www.etan.org/et2003/october/01-6/00parlmnt.htm.

Egonda-Ntende, Frederick (2001) "Building a New Judiciary in East Timor", *Commonwealth Judicial Journal* 14(1), pp. 22–26.

Evans, Gareth (1993) *Cooperating for Peace: The Global Agenda for the 1990s and Beyond*, St Leonards, NSW: Allen & Unwin.

Fairlie, Megan (2003) "Affirming Brahimi: East Timor Makes the Case for a Model Criminal Code", *American University International Law Review* 18(5), pp. 1059–1102.

Fox, Gregory (2008) *Humanitarian Occupation*, Cambridge: Cambridge University Press.

Friedlander, Henry (2002) "The Judiciary and Nazi Crimes in Post-War Germany", available at http://moltc.wiesenthal.com/site/pp.sap?c=gvKVLCMVluG&b=394973.

Friman, Håkan (2004) "Procedural Law of Internationalized Criminal Courts", in Cesare Romano, André Nollkamper and Jann K. Kleffner, eds, *Internationalized Criminal Courts: Sierra Leone, East Timor, Kosovo and Cambodia*, Oxford: Oxford University Press, pp. 317–358.

Fuller, Lon L. (1969) *The Morality of Law*, New Haven, CT: Yale University Press.

Galtung, Johan (1976) "Three Approaches to Peace: Peacekeeping, Peacemaking, and Peacebuilding", in Johan Galtung, *Peace, War and Defense – Essays in Peace Research*, Vol. 2, Copenhagen: Ejlers, pp. 282–304.

Ganzglass, Martin (1997) "The Restoration of the Somali Justice System", in Walter Clarke and Jeffrey Herbst, eds, *Learning from Somalia: The Lessons of Armed Humanitarian Intervention*, Boulder, CO: Westview Press, pp. 20–41.

George, Alexander L. (1979) "Case Studies and Theory Development: The Method of Structured, Focused Comparison", in Paul Gordon Lauren, ed., *Diplomacy: New Approaches in History, Theory, and Policy*, New York: Free Press, pp. 43–68.

Gompert, David (1996) "The United States and Yugoslavia's Wars", in Richard Ullman, ed., *The World and Yugoslavia's Wars*, New York: Council on Foreign Relations, pp. 122–144.

Greenless, Don (2002) *Deliverance: The Inside Story of East Timor's Fight for Freedom*, Crow's Nest, NSW: Allen & Unwin.

Hart, Herbert L. A. (1961) *The Concept of Law*, Oxford: Clarendon Press.

Hartmann, Michael E. (2003) "International Judges and Prosecutors in Kosovo: A New Model for Postconflict Peacekeeping", US Institute of Peace Special Report No. 112, October, available at ww.usip.org./pubs/specialreports/sr112.html.

Hayner, Priscilla B. (1994) "Fifteen Truth Commissions – 1974 to 1994: A Comparative Study", *Human Rights Quarterly* 16(4), pp. 597–655.

——— (2001) *Unspeakable Truths: Confronting State Terror and Atrocities*, New York: Routledge.

Heininger, Janet E. (1994) *Peacekeeping in Transition: The United Nations in Cambodia*, New York: Twentieth Century Fund Press.

Higgins, Rosalyn (1970) *United Nations Peacekeeping, 1946–1967: Documents and Commentary – Volume 2: Asia*, New York: Oxford University Press.

Hohe, Tanja and Rod Nixon (2003) "Reconciling Justice: 'Traditional' Law and State Judiciary in East Timor", US Institute of Peace report, January, available at www.jsmp.minihub.org/Traditional%20Justice%20/Reports/ReconcilingJustice Report.doc.

Holm, Tor Tanke and Espen Barth Eide, eds (2000) *Peacebuilding and Police Reform*, London: Frank Cass.

HRFOR (1996) "The Administration of Justice in Post-Genocide Rwanda", UN Human Rights Field Operation in Rwanda Report, June, Doc. HRFOR/Justice/June 1996/E.

Human Rights Watch (1999) "Federal Republic of Yugoslavia: Abuses against Serbs and Roma in the New Kosovo", HRW 11:10(D), August, available at www.hrw.org/reports/1999/kosov2/.

——— (2002a) *World Report 2002*, New York: Human Rights Watch, available at www.hrw.org/wr2k2/.

——— (2002b) "Justice Denied For East Timor: Indonesia's Sham Prosecutions, the Need to Strengthen the Trial Process in East Timor, and the Imperative of U.N. Action", available at www.hrw.org/backgrounder/asia/timor/etimor1202bg. htm.

——— (2003) "Serious Flaws: Why the U.N. General Assembly Should Require Changes to the Draft Khmer Rouge Tribunal Agreement", briefing paper, April, available at http://hrw.org/backgrounder/asia/cambodia040303-bck. htm.

Huyse, Luc (1995) "Justice after Transition: On the Choices Successor Elites Make in Dealing with the Past", *Law and Social Inquiry* 20(1), pp. 51–78.

ICTY (1999) "Statement by Carla del Ponte Prosecutor of the International Criminal Tribunal for the Former Yugoslavia on the Investigation and Prosecution of Crimes Committed in Kosovo", Press Release PR/P.I.S./437-E, International Criminal Tribunal for the Former Yugoslavia, 29 September.

Ingadottir, Thordis (2004) "The Financing of Internationalized Criminal Courts and Tribunals", in Romano Cesare, André Nollkamper and Jann K. Kleffner, eds, *Internationalized Criminal Courts: Sierra Leone, East Timor, Kosovo and Cambodia*, Oxford: Oxford University Press, pp. 271–287.

International Center for Transitional Justice (2008) "Handbook on the Special Tribunal for Lebanon", Justice Prosecutions Program handbook, available at www.ictj.org/images/content/9/1/914.pdf.

International Commission of Jurists (2002) "Pakistan: The ICJ Condemns the Illegal Exercise of Judicial Power by Tribal Councils in Pakistan", news item, available at www.icj.org/news/php3?id_article=2641&lang=n&pring=true.

International Crisis Group (2002) "Finding the Balance: The Scales of Justice in Kosovo", ICG Balkans Report No. 134, 12 September, available at www.crisisgroup.org/home/index.cfm?id=1609&l=1.

Jeong, Ho-Won (2002) *Approaches to Peacebuilding*, Basingstoke: Palgrave Macmillan.

Johnstone, Ian (1997) "Rights and Reconciliation in El Salvador", in Michael Doyle, Ian Johnstone and Robert C. Orr, eds, *Keeping the Peace: Multidimensional UN Operations in Cambodia and El Salvador*, Cambridge: Cambridge University Press, pp. 312–341.

Judicial System Monitoring Programme (2001) "Justice in Practice: Human Rights in Court Administration", Thematic Report 1, November, Dili, available at http://jsmp.minihub.org/Language_English/reports_english.htm.

———— (2002a) "The General Prosecutor v Joni Marquez and 9 Others (the Los Palos Case)", Trial Report, July, Dili, available at http://jsmp.minihub.org/Language_English/reports_english.htm.

———— (2002b) "The Right to Appeal in East Timor", Thematic Report 2, October, Dili, available at http://jsmp.minihub.org/Language_English/reports_english.htm.

———— (2002c) "Findings and Recommendations: Workshop on Formal and Local Justice Systems in East Timor", Report on Workshop on Community Based Justice, July, Dili, available at http://jsmp.minihub.org/Language_English/reports_english.htm.

———— (2003) "The Court of Appeal Decision on the Applicable Subsidiary Law in Timor-Leste", August, Dili, available at http://jsmp.minihub.org/Language_English/reports_english.htm.

———— (2006) "Overview of Timor Leste Justice Sector 2005", January, Dili, available at http://jsmp.minihub.org/Language_English/reports_english.htm.

Kaldor, Mary (1999) *New and Old Wars: Organized Violence in a Global Era*, Stanford, CA: Stanford University Press.

Kaminski, Matthew (1999) "UN Struggles with a Legal Vacuum in Kosovo: Team Improvises in Effort to Build a Civil Structure", *Wall Street Journal*, 4 August, p. A12.

Katzenstein, Suzanne (2003) "Hybrid Tribunals: Searching for Justice in East Timor", *Harvard Human Rights Journal* 16, pp. 245–278.

Kelly, Michael (2000) "INTERFET Detainee Management Unit in East Timor", paper presented at Swiss Seminar on the Law of Armed Conflict, Chavannes-de-Bogis, Geneva, 27 October, available at http://jsmp.minihub.org/Resources/2000/INTERFET%20DETAINEE%20MANAGEMENT%20UNIT%20(e).pdf.

Knoll, Bernhard (2008) *The Legal Status of Territories Subject to Administration by International Organisations*, Cambridge: Cambridge University Press.

Kondoch, Boris (2001) "The United Nations Administration of East Timor", *Journal of Conflict and Security Law* 6(2), pp. 245–265.

Kritz, Neil, ed. (1995) *Transitional Justice: How Emerging Democracies Reckon with Former Regimes*, 3 vols, Washington, DC: US Institute of Peace.

Kumar, Chetan (1998) *Building Peace in Haiti*, Boulder, CO: Lynne Rienner.

Lau, Martin (2002) "The Compatibility of Afghanistan's Legal System with International Human Rights Standards", Final Report for International Commission of Jurists, available at www.icj.org/IMG/pdf/doc-46.pdf.

Lederach, John Paul (1997) *Building Peace: Sustainable Reconciliation in Divided Societies*, Washington, DC: US Institute of Peace.

Lijphart, Arend (1971) "Comparative Politics and the Comparative Method", *American Political Science Review* 65 (September), pp. 682–693.

Linton, Suzannah (2001a) "Rising from the Ashes: The Creation of a Viable Criminal Justice System in East Timor", *Melbourne University Law Review* 25, pp. 122–180.

—— (2001b) "Prosecuting Atrocities at the District Court of Dili", *Melbourne Journal of International Law* 2(2), pp. 414–458.

—— (2001c) "Cambodia, East Timor and Sierra Leone: Experiments in International Justice", *Criminal Law Forum* 12(2), pp. 185–246.

—— (2002) "New Approaches to International Justice in Cambodia and East Timor", *IRRC* 84(845), pp. 93–119.

Livingstone, Stephen (2002) "International Law Relating to States of Emergency and Derogations from International Human Rights Law Treaties", Human Rights Centre, Queens University Belfast, available at www.interights.org/doc/Livingstone_derogation_final.doc.

Maguire, Robert (1996) "Haiti Held Hostage: International Responses to the Quest for Nationhood, 1986–1996", Occasional Paper No. 23, Providence, RI: Thomas J. Watson Institute for International Studies, Brown University.

Malcolm, Noel (1998) *Kosovo: A Short History*, New York: New York University Press.

Maley, W., C. Sampford and R. Thakur, eds (2003) *From Civil Strife to Civil Society: Civil and Military Responsibilities in Disrupted States*, Tokyo: United Nations University Press.

Malunga, Siphosami and Shyamala Alagendra (2002) "Prosecuting Serious Crimes in East Timor: An Analysis of the Justice System", July, unpublished article.

Mani, Rama (2002) *Beyond Retribution: Seeking Justice in the Shadows of War*, Cambridge: Polity Press.

Marshall, David and Shelley Inglis (2003) "The Disempowerment of Human Rights-Based Justice in the United Nations Mission in Kosovo", *Harvard Human Rights Journal* 16 (Spring), pp. 95–146.

Martin, Ian (2001) *Self-Determination in East Timor: The United Nations, the Ballot, and International Intervention*, Boulder, CO: Lynne Rienner.

Martin, Ian and Alexander Mayer-Rieckh (2005) "The United Nations and East Timor: From Self-Determination to State-Building", *International Peacekeeping* 12(1), pp. 104–120.

Matheson, Michael (2001) "United Nations Governance of Postconflict Societies", *American Journal of International Law* 95(1), pp. 76–85.

Mayall, James, ed. (1996) *The New Interventionism, 1991–1994: United Nations
Experience in Cambodia, Former Yugoslavia and Somalia*, Cambridge: Cambridge University Press.

McAdams, James (1997) *Transitional Justice and the Rule of Law in New Democracies*, Notre Dame, IN: University of Notre Dame Press.

Mearns, David (2002) "Looking Both Ways: Models for Justice in East Timor",
paper for Australian Legal Resources International, November, available at
www.jsmp.minihub.org/Traditional%20Justice/Reports/Mearns/%20Looking%
20Both%20Ways%20Report/Mearns%20Looking%20both%20ways.pdf.

MICIVIH (1994a) "Analysis of the Haitian Justice System with Recommenda-
tions to Improve the Administration of Justice in Haiti", Working Group on
Haitian Justice System of OAS/UN International Civilian Mission to Haiti –
MICIVIH, 17 March, available at www.nchr.org/hrp/jud_reform_eng.htm.

——— (1994b) "Executive Summary: Analysis and Evaluation of the Haitian Justice System", Working Group on the Justice System of the OAS/UN International Civilian Mission to Haiti – MICIVIH, 18 March.

National Parliament, Democratic Republic of Timor-Leste (2003) "Interpretation of Article 1 of Law 2/2002 of 7 August and Sources of Law", proposed
law, 29 July, available at www.jsmp.minihub.org/Legislation/LegEng/Proposed
01Law%20on%20Applicable8Law%2029%20July.03pdf.pdf.

Neier, Aryeh (1998) *War Crimes: Brutality, Genocide, Terror and the Struggle for
Justice*, New York: Times Books.

Neild, Rachel (1995) *Policing Haiti: Preliminary Assessment of the New Civilian
Security Force*, Washington, DC: Washington Office on Latin America.

No Peace Without Justice (2003) "Special Panel Delivers Its Own Decision on
the Applicable Law", news item, 28 July, available at www.npjw.org/modules.
php?name=News&file=article&sid=1360.

Nouwen, Sarah M. H. (2006) "Hybrid Courts: The Hybrid Category of a New
Type of International Crimes Courts", *Utrecht Law Review* 2(2), pp. 190–214,
available at www.utrechtlawreview.org.

OCHA (2006) "Justice for a Lawless World? Rights and Reconciliation in a
New Era of International Law – Part I", UN Office for the Coordination of
Humanitarian Affairs, July, available at www.irinnews.org/pdf/in-depth/Rights
AndReconciliationPart1.pdf.

O'Connor, Vivienne (2005) "Traversing the Rocky Road of Law Reform in Conflict and Post Conflict States: Model Codes for Post Conflict Criminal Justice as
a Tool of Assistance", *Criminal Law Forum* 16(3/4), pp. 231–255.

O'Connor, Vivienne and Colette Rausch (2005) "A Toolbox to Tackle Law Reform in Post Conflict States: The Model Codes for Post Conflict Criminal Justice", in Harvey Langholtz, Boris Kondoch and Alan Wells, eds, *International
Peacekeeping: The Yearbook of International Peace Operations*, Vol. 10, Leiden
and Boston, MA: Martinus Nijhoff, pp. 71–92.

——— eds (2007) *Model Codes for Post-Conflict Criminal Justice*, Washington,
DC: US Institute of Peace.

OHCHR (2006a) *Rule-of-Law Tools for Post-Conflict States: Truth Commissions*, Doc. HR/PUB/06/1, New York and Geneva: United Nations, available at www.ohchr.org/english/about/publications/docs/ruleoflaw-TruthCommissions_en.pdf.

—— (2006b) *Rule-of-Law Tools for Post-Conflict States: Mapping the Justice Sector*, Doc. HR/PUB/06/2, New York and Geneva: United Nations, available at www.ohchr.org/english/about/publications/docs/ruleoflaw-Mapping_en.pdf.

—— (2006c) *Rule-of-Law Tools for Post-Conflict States: Monitoring Legal Systems*, Doc. HR/PUB/06/3, New York and Geneva: United Nations, available at www.ohchr.org/english/about/publications/docs/ruleoflaw-Monitoring_en.pdf.

—— (2006d) *Rule-of-Law Tools for Post-Conflict States: Prosecution Initiatives*, Doc. HR/PUB/06/4, New York and Geneva: United Nations, available at www.ohchr.org/english/about/publications/docs/ruleoflaw-Prosecutions_en.pdf.

—— (2006e) *Rule-of-Law Tools for Post-Conflict States: Vetting – An Operational Framework*, Doc. HR/PUB/06/5, New York and Geneva: United Nations, available at www.ohchr.org/english/about/publications/docs/ruleoflaw-Vetting_en.pdf.

Ombudsperson Institution in Kosovo (2001a) "On the Conformity of Deprivations of Liberty Under 'Executive Orders' with Recognized International Standards", Special Report No. 3, 29 June, available at www.ombudspersonkosovo.org.

—— (2001b) "On Certain Aspects of UNMIK Regulation 2001/18 on the Establishment of a Detention Review Commission for Extra-Judicial Detentions Based on Executive Orders", Special Report No. 4, 25 August, available at www.ombudspersonkosovo.org.

O'Neill, William G. (1995) *No Greater Priority: Judicial Reform in Haiti*, New York: National Coalition for Haitian Rights.

—— (2002) *Kosovo: An Unfinished Peace*, Boulder, CO: Lynne Rienner.

Orentlicher, Diane F. (1991) "Settling Accounts: The Duty to Prosecute Human Rights Violations of a Prior Regime", *Yale Law Journal* 100(2537), pp. 2541–2542.

OSCE Mission in Kosovo (1999a) "Part I – Framework for the Report", draft report, available at www.osce.org/publications/odihr/1999/11/17756_516_en.pdf.

—— (1999b) "The Development of the Kosovo Judicial System (10 June Through 15 December 1999)", Observations and Recommendations of OSCE Legal System Monitoring Section, Human Rights Division, Department of Human Rights and Rule of Law, Report No. 2, 17 December, available at www.osce.org/kosovo/documents.html.

—— (2000a) "Extension of Custody Time Limits and the Rights of Detainees: The Unlawfulness of Regulation 1999/26", Observations and Recommendations of OSCE Legal System Monitoring Section, Department of Human Rights and Rule of Law, Report No. 6, 29 April, available at www.osce.org/kosovo/documents.html.

—— (2000b) "Access to Effective Counsel – Stage 1: Arrest to the First Detention Hearing", Observations of OSCE Legal System Monitoring Section, Department of Human Rights and Rule of Law, Report No. 7, 23 May, available at www.osce.org/kosovo/documents.html.

—— (2000c) "A Review of the Criminal Justice System (1 February – 31 July 2000)", Department of Human Rights and Rule of Law, Review 1, 10 August, available at www.osce.org/kosovo/documents.html.

—— (2001a) "A Review of the Criminal Justice System (1 September 2000 – 28 February 2001)", Department of Human Rights and Rule of Law, Review 2, 28 July, available at www.osce.org/kosovo/documents.html.

—— (2001b) "Review of the Criminal Justice System (March 2001 – August 2001)", Department of Human Rights and Rule of Law, Review 3, 8 November, available at www.osce.org/kosovo/documents.html.

—— (2002) "Review of the Criminal Justice System: September 2001 – February 2002", Department of Human Rights and Rule of Law, Review 4, 29 April, available at www.osce.org/kosovo/documents.html.

—— (2003) "Parallel Structures in Kosovo", Department of Human Rights and Rule of Law, 7 October, available at www.osce.org/kosovo/documents.html.

Osiel, Mark (2000) "Why Prosecute? Critics of Punishment for Mass Atrocity", *Human Rights Quarterly* 22(3), pp. 347–361.

Oswald, Bruce (2000) "INTERFET Detainee Management Unit in East Timor", *Yearbook of International Humanitarian Law* 3.

—— (2004) "Model Codes for Criminal Justice and Peace Operations: Some Issues", *Journal of Conflict and Security Law* 9(2), pp. 253–275.

Paris, Roland (2004) *At War's End: Building Peace After Civil Conflict*, Cambridge: Cambridge University Press.

Pellet, Alain (2004) "Internationalized Courts: Better than Nothing ...", in Cesare Romano, André Nollkamper and Jann K. Kleffner, eds, *Internationalized Criminal Courts: Sierra Leone, East Timor, Kosovo and Cambodia*, Oxford: Oxford University Press, pp. 437–444.

Perriello, Tom and Marieke Wierda (2006) "Lessons from the Deployment of International Judges and Prosecutors in Kosovo", *Prosecutions Case Studies Series*, New York: International Center for Transitional Justice.

Plunkett, Mark (1994) "The Establishment of the Rule of Law in Post-Conflict Peacekeeping", in Hugh Smith, ed., *International Peacekeeping: Building on the Cambodian Experience*, Canberra: Australian Defence Studies Centre, pp. 65–78.

—— (1998) "Re-establishing Law and Order in Peace-Maintenance", in Jarat Chopra, ed., *The Politics of Peace-Maintenance*, Boulder, CO: Lynne Rienner, pp. 61–80.

—— (2003) "Rebuilding the Rule of Law", in W. Maley, C. Sampford and R. Thakur, eds, *From Civil Strife to Civil Society: Civil and Military Responsibilities in Disrupted States*, Tokyo: United Nations University Press, pp. 207–228.

Politi, Mauro and Giuseppe Nesi, eds (2001) *The Rome Statute of the International Criminal Court: A Challenge to Impunity*, Aldershot: Ashgate.

Popkin, Margaret (2000) *Peace Without Justice: Obstacles to Building the Rule of Law in El Salvador*, University Park, PA: Pennsylvania State University Press.

Pritchard, Sarah (2001) "United Nations Involvement in Post-Conflict Reconstruction Efforts: New and Continuing Challenges in the Case of East Timor", *University of New South Wales Law Journal* 24(1), pp. 183–190.

Pugh, Michael (2000) "Introduction: The Ownership of Regeneration and Peacebuilding", in Michael Pugh, ed., *Regeneration of War-Torn Societies*, Basing-stoke: Macmillan, pp. 1–14.

Ratner, Steven (1995) *The New UN Peacekeeping: Building Peace in Lands of Conflict After the Cold War*, New York: St Martin's Press.

——— (1999) "New Democracies, Old Atrocities: An Inquiry in International Law", *Georgetown Law Journal* 87, pp. 707–748.

Rausch, Colette, ed. (2006) *Combating Serious Crimes in Post-Conflict Societies: A Handbook for Policymakers and Practitioners*, Washington, DC: USIP Books.

Roberts, Adam and Richard Guelff, eds (1989) *Documents on the Laws of War*, 2nd edn, Oxford: Clarendon Press.

Robertson, Geoffrey (1999) *Crimes Against Humanity: The Struggle for Global Justice*, London: Allen Lane.

Roht-Arriaza, Naomi (1996) "Combating Impunity: Some Thoughts on the Way Forward", *Law and Contemporary Problems* 59(4), pp. 93–102.

Romano, Cesare, André Nollkamper and Jann K. Kleffner, eds (2004) *Internationalized Criminal Courts: Sierra Leone, East Timor, Kosovo and Cambodia*, Oxford: Oxford University Press.

Ruffert, Matthias (2001) "The Administration of Kosovo and East Timor by the International Community", *International and Comparative Law Quarterly* 50(3), pp. 613–631.

Schabas, William (2003) "The Relationship between Truth Commissions and International Courts: The Case of Sierra Leone", *Human Rights Quarterly* 25, pp. 1035–1066.

Scharf, Michael P. (1996) "Swapping Amnesties for Peace: Was There a Duty to Prosecute International Crimes in Haiti?", *Texas International Law Journal* 3(1), pp. 1–41.

Schoups, Johan (2001) "Peacekeeping and Transitional Administration in Eastern Slavonia", in Luc Reychler and Thania Paffenholz, eds., *Peacebuilding: A Field Guide*, Boulder, CO: Lynne Rienner, pp. 389–396.

Shoichi, Koseki (1997) *The Birth of Japan's Postwar Constitution*, trans. Ray A. Moore, Boulder, CO: Westview Press.

Shraga, Daphna (2004) "The Second Generation UN-Based Tribunals: A Diversity of Mixed Jurisdictions", in Romano Cesare, André Nollkamper and Jann K. Kleffner, eds, *Internationalized Criminal Courts: Sierra Leone, East Timor, Kosovo and Cambodia*, Oxford: Oxford University Press, pp. 15–38.

Silber, Laura and Allen Little (1997) *Yugoslavia: Death of a Nation*, New York: TV Books.

Special Panel for Serious Crimes, Democratic Republic of Timor-Leste (2002) "Judgement", *Prosecutor General v Armando Dos Santos*, 10 September, available at www.minihub.org/Language_English/spsc2001_english.htm.

——— (2003) "Decision on the Defense (Domingos Mendonca) Motion for the Court to Order the Prosecutor to Amend the Indictment", *The Public Prosecutor v Joao Sarmento, Domingos Mendonca*, Case No. 18a/2001, 24 July, available at www.jsmp.minihub.org/judgmentspdf/Domingos_Mendonca28703.pdf.

Special Panel for Serious Crimes, East Timor (2001) "Judgement", *The Prosecutor v Joseph Leki*, Case No. 05/2000, 11 June, available at www.jsmp.minihub.org/judgmentspdf/JOSEPH%20LEKI%20SENTENCE.pdf.

Stahn, Carsten (2001) "The United Nations Transitional Administration in Kosovo and East Timor: A First Analysis", *Max Planck Yearbook of United Nations Law* 5, pp. 105–184.

—— (2008) *The Law and Practice of International Territorial Administration: Versailles to Iraq and Beyond*, Cambridge: Cambridge University Press.

Strohmeyer, Hansjoerg (2000) "Building a New Judiciary for East Timor: Challenges of a Fledgling Nation", *Criminal Law Forum* 11, pp. 259–285.

—— (2001a) "Making Multilateral Interventions Work: The United Nations and the Creation of Transitional Justice Systems in Kosovo and East Timor", *Fletcher Forum of World Affairs* 25(2), pp. 107–128.

—— (2001b) "Collapse and Reconstruction of a Judicial System: The United Nations Mission in Kosovo and East Timor", *American Journal of International Law* 95(1), pp. 46–63.

—— (2001c) "Policing the Peace: Post-Conflict Judicial System Reconstruction in East Timor", *University of New South Wales Law Journal* 24, pp. 171–182.

Tanaja, Vanja (2001) "East Timor: UN Lets Indonesian Military Off the Hook", *Green Left Weekly* 447, 9 May.

Thier, Alexander J. (2004) "Reestablishing the Judicial System in Afghanistan", Working Paper No. 19, Centre on Democracy, Development, and the Rule of Law, Stanford Institute for International Studies, 1 September, available at http://iis-db.stanford.edu/pubs/20714/Reestablishing_the_Judiciary_in_Afghanistan.pdf.

Trenkov-Wermuth, Calin (2001) "Bulgarian Foreign Policy Towards the Balkan Crises 1991–1999", MPhil dissertation, University of Cambridge.

Uhler, Oscar, Henri Coursier with F. Siordet, C. Pilloud, J.-P. Schoenholzer, R.-J. Wilhelm and R. Boppe (1958) *Commentary on the Geneva Conventions of August 12, 1949*, Geneva: International Committee of the Red Cross.

UN Commission on Human Rights (1997) "Report of the Special Rapporteur on the Independence of Judges and Lawyers", UN Doc. E/CN.4/1997/32, 18 February, available through the UN Bibliographic Information System (UNBISNET) at http://unbisnet.un.org/.

UN Department of Peacekeeping Operations (2006) "Primer for Justice Components in Multidimensional Peace Operations: Strengthening the Rule of Law", Peacekeeping Best Practices Series, New York: United Nations.

UN General Assembly (1996) "General Assembly Resolution 51/197", situation in Central America; procedures for establishment of a firm and lasting peace and progress in fashioning a region of peace, freedom, democracy and development, UN Doc. A/RES/51/197, 17 December.

—— (1999) "Question of East Timor: Progress Report of the Secretary-General", UN Doc. A/54/654, 13 December.

UN General Assembly and Security Council (1992) "An Agenda for Peace: Preventive Diplomacy, Peacemaking and Peacekeeping", report of the Secretary-General pursuant to statement adopted by Summit Meeting of the Security Council on 31 January 1992, UN Doc. A/47/277-S/24111, 17 June.

—— (1995) "Supplement to An Agenda for Peace: Position Paper of the Secretary-General on the Occasion of the Fiftieth Anniversary of the United Nations", UN Doc. A/50/60-S/1995/1, 3 January.

—— (2000a) "Report of the International Commission of Inquiry on East Timor to the Secretary-General", UN Doc. A/54/726-S/2000/59, 31 January.

—— (2000b) "Report of the Panel on United Nations Peace Operations" (Brahimi Report), UN Doc. A/55/305-S/2000/809, 21 August.

—— (2000c) "Report of the Secretary-General on the Implementation of the Report of the Panel on United Nations Peace Operations", UN Doc. A/55/502-S2000/1081, 20 October.

—— (2002) "Report of the Secretary-General on the Situation in Afghanistan and its Implications for International Peace and Security", UN Doc. A/56/875-S/2002/278, 18 March.

UN Human Rights Committee (1996) "Consideration of Reports Submitted by States Parties under Article 40 of the Covenant: Preliminary Observations of the Human Rights Committee: Peru", UN Doc. CCPR/C/79/Add.67, 25 July.

UN News Service (2007) "International Judges at UN-backed Khmer Rouge Trials Welcome Breakthrough on Fees", 30 April, available at www.un.org/apps/news/story.asp?NewsID=22398&Cr=cambodia&Cr1.

UN Security Council (1975) "Security Council Resolution 384 (1975)", on East Timor, UN Doc. S/RES/384(1975), 22 December.

—— (1976) "Security Council Resolution 389 (1976)", on East Timor, UN Doc. S/RES/389(1976), 22 April.

—— (1993a) "Security Council Resolution 814 (1993)", on expansion of size and mandate of UN Operation in Somalia II, UN Doc. S/RES/814(1993), 26 March.

—— (1993b) "From Madness to Hope: The 12 Year War in El Salvador", report of Commission on the Truth for El Salvador, UN Doc. S/25500, 1 April.

—— (1993c) "Report of the Secretary-General on the United Nations Observer Mission in El Salvador" (contains an analysis of recommendations of Commission on the Truth for El Salvador), UN Doc. S/25812/Add.3, 25 May.

—— (1998) "Security Council Resolution 1184 (1998)", on establishment by UN Mission in Bosnia and Herzegovina of a programme to monitor and assess the court system in Bosnia and Herzegovina, UN Doc. S/RES/1184(1998), 16 July.

—— (1999a) "Security Council Resolution 1244 (1999)", on deployment of international civil and security presence in Kosovo, UN Doc. S/RES/1244(1999), 10 June.

—— (1999b) "Report of the Secretary-General on the United Nations Interim Administration Mission in Kosovo", UN Doc. S/1999/779, 12 July.

—— (1999c) "Report of the Secretary-General on the Situation in East Timor", UN Doc. S/1999/1024, 4 October.

—— (1999d) "Report of the Secretary-General on the United Nations Interim Administration Mission in Kosovo", UN Doc. S/1999/1250, 23 December.

—— (1999e) "Security Council Resolution 1272 (1999)", on establishment of UN Transitional Administration in East Timor, UN Doc. S/RES/1272(1999), 25 October.

—— (2000a) "Report of the Secretary-General on the United Nations Transitional Administration in East Timor", UN Doc. S/2000/53, 26 January.

—— (2000b) "Report of the Secretary-General on the United Nations Interim Administration Mission in Kosovo", UN Doc. S/2000/177, 3 March.

————— (2000c) "Report of the Secretary-General on the United Nations Interim Administration Mission in Kosovo", UN Doc. S/2000/538, 6 June.

————— (2000d) "Report of the Security Council Mission to East Timor and Indonesia", UN Doc. S/2000/1105, 21 November.

————— (2002) "Security Council Resolution 1410 (2002)", on establishment of UN Mission of Support in East Timor, UN Doc. S/RES/1410(2002), 17 May.

————— (2003) "Justice and the Rule of Law: The United Nations Role", verbatim record of debate, UN Doc. S/PV.4833, 24 September.

————— (2004) "The Rule of Law and Transitional Justice in Conflict and Post-conflict Societies: Report of the Secretary-General", UN Doc. S/2004/616, 3 August.

UNDP (2002) *National Human Development Report: Timor Leste*, May, New York: UN Development Programme.

————— (2006) "UNDP and Transitional Justice – An Overview", UN Development Programme, January, available at www.undp.org/bcpr/documents/jssr/trans_justice/UNDP_Transtional_Justice_Overview_2006.doc.

UNMIK (1999a) "Providing Legal Basis for the Establishment of the Joint Advisory Council for Provisional Judicial Appointments (JAC/PJA)", UNMIK Emergency Decree No. 1999/1, 28 June.

————— (1999b) "Appointing Members of the Joint Advisory Council", UNMIK Emergency Decree No. 1999/2, 28 June.

————— (1999c) "On the Authority of the Interim Administration in Kosovo", UNMIK Regulation No. 1999/1, 25 July, available at www.unmikonline.org/regulations/index.htm.

————— (1999d) "On the Prevention of Access by Individuals and Their Removal to Secure Public Peace and Order", UNMIK Regulation No. 1999/2, 12 August, available at www.unmikonline.org/regulations/index.htm.

————— (1999e) "On the Establishment of an Ad Hoc Court of Final Appeal and an Ad Hoc Office of the Public Prosecutor", UNMIK Regulation No. 1999/5, 4 September, available at www.unmikonline.org/regulations/index.htm.

————— (1999f) "On Recommendations for the Structure and Administration of the Judiciary and Prosecution Service", UNMIK Regulation No. 1999/6, 7 September, available at www.unmikonline.org/regulations/index.htm.

————— (1999g) "On Appointment and Removal from Office of Judges and Prosecutors", UNMIK Regulation No. 1999/7, 7 September, available at www.unmikonline.org/regulations/index.htm.

————— (1999h) "On the Law Applicable in Kosovo", UNMIK Regulation No. 1999/24, 12 December, available at www.unmikonline.org/regulations/index.htm.

————— (1999i) "Amending UNMIK Regulation No. 1999/1 on the Authority of the Interim Administration in Kosovo", UNMIK Regulation No. 1999/25, 12 December, available at www.unmikonline.org/regulations/index.htm.

————— (1999j) "On the Extension of Periods of Pre-Trial Detention", UNMIK Regulation No. 1999/26, 22 December, available at www.unmikonline.org/regulations/index.htm.

————— (2000a) "On the Kosovo Joint Interim Administrative Structure", UNMIK Regulation No. 2000/1, 15 January, available at www.unmikonline.org/regulations/index.htm.

——— (2000b) "On the Appointment and Removal from Office of International Judges and International Prosecutors", UNMIK Regulation No. 2000/6, 15 February, available at www.unmikonline.org/regulations/index.htm.

——— (2000c) "First International Prosecutor Appointed in Mitrovica", Press Release UNMIK/PR/162, 17 February.

——— (2000d) "Amending UNMIK Regulation No. 2000/6 on the Appointment and Removal from Office of International Judges and International Prosecutors", UNMIK Regulation No. 2000/34, 27 May, available at www.unmikonline. org/regulations/index.htm.

——— (2000e) "Hague Tribunal and War Crimes Court to Work Together", press summary, 3 June, available at www.unmikonline.org/press/mon/lmm030600.htm.

——— (2000f) "On Assignment of International Judges/Prosecutors and/or Change of Venue", UNMIK Regulation No. 2000/64, 15 December, available at www.unmikonline.org/regulations/index.htm.

——— (2001a) "On the Prohibition of Trials in Absentia for Serious Violations of International Humanitarian Law", UNMIK Regulation No. 2001/1, 12 January, available at www.unmikonline.org/regulations/index.htm.

——— (2001b) "On the Prohibition of Trafficking in Persons in Kosovo", UNMIK Regulation No. 2001/4, 12 January, available at www.unmikonline.org/ regulations/index.htm.

——— (2001c) "On a Constitutional Framework for Provisional Self-Government in Kosovo", UNMIK Regulation No. 2001/9, 15 May, available at www. unmikonline.org/regulations/index.htm.

——— (2001d) "UNMIK Refutes Allegations of Judicial Bias and Lack of Strategy", *UNMIK News* No. 98, 25 June, available at www.unmikonline.org/pub/ news/nl98.html.

——— (2001e) "On the Establishment of a Detention Review Commission for Extra-Judicial Detention Based on Executive Orders", UNMIK Regulation No. 2001/18, 25 August, available at www.unmikonline.org/regulations/index.htm.

——— (2001f) "On the Rights of Persons Arrested by Law Enforcement Authorities", UNMIK Regulation No. 2001/28, 11 October, available at www. unmikonline.org/regulations/index.htm.

——— (2003a) "Amending the Applicable Law on Criminal Offences Involving Sexual Violence", UNMIK Regulation No. 2003/1, 6 January, available at www. unmikonline.org/regulations/index.htm.

——— (2003b) "On the Provisional Criminal Code of Kosovo", UNMIK Regulation No. 2003/25, 6 July, available at www.unmikonline.org/regulations/index.htm.

——— (2003c) "On the Provisional Criminal Procedure Code of Kosovo", UNMIK Regulation No. 2003/26, 6 July, available at www.unmikonline.org/ regulations/index.htm.

——— (2005) "On the Establishment of the Kosovo Judicial Council", UNMIK Regulation No. 2005/52, 20 December, available at www.unmikonline.org/ regulations/index.htm.

UNMISET (2003) "Serious Crimes Process in Timor-Leste", press release, Public Information Office, 25 February.

UNTAET (1999a) "On the Authority of the Transitional Administration in East Timor", UNTAET Regulation No. 1999/1, 27 November, available at www. un.org/peace/etimor/UntaetN.htm.

————— (1999b) "On the Establishment of a National Consultative Council", UNTAET Regulation No. 1999/2, 2 December, available at www.un.org/peace/etimor/UntaetN.htm.

————— (1999c) "On the Establishment of a Transitional Judicial Service Commission", UNTAET Regulation No. 1999/3, 3 December, available at www.un.org/peace/etimor/UntaetN.htm.

————— (1999d) "On the Establishment of the Official Gazette of East Timor", UNTAET Regulation No. 1999/4, 29 December, available at www.un.org/peace/etimor/UntaetN.htm.

————— (2000a) "On the Organization of Courts in East Timor", UNTAET Regulation No. 2000/11, 6 March, available at www.un.org/peace/etimor/UntaetN.htm.

————— (2000b) "Amending Regulation No. 2000/11", UNTAET Regulation No. 2000/14, 10 May, available at www.un.org/peace/etimor/UntaetN.htm.

————— (2000c) "On the Establishment of Panels with Exclusive Jurisdiction over Serious Criminal Offences", UNTAET Regulation No. 2000/15, 6 June, available at www.un.org/peace/etimor/UntaetN.htm.

————— (2000d) "On the Organization of the Public Prosecution Service in East Timor", UNTAET Regulation No. 2000/16, 6 June, available at www.un.org/peace/etimor/UntaetN.htm.

————— (2000e) "On the Establishment of the Cabinet of the Transitional Government in East Timor", UNTAET Regulation No. 2000/23, 14 July, available at www.un.org/peace/etimor/UntaetN.htm.

————— (2000f) "On Transitional Rules of Criminal Procedure", UNTAET Regulation No. 2000/30, 25 September, available at www.un.org/peace/etimor/UntaetN.htm.

————— (2001) "On the Amendment of UNTAET Regulation No. 2000/11 on the Organization of Courts in East Timor and UNTAET Regulation No. 2000/30 on the Transitional Rules of Criminal Procedure", UNTAET Regulation No. 2001/25, 14 September, available at www.un.org/peace/etimor/UntaetN.htm.

Vicovac, R. Dule (2004) "Justice Reaches Out to the Communities", *Focus Kosovo*, August, available at www.unmikonline.org/pub/focuskos/aug04/focusklaw1.htm.

Vieira de Mello, Sergio (2000) "How Not to Run a Country: Lessons for the UN from Kosovo and East Timor", available at http://jsmp.minihub.org/Resources/2000/INTERFET%20DETAINEE%20MANAGEMENT%20UNIT%20(e).pdf.

————— (2001) "United Nations Transitional Authority in East Timor", in Nassrine Azimi and Chang Li Lin, eds, *The Reform Process of United Nations Peace Operations*, London: Kluwer Law International, pp. 93–100.

Weller, Marc (1999) "The Rambouillet Conference on Kosovo", *International Affairs* 75(2), pp. 211–251.

White House (2001) "President Issues Military Order: Detention, Treatment, and Trial of Certain Non-Citizens in the War Against Terror", Office of the Press Secretary, The White House, 13 November, available at www.whitehouse.gov/news/releases/2001/11/20011113-27.html.

Whitman, Jim, ed. (1999) *Peacekeeping and the UN Specialized Agencies*, London: Frank Cass.

Wilde, Ralph (2001a) "From Danzig to East Timor and Beyond: The Role of International Territorial Administration", *American Journal of International Law* 95(3), pp. 583–606.

—— (2001b) "The Complex Role of the Legal Adviser When International Organizations Administer Territory", paper presented at annual meeting of American Society of International Law, Washington, DC.

—— (2003) "The Administration of Territory by International Organizations: Conceptualizing a Policy Institution", PhD dissertation, University of Cambridge.

—— (2004) "Representing International Territorial Administration: A Critique of Some Approaches", *European Journal of International Law* 15(1), pp. 71–96.

—— (2008) *International Territorial Administration: How Trusteeship and the Civilizing Mission Never Went Away*, Oxford: Oxford University Press.

Wilkins, Timothy A. (1997) "The El Salvador Peace Accords: Using International and Domestic Law Norms to Build Peace", in Michael Doyle, Ian Johnstone and Robert Orr, eds, *Keeping the Peace: Multidimensional UN Operations in Cambodia and El Salvador*, Cambridge: Cambridge University Press, pp. 255–281.

Yannis, Alexandros (2004) "The UN as Government in Kosovo", *Global Governance* 10(1), pp. 67–81.

Zaum, Dominik (2007) *The Sovereignty Paradox: The Norms and Politics of International Statebuilding*, Oxford: Oxford University Press.

Treaties

"African Charter on Human Rights and Peoples' Rights", adopted at Banjul, 27 June 1981, OAU Doc. CAB/LEG/67/3 rev. 5, 21 I.L.M. 58 (1982), available at www.hrcr.org/docs/Banjul/afrhr.html.

"Agreement between the Republic of Indonesia and the Portuguese Republic on the Question of East Timor", done at New York, 5 May 1999, available at www.usip.org/library/pa/et/Ieast_timor_05051999_toc.html.

"Agreement on a Comprehensive Political Settlement of the Cambodia Conflict", 23 October 1991, UN Doc. A/46/608-S/23177, 30 October 1991, Annex, available through the UN Bibliographic Information System (UNBISNET) at http://unbisnet.un.org/.

"Agreement on Provisional Arrangements in Afghanistan Pending the Re-establishment of Permanent Government Institutions" (Bonn Agreement), done at Bonn, 5 December 2001, UN Doc. S/2001/1154, available through the UN Bibliographic Information System (UNBISNET) at http://unbisnet.un.org/.

"Basic Agreement on the Region of Eastern Slavonia, Baranja and Western Sirmium, or Erdut Agreement", 12 November 1995, UN Doc. S/1995/951, Annex, available through the UN Bibliographic Information System (UNBISNET) at http://unbisnet.un.org/.

"Basic Principles on the Role of Lawyers", adopted by Eighth UN Congress on Prevention of Crime and Treatment of Offenders, Havana, Cuba, 27 August–7 September 1990, available at www.unhchr.ch/html/menu3/b/h_comp44.htm.

"Charter of the United Nations", signed at San Francisco, 26 June 1945, available at www.un.org/aboutun/charter/.

"Convention (IV) Respecting the Laws and Customs of War on Land and Its Annex: Regulations Concerning the Laws and Customs of War on Land" (1907 Hague Regulations), done at The Hague, 18 October 1907, available at www.icrc.org/ihl.

"Convention on the Prevention and Punishment of the Crime of Genocide", adopted by UN General Assembly Resolution 260A (III), 9 December 1948, available at www.hrweb.org/legal/genocide.html.

"Convention Relative to the Protection of Civilian Persons in Time of War" (Fourth Geneva Convention), done at Geneva, 12 August 1949, available at www.icrc.org/ihl.

"European Convention on Human Rights", done at Rome, 4 November 1950, available at www.hri.org/docs/ECHR50.html.

"International Covenant on Civil and Political Rights", adopted by UN General Assembly Resolution 2200A (XXI), 16 December 1966, available at www.unhchr.ch/html/menu3/b/a_ccpr.htm.

"Mexico Agreement" between the Government of El Salvador and the Frente Farabundo Marti para la Liberacion Nacional, done at Mexico City, 27 April 1991, available at www.usip.org/library/pa/el_slavador/pa_es_04271991_mexico.html.

"Military Technical Agreement between the International Security Force ('KFOR') and the Governments of the Federal Republic of Yugoslavia and the Republic of Serbia", 9 June 1999, available at www.nato.int/kosovo/docu/a990609a.htm.

"Peace Agreement between the Government of the Republic of Sierra Leone and the Revolutionary United Front (RUF/SL)" (Abidjan Agreement), done at Abidjan, 30 November 1996, available at www.sierra-leone.org/abidjanaccord.html.

"Universal Declaration of Human Rights", adopted by UN General Assembly Resolution 217A (III), 10 December 1948, available at www.un.org/overview/rights.htm.

Index

Special Tribunal for Lebanon (STL),
180n90, 185, 188, 196
SRSG. *See* Special Representative of the
Secretary-General (SRSG)
State of Cambodia (SOC), 18
STL. *See* Special Tribunal for Lebanon
(STL)
Strohmeyer, Hansjoerg
"creation of an immediately applicable
legal framework," 153
East Timor, observations on, 103–7, 109
interview with, 178n15
Kosovo, observations on, 67, 78
laws in East Timor, application of, 24
laws in Kosovo, application of, 24, 55
legal adviser to the SRSG in Kosovo,
31n69, 92n136
"'quick-start package' for UN
administered territories," 153
references, 31n71, 88n25, 90n63, 90n68,
94n194, 144n33, 144n35, 145n63,
145n67, 145n69–71, 145n73–74, 145n76,
145n78, 145n84, 146n65, 146n98,
149n212, 150n216–17, 178n11–12,
181n118, 202
SRSG legal adviser, 31n69, 67, 78,
92n136–37
standby network of experienced and
qualified international jurists, 176–77,
184–85
UNTAET's principal legal adviser in
East Timor, 31n69, 150n216
Suharto, President, 96
Supreme National Council [Cambodia],
18

TA. *See* Transitional Administrator (TA)
[East Timor]
TJSC. *See* Transitional Judicial Service
Commission (TJSC) [East Timor]
Tokyo war crimes trials, 26–27, 167
Transitional Administrator (TA) [East
Timor]. *See also* UN Transitional
Administration in East Timor
(UNTAET)
eight district courts and one Court of
Appeal, 101
eight judges and two prosecutors,
appointed, 106
jurists, appointed first, 110
legal framework, transitional, 159

mandate of, 98, 144n37, 150n240
National Consultative Council (NCC),
98
panels of both East Timorese and
international judges for trials of serious
offences, 102
panels of judges to operate in district
court in Dili, 102
Regulation 2000/11, 101
Regulation 2000/15, 102
Resolution 2000/11 "On the Organization
of Courts in East Timor," 110
UN regulations or directives issued by,
100
Transitional Criminal Code, 154–55
Transitional Detention Act, 154
Transitional Judicial Service Commission
(TJSC) [East Timor], 105–6, 116,
120–21, 149n190, 206
Transitional Law Enforcement Powers Act,
154
transitional model legal codes [Brahimi
Report], 154, 178n18
Treaty of Lisbon, 95
tribal-level justice mechanism, 164, 186

UCK. *See* Ushtria Clirimtare E Kosoves
(UCK) [Kosovo Liberation Army]
UDT. *See* Uniao Democratica Timorense
[Timorese Democratic Union] (UDT)
Ugandan Amnesty Commission, 167
UNAMET. *See* UN Mission in East Timor
(UNAMET)
UN Charter
Article 1(3) (human rights), 25
Article 55, 31n73
references, 31n72, 208
UN Department of Peacekeeping
Operations (DPKO), 14n44, 20, 159,
180n72, 202
UN Development Programme (UNDP), 11,
14n48, 14n51, 114–15, 147n128, 189n4,
204
UNDP. *See* UN Development Programme
(UNDP)
UNHCR. *See* UN High Commissioner for
Refugees (UNHCR)
UN High Commissioner for Refugees
(UNHCR), 53, 98
UN Human Rights Committee, 27–28,
32n91, 203